The Empowered

Imperative

The Empowered Imperative

Assertively Managing Yourself for Optimum Success

Nicholas Smeed

PARAGONHOUSE

St. Paul, Minnesota

First Edition, 2002

Published in the United States by
Paragon House
2285 University Avenue West
St. Paul, MN 55114

Manufactured in the United States of America.

Library of Congress Cataloging-in-Publishing data

Smeed, Nicholas, 1945-
  The empowered imperative : assertively managing yourself for optimum success / Nicholas Smeed.-- 1st ed.
    p. cm.
  ISBN 1-55778-814-6 (pbk. : alk. paper)
  1. Success--Psychological aspects. 2. Success in business. 3. Self-management (Psychology) I. Title.
  BF637.S8 S56 2002
  646.7--dc21
                              2002010146

10 9 8 7 6 5 4 3 2 1

For current information about all releases from Paragon House,
visit the web site at http://www.paragonhouse.com

DEDICATED TO MY DEPARTED PARENTS, PETER AND ANNA.

With an acknowledgment of Mrs. Ashley, my second through fourth grade teacher at the former Crowfoot Elementary School in Pontiac, Michigan. Many, many years ago she gave me the best encouragement anyone ever could, whether she knew it or not. She walked around the class, telling each student what she thought each would do when they grew up. When she came to me, she said that I could be anything that I wanted to be. This book also acknowledges all other teachers who care enough about their students to have that level of interest and that kind of an impact.

A book of essays on the economics of practical, critical thinking and the art of continuously improving your organization, your career, and yourself.

CONTENTS

SECTION I: ORGANIZATIONAL REALITIES

Chapter 1

Each organization undergoes change on a continuous basis, and must reexamine itself regularly to be sure the architecture (or structure) is consistent with its purpose and needs. As any organization matures, continuous improvement will occur only if the management of change is built into the organization's culture.

Chapter 2

Decisions involving people are critical to the success of any organization (or individual), and managers spend much of their time dealing with these and closely related matters. The impact of people decisions on an organization can be substantial from many perspectives, and underestimating, trivializing, or overlooking their importance can be a critical and expensive mistake.

Chapter 3

A review of how an acquired company can be inadvertently undermined with excessive/superficial corporate attention, demands for unnecessary information, formulated performance expectations/measurements, and an incompatible style. The commentary illustrates the difference between corporate and entrepreneurial cultures, and provides insights on why many mergers/acquisitions fail.

Chapter 4

More than hypothetical, this primer on M&As addresses several practical issues important to both parties before, during, and after a deal. Anyone acquiring or considering being acquired will likely gain a few insights and tips from these notes to help avoid residual problems. Cultural issues, integrations, business interests, and people-management issues are discussed.

Chapter 5

Incompatible leadership styles can have a deleterious effect on an organization. The discussion attacks the notion that once someone has been in an executive position, they are necessarily capable and/or effective in other high-level positions in different organizations, environments, or times. The discussion addresses the many ways recruitment/selection practices fail when pursuing a high level leader and sums up with a better way to go about it. The commentary applies to every industry and every type of organization.

Chapter 6

Bureaucrats are the antithesis of being empowered. This is a critical examination of the bureaucratic mind-set and how detrimental it can be to an organization. While there may be a place for this type of person, careful control must be exercised or they will "wag the dog" (organization) and redefine excellence in their own marginal terms: the lowest common denominator. Are you a bureaucrat?

Chapter 7

The discussion focuses on the importance of creating and maintaining a clean organization with ethical staff and integrity in all of its operations. Topics also include individual acts that should not be tolerated, that occur often, and that are usually overlooked: but which serve to define the organizational culture (negatively). Removing individuals who have marginal ethics/integrity can be an effective improvement measure.

Chapter 8

The term "trust" has many applications: ranging from having full faith in someone to confiding corporate strategies, to entrusting someone with an important assignment, to suspecting someone of industrial espionage. The concept of trust is often more of an abstraction than people realize. Trust and truth are inseparable, it's a matter of facts vs. opinions, but then "spin" confuses reality. Duplicity is sometimes unavoidable, and it can produce a minefield of problems if it isn't handled well.

Chapter 9

Results are a calculated compromise of cost, time, and quality. This chapter examines misconceptions often associated with quality programs and asserts that quality emanates from an individual's style, competence, and attitude (a rare combination of traits). The most effective methods for developing and maintaining a true quality culture are explored.

Chapter 10

This discussion takes on thirteen (13) areas of the human resources field that are often overbureaucratized, poorly executed and/or unnecessary. The observations are critical of an occupation that has outsourced many of its essential aspects and has yet to establish its credibility. The focus is on how to improve this administrative area.

Chapter 11

A reality check for anyone currently managing or about to go into management. The discussion touches on leaders/managers being born vs. made, and illustrates the shortcomings of most management development programs. The chapter also outlines effective and useful assessment/development approaches for individuals and for groups.

Chapter 12

Organizational Development is defined in the terms and breadth it should ideally encompass, instead of the narrow focus it has evolved into. A very direct and practical approach to starting an internal people-development program is examined: providing an interface with several normally independent systems/processes, allowing for compliance with ISO 9000 (and similar) requirements, and creating a framework for assessing effectiveness.

SECTION II: INDIVIDUAL REALITIES

Chapter 13

This series of observations on how one becomes competent also provides a few soul-searching ideas on what it takes to become successful. A simple chart illustrating cost vs. competence will drive the point home that obsolescence will occur unless you continuously develop yourself.

Chapter 14

Individuals who are good at managing themselves, their play, their profession, who have common sense, and who are grounded with a good technical capability are likely capable of managing almost anything they are faced with at work and in their personal lives (regardless of if they've had the specific experience or not). Planning, leadership, execution, empowered mind-set, and managing different types of people are discussed.

Chapter 15

Being overly positive or negative can have upsides and downsides. For many people, finding the right balance can be tricky, if not impossible. Your tendency for optimism or pessimism may be the source of your motivations, goals, and aspirations. The discussion also explores other components and sources of motivation.

Chapter 16

This chapter focuses on how to reengineer ones self to optimize effectiveness, impact, and how to develop a "presence" leading to the self-confidence and pride needed for motivation. An old but true concept is explored that suggests the more roles you play, the better adjusted and more complete you will be, contributing to better performance.

Chapter 17

The Zone is a transient experience in which performance is effortless and exceptional. All of the elements of what it takes to be perfect converge, and the result is awesome; but then it goes away. There are ways to facilitate and maximize repeating the adventure of being in the Zone, and this chapter provides a few hints on how to improve your chances of "being there." Empowered mind-sets and attitudes are discussed.

Chapter 18

The illusion of intelligence and leadership often created by articulate individuals. The article also looks at how less-articulate people can retain or regain control in a variety of situations: from social settings through interactions with many different occupations where very articulate and often persuasive pretenders are found. Most readers will identify with all or most of the observations, and may find a few useful insights.

Chapter 19

This chapter deals with a very critical relationship, second only to one with your spouse. The motivations/interests of the respective parties are explored, and suggestions are provided for managing one another.

Chapter 20

An in-depth exploration of how to apply negotiating principles at work and in one's personal life. The discussion provides exceptionally useful insights into a very delicate and often mysterious area that is difficult for some people, but where empowered individuals are in their element.

SECTION III: PERSONAL REALITIES

Chapter 21

This chapter looks at practical ways to keep your stress levels under reasonable control without resorting to the psychobabble and medications often associated with this prevalent and troubling ailment. Stressed individuals are fundamentally handicapped, cannot perform optimally in any aspect of their life, and must actively address this dilemma.

Chapter 22

Once you have acquired a certain level of wealth, assets, and family stability protecting them from financial advisers and other invaders can be more difficult than it seems, unless you're willing to put full trust in people and perhaps learn (pay the price) the hard way. Discussions include: personal security, insurance fraud, crime, potential liabilities; and protecting your family, yourself, your property, and your future.

Chapter 23

This topic provides a framework for proactively managing a high-stress aspect of your life: entertaining visitors in your home and still having an enjoyable experience. The discussion places the burden for a positive outcome onto the houseguest, and provides an excellent example of correct, empowered expectations.

Chapter 24

A pervasive, important and compelling aspect of most people's lives is explored. Discussions include belief systems, the effects of organized religion, and spirituality; making the point that religious influence, while probably not the total answer to being a good person, can help many people maintain integrity, find stability and at least vicariously experience "the Zone."

Chapter 25

This discussion briefly looks at the male-female relationship and its respective needs. The chapter then emphasizes the importance of continuously improving, attending to, and mustering all of your talents and resources to manage this very complex, emotional/demanding/need-ridden, and often tenuous relationship in an assertive manner to keep it interesting and mutually satisfying.

Chapter 26

Information in its many forms can create misconceptions and unanticipated problems if not executed effectively and interpreted accurately. Development of basic skills, knowing when there is enough information, expanding conceptual range, understanding reality, and dealing with information constraints are explored. The chapter ends with observations on use of information in business operations.

Chapter 27

Individuals experience a plethora of ongoing changes, but are often reluctant to change and improve themselves: inadvertently becoming obsolete. The discussion encourages continuous revitalization through constructive personal improvements and provides practical examples for trying new and empowering activities.

Chapter 28

"Power" emanates from the individual. Influence and persuasiveness are by-products of being empowered, and it is important to understand how power, influence, and persuasion are used to protect against being manipulated.

Chapter 29

"Happiness" is examined theoretically and practically, concluding that real, meaningful happiness emanates from the individual and that a quest for it isn't the best approach.

Chapter 30

Practical day-to-day perfection is synonymous with truth, fairness, honesty and attaining a comfortable balance between competing demands (i.e., conflicts). The discussion addresses how to resolve conflicts, irresolvable issues such as war, and suggests what we should consider and understand to be "perfection."

A series of questions and answers on applying an empowered mind-set.

Prologue

The purpose of this book is to encourage the development and use of a conceptual framework and mind-set that will enable optimum results within organizations, with individual careers, and in one's personal life. The commentaries challenge individuals and organizations to explore, assess, and refine themselves, and cast off useless (often institutionalized) habits, constraints, and impediments to assimilating knowledge, making good judgments, embracing reason and objectivity, and taking effective actions. Those elements are *imperative* if one's purpose is to excel, successfully resolve conflicts, or simply feel satisfied if not happy.

Although the chapters can be read individually, in the aggregate the book provides a compelling argument for continuous change and improvement in all areas, on a foundation of ethics and integrity.

Throughout the chapters, ideas and thoughts are provided on how individuals may improve the way they manage or navigate their way through a variety of personal, career, and business environments while gaining more power, confidence, and control by using simple, effective, logical, and assertive actions.

THE EMPOWERED MIND-SET AND "ZONE"

When you (as an individual or organization) are functioning in *the Zone*, you are in your element, you are at your best, you are prepared, you have passion and a purpose, and you are performing effortlessly (at work, play, or anywhere). During that transient experience your energies are focused and results are exceptional. At that point you are alert and have considerable faith in your actions.

Being *empowered* is a mind-set that gives you the confidence and self-assurance to eliminate distractions and get a glimpse of how good, capable, and competent you can be. Each time you flirt with and function in *the Zone* you get a little better: your expectation of optimum results and your personal best ratchet up another notch, encouraging you to keep trying to repeat and improve upon that higher level of excellence, achievement, and impact.

Operating in an empowered mode mandates a predilection for conscious control without reliance on fate. There is a resistance to being "wagged" by events, and an avoidance of "going with the flow." *Empowered* individuals and organizations recognize (if not make) opportunities, thereby creating their own "luck." Individuals and organizations that feel *empowered* take calculated, but not irresponsible risks, and they have an intuitive sense for knowing when it's time to move on, divesting themselves of losing propositions efficiently. *Empowered* individuals are exceptional negotiators; and their innovativeness and action-orientation comes from a need to expediently solve problems.

The *Empowered Zone* is a convergence of the conscious and subconscious where endless *preparation*, effective *attitude (or mind-set)*, and exceptional *execution* converge, resulting in truly peak, optimum results.

Briefly defined, being e*mpowered* means: *having a purpose, being proactive in pursuing that purpose, assertively addressing problems encountered along the way, doing it not just with motivation and passion, but with a sense of urgency, and believing you can make it happen.*

Empowerment is a product of motivation. More specifically, empowerment stems from individual expectations of *excellence, emendation, exigency,* and *effectiveness. Energy* and *momentum* emanate from achievements, and *epiphanies* occur when individuals are receptive to and willing to assimilate information objectively. These are the ingredients needed for being *empowered.* References to "*the Zone*" throughout this book mean "*the Empowered Zone.*"

INTERTWINED REALITIES

Organizational, individual, and personal lives, or *realities*, are totally interdependent, and the effect of one on another must not be underestimated. Change/evolution is inevitable in each area, and each area requires affirmative attention and management to be successful. This means recognizing and preempting problems early and quickly, before they dominate or become overwhelming. Continuous alertness and an inclination to assess and act provide a basis for controlling events and interactions that could otherwise adversely affect and influence you.

REALITY AND REASONING

As in quantum mechanics, *reality* is very much a perception of the relationship of a set of facts to other things and events. Most certainly, facts that appear to indicate one thing may easily be interpreted to mean something else, and *reality* may be something altogether different from that.

Broadening often fragile, limited individual perceptive constraints: personal experiences and frames of reference (what we've learned, what we think we know, and what we've been conditioned to believe) is another *imperative*. The more narrow the frame of reference, the more impressionable and less accurate the individual's sense of *reality* will be. It is logical to conclude that ignoring reality (including not searching for it) is embracing mediocrity; and that an ignorant person has no understanding of, little use for, and no interest in *reality*. These people tend to react to stimuli without a logical game plan, and they have difficulty understanding how to influence events favorably.

Even attempting to accurately determine what is real is an *empowering* (although often frustrating) process. Unfortunately many of us function consistently and primarily on our assumptions, belief in illusions and reliance on embedded opinions and biases, while dwelling in our proverbial comfort zones. As a result, nothing new is learned or put to use, and no improvement occurs. You can do better than that!

We all have the ability, *if we choose*, to use reason for objectively sorting out and determining what is likely to be real, logical, and beneficial using informed, open-minded judgment vs. what is fantasy (wishful thinking, opinion, conjecture, blind faith/obedience, reliance on others' influence, and/or habit). To continuously improve, progress, and be successful, it is *imperative* to nurture, develop, enable, allow, and demand the use of reason. Objective reasoning takes practice and effort, it's not always easy or popular, but it is incredibly *empowering*.

HAVING A PURPOSE

In either the individual or organizational realm, before you can even think about discovering realities, you must *have* a purpose and you must be interested in actively seeking ways to achieve one or more purposes. The term *purpose* is used instead of "goal" because it infers more depth, intent, urgency, significance, and passion. A philosophical and graceful description of *purpose* can be found in the Koran. Poetically interpolated, it suggests:

> If you don't know where you're going,
> It won't matter which road you take.
>
> If you don't know where you're going,
> It won't matter if you ever get lost.
>
> If you don't know where you're going,
> It won't matter how long it takes.
>
> If you don't know where you're going,
> It won't matter how you get there.
>
> If you don't know where you're going,
> You won't know when you get there (no where).

Finding your purpose(s) is up to you, because only you know what you want to achieve and only you can motivate yourself. When you are motivated, you will discover your purpose(s). After that, efficient pursuit of interim steps and aggressive mitigation of constraints and conflicts is *imperative* for success. Even small accomplishments along the way are *empowering*, energizing and motivating.

THE INDIVIDUAL

Success in anything requires self-confidence and an inherent or developed ability to handle difficulties and competing influences/ interests. An *empowered* mind-set provides a foundation to do exactly that. The total of a person's experiences and attributes determines what that person will do for work, how they personally define themselves, how motivated they are and how successful they will be. Ultimately, each person usually succeeds (and becomes at least competent) at something they consider important. An individual's success in his/her personal life often directly impacts their occupational effectiveness. Has a person made rational choices and decisions in his/her personal life? Are they the right fit for their profession and their organization? Are they continuing to improve themselves?

There are finite jobs and infinite aspirations. In a less than ideal world, people must work to pay their bills but many aren't where they feel they deserve to be. The result is often a less than optimum effort, no clear purpose, and marginal results. The individual, the person's career aspirations, personal needs, and the organization must all compliment each other to achieve the best results.

Surprisingly few people perform the kind of work they really want, or for which they are best suited. As a result, all occupations tend to have similar competence distributions: 5 to 10 percent overachievers (if you're lucky), 40 to 50 percent "OK" at what they do (at least their heart is in the right place), +/- 30 percent just get by (perhaps burned out, disinterested, or stressed: but still hanging on), and the rest are useless (if not dangerous) misfits in some way, shape or form. Are you one of the detractors or a contributor to your own and your organization's success?

THE ORGANIZATION

Organizations suffer immensely from this competence profile. Reporting structures, management, and process controls may offset less than optimum performance, output, quality, and overall results, but only to a degree. Restructurings, reengineering, changing management, training, motivational, and team-building sessions, pay-for-performance, and similar initiatives all try to compensate for, and try to keep the aggregate competence curve on the plus side. Sadly, organizational failures occur when the organization itself suffers from a lack of practical intelligence and/or motivation, much like individuals; or when the culture can't keep the staff in sync. The successful organization is a convergence of: correct structure; effective culture; more than its fair share of motivated, competent individuals; and top-notch leadership.

Organizations experience life cycles that ebb and flow, fail and succeed in varying degrees at different times. Their success or failure is significantly influenced by how well they handle change, much like individuals.

An organization's *preparation* is its architecture or structure, and its *attitude* is its culture. *Empowered* organizations control market share and their competition by being better. They *execute* by: having the best talent representing their interests; not wasting time, money, or effort on bureaucracy; and not engaging in encumbering or useless practices. The least "fit" methods and processes are not allowed to survive. They are ethical and legal, but they will promote and protect themselves aggressively. They have consciously built "change" into their culture, allowing continuous reengineering and improvement without isolated change initiatives. If the organization has enough competent individuals with *empowered* mind-sets, they and the individual(s) will succeed.

In Summary

This book of essays/opinions is based on real experiences and observations. It is not a scholarly academic thesis and it is not pedantic: much is offered, asserted, emphasized, exaggerated, omitted, deduced, inferred, implied, and/or anecdotal. Having said that without remorse, many practical matters are addressed and logical perspectives are offered with potential solutions and improvements. Some observations may seem obvious to the reader, but consider how often the "obvious" is overlooked or denied. A refresher on getting *back to basics* can be surprisingly insightful and useful. If the basics elude you, then handling advanced concepts and complex issues may be well beyond your reach.

The diverse chapters describe many organizational and individual symptoms that detract from achieving optimum results, and suggestions are given for making things better. If anything in this book stimulates other, creative, or more appropriate/effective theories, solutions, methods, and/or practices, then another purpose of this book has been achieved.

A formula for success is consistently suggested through development and use of an *empowered* mind-set. A fundamental message is: *Pursue your vision/purpose with enthusiasm, demand and produce excellence, and enjoy the victories along the way.*

SECTION 1

ORGANIZATIONAL REALITIES

1

Organizational Change, Structures, Cultures

ALL ORGANIZATIONS CHANGE on a continuing basis, it's just a matter of how quickly and in what manner. Customers come and go, business activity expands and contracts, the *mix* of products/services is dynamic, and the organization must reshape itself to meet demands and expectations. In a rapid-growth environment, some staff members simply can't keep up and are often outgrown. Organizations that don't realize that their structure may be obsolete will eventually pay the price. Significant problems can also occur when downsizing is needed, and the need is denied or isn't handled well.

In any event, how change is managed (and how responsive the organization is to all manner of stimuli influencing it) ultimately determines how healthy the organization will be. Will it be nimble, quick, light of foot, and will it seamlessly continuously improve, or will it tough it out with the stops and starts associated with change initiatives? If an organization agonizes over *change*, the organization and its leadership will indeed be slow and sluggish. The organization that embraces change and expects responsiveness to customers has the *empowered* attitude needed to outperform the competition and earn the business. Change management must be built into the organization through its culture with constant reinforcement by its leadership.

Message: *Without a righteous cause, assertive actions inspire change much more effectively than rhetoric. People must see their leaders taking action, and they need to know what they must actually do differently.*

TYPICAL BUSINESS SCENARIO

As any organization grows and matures, it reaches capacity or capability constraints that typically require a significant capital and/or additional staff investment to continue progressing. The investments are usually needed to keep up with product refinements, machine obsolescence, automation needs, increased business, technology changes, or to prepare for the next level of growth. Investments may be needed as well if the business is downsized, to focus on core competencies with improved efficiencies. A smaller business can be surprisingly profitable if executed well.

When capacity or capabilities are stretched and not dealt with early, failures, omissions, oversights, quality, and staff problems all start creeping in and outcomes suffer. Symptoms begin with minor problems (usually ignored) and then larger issues surface with increasing frequency. A typical repertoire of stresses associated with growth include: various forms of denial, lack of competence accusations, finger-pointing, tension between staff members, and staff turnover.

Adding to the conundrum may be a heavy debt load, possible cash flow concerns, and investors expecting a more rapid return (along with a strong resistance to approving any capital or staff expenditures until profitability is where it was promised.) In the meantime, price pressures from suppliers and customers continue to squeeze profit margins, just when investing in the company is most important.

In other words, the pressure on the owners from customers, investors/lenders, and internal needs typically generates a *"We can't afford better equipment, and there's no way we can justify additional staff until inventories are down and profits are up"* response, along with *"We all need to suck it up and crank out more while we work through this period," "Business is looking good and things will get better soon."* Sound familiar?

The real question that the owners (or board) should be asking themselves is: *"Can I really afford <u>not</u> to invest in people or equipment?"* The responses noted above may be a reasonable short-term approach (one to three months), but if systemic problems aren't addressed, they will only become exacerbated and profitability will *not* improve. The correct midterm approach (two to twelve months) is to begin preparing to make appropriate investments and capital plans, starting *now*, since it will take months to find good staff and order/receive the right equipment/systems/machinery. Long-term projections will only have a chance if needed investments are made sooner rather than later!

Further Growth and Development

As a company moves toward or into the midsize realm (typically five hundred +/- employees), the owners need to assess the efficiency of the architecture or structure: does it help or hurt responsiveness, efficiency, productivity, and profitability? There's no easy answer here. The company grew successfully, and the original board or owner(s) will feel a loss of control and a shift from the culture that has served the organization so well to date. Notwithstanding *feelings* of loss, in reality the board/owners *will* lose control by keeping structures as they are. There is just too much work for the same entrepreneurs to handle by themselves, and something must change, or inefficiencies will escalate. The key consideration is to have the vision and courage to see the situation objectively, and to proceed without hesitation.

Message: *The single most effective action to take is to bring on competent, effective leaders and make sure they learn the business inside out!*

But that's tough for successful entrepreneurs to do (initially), so, enter the consultants and the change management experts. Be very careful here. Outsiders can provide guidance, but they can't guarantee improvements. The important question is: what do you hope to achieve with a structural or cultural shift?

If a rapid cultural change is indicated (to improve efficiency, productivity, profitability, and to expand markets), it is very difficult without changing out current skill-sets and a substantial portion of the staff. If you just need the staff "motivated" to do more work, that will take time, and often different staff as well. You'll probably quickly come to the realization you need better leaders, and you'll have to hire them: training present staff won't get you there very quickly if at all.

CHANGE MANAGEMENT

In a word, too much is made of this concept and too many training gurus overpromote the need to change the culture *as a process or event* outside the normal workings of the company. To the employees, new change initiatives boil down to "*Will I keep my job or not?*" and everything else only serves to make senior management feel better about all the people they're about to fire or reassign. Employees are pretty tuned in to how well the business is doing, so announcing "change" initiatives is tantamount to taunting many of them with the ax. Be careful that you're not patronizing and not giving them enough credit for knowing the state of the business.

A better approach is to weed out the marginal to poor performers as needed and as the company outgrows them. Then pump up the ones who remain (with rah-rahs if you must, but more money is better), since they'll be taking on more responsibilities.

Another key consideration in the change management arena revolves around the fact that subordinates emulate their leaders. This in turn defines the corporate culture. If you have turkeys on top, there'll be lots of gobbling below as well. Unless your change management *project* reengineers those on top, don't expect much in the way of *lasting* change. You can preach, motivate, hoot, holler, stomp your feet and team-build all you want, but subordinates will still act in a manner they feel will ingratiate them to their immediate manager (cloning). This alone makes the case for ensuring your leadership is as top-notch as possible.

BUILDING "CHANGE" INTO THE CULTURE

Making continuous change, and thereby enabling continuous improvement an organizational mind-set is directly related to the organization's leadership style. The following points provide a good definition of an *empowered* leader.

- The leader needs to be self-sufficient and confident in his/her own abilities. The fewer consultants the better. When consultants are used excessively, staff sees it as delegation of important matters and an indication that management doesn't know enough to deal with the situation.

- The leader must be perceived as being ahead of significant events, acting in the best interest of the organization in anticipation and ahead of changing conditions (laying off, staffing-up, cutting back, increasing supply-chain activities, renegotiating contracts, etc).

- The leader must be seen personally acting on issues and problems: doing it themselves and not delegating excessively (especially where delegation keeps cascading down to the lowest and often least capable person).

- The leader must not be into pontificating and philosophizing, ostensibly to motivate others. As much as possible, the leader must be available to staff, solving or improving situations on the spot: where the work is being done and not in meeting rooms.

- The leader must have a sense of urgency to act immediately, and expect the same of the staff.

- The leader must expect the best work and quality results in everything that is undertaken.

LEADERS AND CHANGE

Anyone naïve enough to think that leaders (CEOs with considerable hubris for example) as individuals can reshape an organization primarily with their personality and rhetoric need only to look at the history of mass movements. Leaders in those situations have generally been spawned by evolving socioeconomic conditions: they didn't precipitate the conditions, and if they tried to preach change ahead of the *perceived* "need," they were ignored. In other words, you can't "talk-in" change, it must happen through effective, obvious, continuing *action*.

Accordingly, change agents must be perceived as *action* figures, not philosophers. And, actions need to be evident at the micro level (involving each individual, with each person realizing what the change will do for *them*), or there will be little impact. *Leadership must be apparent where the work is being done*, making visible/useful changes on a continuing basis! Otherwise, constructive change won't occur readily, and if it does occur, it probably won't last.

Another common practice, especially by CEOs in difficult times, is to restructure the organization to purportedly rejuvenate it. If one restructuring doesn't work, they try another, and another: usually creating more confusion than results. If restructurings don't increase profitability, the board may start changing out the leaders. If there is significant turnover in the senior management ranks, and especially if employees don't sense stability in the top ranks, the organization takes on a life of its own. It learns to ignore leadership changes, resists changes of any kind (if only because the next bunch of leaders will change things again) and it becomes a playground for bureaucrats (see chapter on *"Bureaucrats"*).

ELEMENTS OF EFFECTIVE CHANGE

For any significant change to be implemented effectively, either on a continuing basis or, heaven forbid, as an initiative, the following elements need to be in place:

- The participants need to have some discontent with the practices or procedures about to be changed; otherwise changes will be resisted;

- The participants must believe that the new procedure, practice, or philosophy will be eminently better for them. They must know how, when, and why changes will benefit them;

- The participants need to be at least a little ignorant about the implementation, especially if it may be difficult, otherwise they will have all the more reasons to be critical of and resistant to new programs;

- The new policy, procedure, or system must be implemented as quickly as possible. Move hard, fast, and don't let up;

- It would help to have some bigger goal, purpose, or mission associated with the implementation, giving it extra weight, credence, and emphasis.

- Be prepared to force-feed implementation if there is undue resistance, and to replace noncompliant staffers if necessary.

EMPOWERED CHANGE AGENTS

Once the conditions are right and the stage is set for change to take place (especially cultural shifts), a *champion* devoted (and authorized) to making it happen becomes the indispensable component. If the change agent doesn't have the characteristics outlined below, only a modicum of success can be expected. Don't make the mistake of assigning a soft, likable, nonthreatening staffer to a significant change assignment, it simply won't work! Here are a few traits of effective *empowered* leaders in an environment where significant change is about to be initiated, or in an environment where change is a way of life:

- To be a change leader, the individual must have shown an ability to conform when needed, but must also be distinguished by occasionally taking a risk, making independent judgments and taking independent actions that worked;

- The leader must be flexible, intelligent, reasonably diplomatic, ethical, capable of having several contingency plans ready to act on as needed, and have a good dose of innovation;

- Digging deeper into the character, the change leader: wants to succeed at all costs (a *competitor* and *winner*), may be a little arrogant (others' opinions tend to be distractions), is more of a nonconformist (defiant) than their diplomacy suggests, and has no use for the old way of doing things;

- The leader must have a knack for getting people to rally around the change because of an *action-orientation*. The leader's enthusiasm/drive/purpose and total commitment to making things work, and others having faith that they will, all tend to keep staff in line throughout the process. Key players *must* be kept focused.

- Once the project is completed, the leadership personality that made it successful will be an unlikely and probably unwilling "maintenance" person, unless (ideally) continuous change is built into the organization and the challenges continue to be stimulating. Otherwise, the individual's talents would be underutilized and misappropriated.

DOMINANCE OF LEADERSHIP

Usually in small operations, but sometimes in larger ones as well, the culture of an organization can be that of the owner or other dominant personality who is everpresent and makes every decision. When that leader leaves (even for a vacation), everything locks up until that person returns. By all means capitalize on a personality if it works, but also understand that everything has a life cycle, including any individual and the impact they make.

TAKING RISKS

This has been said before, but it's worth repeating if only as a check-list and reminder of situations where an organization can easily and inadvertently run into trouble. Some of the most common risks facing any organization during growth or change cycles, and even on a continuing basis, include:

- Bringing on new leadership, and trusting that the new vision and style will be compatible with what the organization needs; believing that any new structure will improve the organization (invariably a new leader will reorganize); and trusting that the new leadership will understand the business as a whole;

- Believing that revenue projections are accurate and can be sustained throughout the forecasted period;

- Believing that new products, services, and/or customers will support revenue projections and that focus on current profitable programs/customers will not be diluted;

- Believing that current customers will remain committed and that the competition will not consume market share;

- Believing that margins, earnings, and market share trends have been assessed and evaluated accurately; and that competitors will not present significant surprises (such as predatory pricing);

- Believing that there will be no significant unforeseen risks, liabilities, potential economic downturns, wars, or political turmoil affecting trade, and/or new costly legislation (locally or internationally);

- Having confidence that new and existing programs will be

executed (produced, distributed, and marketed) effectively, efficiently, without quality glitches, and reasonably on schedule;

- Believing that the organization has the capacity, people, and equipment to produce the promised product(s)/services at a competitive price;

- Believing that the technology utilized will not become obsolete, and having invested enough in research and development to have that confidence;

- Knowing when to discard programs, services, and/or customers that aren't profitable or that won't lead to profitability in the visible future.

- Believing that new, comprehensive (and expensive) information systems will improve operations and help control costs. *Note: synthesizing, analyzing, and disseminating information is a costly proposition and should not be underestimated. The quality of output/ results from a new information system shouldn't be overestimated.*

- Believing that certain performance measurements, if emphasized, will improve *financial* performance. *Note: focusing on back-to-basics operations management (including visual inventories) in addition to any systems can be reassuring and great for troubleshooting.*

- Believing that the organization is "in sync" philosophically and focused on its purpose throughout the ranks, without detracting factions or personal agendas. *Note: Don't underestimate the "law of the shop floor" aspect of the organization. What happens where the work is done can be very different from the "values" touted at the higher levels. It pays for leaders to know what's really going on throughout the organization.*

- Assuming additional debt load.

Accuracy and responsiveness in these and related areas are where good *empowered* leaders are quickly sorted out from the rest.

CENTRALIZED OR DECENTRALIZED?

As change (growth, contraction, development, diversification, or any combination thereof) continues to take place, the organizational leadership will need to decide if the structure currently in place can handle the existing conditions efficiently, or whether the organization needs to be refocused.

One of the key decisions facing the leaders will invariably be: should the company continue to be centralized or would some form of divisional structure be a better alternative? If the organization needs to be downsized, then centralizing as much as possible probably makes sense. If it's growing, developing freestanding units often makes a great deal of sense in order to remain responsive and reactive to the markets.

As discussed in detail in the chapter on "*Who's Doing the Real Work?*" a growing and large centralized organization runs the strong risk of overemphasizing the administrative functions (accounting, information technology, human resources, facilities, safety/environmental, legal, quality improvement, insurance, import-export, and a multitude of subcategories).

Administrative staffers, when left to their own devices and tendencies, look for problems in order to justify their existence. They'll impose on the divisions to gather innocuous data for them, detracting from focusing on and improving business matters. Administrative types tend to delegate excessively, specialize unnecessarily, and use expensive outside help when they are in a quandary, rather than researching alternate solutions themselves. In a growing centralized organization, administrative costs don't creep up, they *explode!*

On the upside, if you can keep staff numbers in check with fewer but excellent (and well paid) multitaskers who can actually help the divisions do their work better, you may just have something going for you. Some administrative standardization can be very helpful: health and risk insurances, strategic and financial coordination, investor relations, R&D, and in-house "consulting" in legal, HR, labor, and environmental areas. Issues such as quality, sales/marketing, day-to-day accounting and information systems, human resources, and safety issues are usually best kept at the plant level.

Decentralized structures can be useful if a holding company model and mentality is employed, where a few high-level execs and technical experts oversee very lean companies: letting them operate on their own, but making sure their earnings are at forecasted (or better) levels. There is much to be said for local management of a "complete" company vs. getting into corporate-local jurisdictional tug-of-wars.

In any approach, the temptation to hire too many chiefs (VPs) must be ardently resisted. After a short time, all these chiefs need armies of underlings to do the real work, and none of these folks do much to increase profits. The more chiefs you have, the more they bump into each other, vying for influence, control, and power. The mission of the organization quickly becomes secondary. The rule of thumb is keep the number of chiefs to an absolute minimum, surround yourself with energetic, enthusiastic, committed, multiskilled doers, and your organization will thrive (unless your service, pricing, and/or products aren't very good).

CULTURE AND PERSONALITY CHANGE

All organizations are political in some way. The quickest way to realize a true culture change (political or other) is to sell the organization to a conglomerate. Whoever takes over would certainly not have the same way of doing business as the original owner(s). The priorities will change, and the debt burden on the company will force many efficiencies and cost-cutting initiatives. If the company's personality emulated the original owner's, then the company will change most radically to: being more corporate, providing many new standardized reports, having a new company man/woman in the top spot, conforming the business to a group or division of like businesses; and the personal touch will go away. There's nothing wrong with that kind of a change, it's the way it works, and the business will have morphed into its next developmental stage. The upshot: some people will be able to work in the new environment and some will leave. The prognosis for continued success: historically, don't bet on it.

2

People Decisions: Don't Underestimate Them

FOUNDATION FOR EXCELLENCE

THE *PEOPLE*-DECISIONS you make will in large part determine your level of success or failure and your profitability or losses. You must surround yourself with *empowered* individuals on all fronts, not just in the employment arena. As you will see in later chapters, when it comes to decisions regarding key staff members, making invalid assumptions (level of competence and extent of knowledge, skills, and abilities) and relying on stereotypes (such as liking or being uncomfortable with a potential colleague) can produce unexpected and usually disappointing results.

People decisions involve practically everything that happens, is about to happen, or has happened in or to an organization. It involves trusting your partners to contribute their fair share to the organization's development, it involves hoping that the individual working on your tool somewhere in Asia is competent, it involves your banker who must be advised of your credit needs, it involves who you choose as a supplier and/or customer, it involves legal actions you may or may not choose to take against others, and it involves almost everything else going on within your organization (who is assigned that most important design project; who is promotable and who isn't; who has been trained in new technologies, protocols, and methods; etc.).

All too often, price is the governing consideration in making people decisions. But is price worth the risk of differences in operating styles and cultures, the possible adverse impact on your reputation, and whether or not your business colleagues can deliver and meet your needs/expectations?

All levels of managers spend an extraordinary amount of time dealing with people issues on a constant basis. In addition to surrounding yourself with quality staff, examine your entire supply chain, your distribution channels, as much as possible your customers, and try to be collaborating with and servicing quality individuals (talented, knowledgeable, ethical, resourceful, flexible, capable, multifaceted, and successful). Everything works better if that is the case. Surround yourself with marginal performers on any front, and you'll pay the price in lost time, poor quality, redoing work, compensating for poorly constructed tools, excess staff, excess delivery fees, and extra stress on *you*: it all ties together.

On the employment side, having fewer, more capable, and motivated individuals who are compensated well is a quantum leap (in real costs and effectiveness) from surrounding yourself with bureaucrats and inexpensive slugs. If you want to be the best at what you do and you want to be successful, you must surround yourself with excellence and expect it in all areas.

FROM THE BEGINNING

An organization at its inception is often faced with one of the most important people-issues: will you build the organization alone (pretty hard unless you're a craftsman, writer, or independent consultant), will you involve family, or will you partner with one or more people? If you involve anyone else, there will be upsides and downsides, and unexpected issues to contend with.

In a business partnership, the compatibility and strengths of the partners should compliment one another's and the purpose and eventual outcomes should, ideally, be mutual goals. Disagreements can often be preempted by thinking through the corporate/partnership bylaws, decision-making authority, and/or ownership proportions vis-à-vis initial investments in some detail (kind of like a prenuptial). Creating a good, diverse board to keep strategies and ideas from getting a little crazy wouldn't hurt either. Too bad that couldn't work in a marriage. In any case, these types of precautions serve to keep people managed, organized, and focused.

Case in point: *My first venture into the partnership realm involved opening a coffeehouse. My one potential partner was a coworker with lots of enthusiasm and interest in making money, as I was. We reached the point of finding a location to lease and then began drawing up the plans. Everything stopped and cratered when a decision was needed on whether or not we should serve beer, wine, and/or other alcohol. I contended it was the best way to make money, albeit with some additional risk and more upfront work. My partner checked with his highly religious wife, who would not let him have any part of dealing in alcohol. That venture dissolved, my partner didn't do anything on his own, and I became a solo entertainer (part-time). My solo mini-entrepreneurship had a fun-filled, ten-year run. My partner didn't pursue any business ventures, but he protected his marriage and his wife's principles. Our personal relationship was never quite as good after that.*

IT INVOLVES YOU, TOO

On the individual level, how you handle yourself, the hourly decisions you make, and the long-term plans you envision for yourself and your family are all people-decisions. Not much happens without people (unless you withdraw from yourself, and even then you'll probably alarm someone with your behavior). Just make absolutely sure that your priorities with relationships, time, money, and financial security are where they should be and where you want them to be.

EPIPHANIES

The following *epiphanies* (people-related realizations based on actual experiences) illustrate real-world situations that could benefit from substantial doses of logic, reasonableness, and continuous improvement.

EPIPHANY #1: DETACHED "HIGHER" EDUCATION

A few years ago I had the privilege of preparing a graduate course outline for a class in human resources and labor relations at a major midwestern university. It was the first time a grad-level course was being offered in the school of business on this subject, and (interestingly) it still was not a requirement. A lower-level course was available with the usual personnel-related information, and a largely theoretical/historical undergraduate class in labor relations was also offered. The first graduate class dedicated to people-related issues, and it was still an elective! Perhaps that was the best indicator of how far the HR profession had *not* come to date. It was an epiphany.

That being said, the people-side of most organizations (labor, training, safety, worker's comp, and benefit costs) has always constituted a substantial portion of the financial plan. What had been going on, and what is often still the case, is that HR practitioners are insulated from the financial side of their activities: relegating their occupation to an elective status. They usually don't understand accruals or balance sheets, they don't become involved with funding mechanisms, they don't understand actuarial projections, they can't project the costs of a class-action legal settlement or distribution of a labor department penalty, they can't tell if a pension plan is adequately funded, they don't understand payroll accounting, and they can't accurately cost out the impact of an across-the-board salary increase (unless someone sets up a computer model for them). *See chapter on "HR myths" for much more on this subject.*

EPIPHANY #2: PERCEIVED IMPACT

Early in my career I worked as a human resources and labor relations director for a medium-sized municipal government in a prominent university town. I reported to a well-respected PhD-degreed city manager for over five years. When the city manager resigned for another position, he presented the city council and the media with a list of achievements during his tenure. Two-thirds of his accomplishments directly involved people-related matters. The HR and labor relations programs apparently had more impact on the community than bond issuances, public works/utility projects, police and fire initiatives, and university/municipal relations; at least as he chose to highlight his many years of effort and activity.

This achievement list was probably a result of the city manager's perception that the community tends to understand people-related issues better than other matters, and empathize with their importance.

In other words, it was a calculated political strategy that emphasized the positive and avoided the controversial. Most people think they have a good grasp of HR matters, understand them, are interested in them, and most everyone has an opinion on them. HR matters are politically visible and addressable and generally safe. More complex issues are not given as much time or visibility when they are the least bit controversial or not generally understood. The realization: don't underestimate just how politically important and effective representing people-issues as an upside really is (labor-management cooperation, staff efforts and dedication, public safety/security, and fundamentally the *human* side of the business).

EPIPHANY #3: EASY MONEY FOR THE PLAINTIFFS

HR decisions can be costly and disastrous on several fronts if not managed and handled well.

Over the years I completed several consults where I worked as an expert witness representing plaintiffs suing organizations for various forms of discrimination. In each case an individual was pursuing the complaint (not class actions), and the EEOC had already given the organizations tacit absolution with no probable cause findings. This meant that the feds weren't interested in following up on their initiative—the complaining party would have to by themselves.

The role of the expert witness is to review the case in its entirety, read depositions taken to date, and render an opinion as to whether or not the individual was illegally treated. In each case (in my opinion) there were illegalities. I was deposed extensively, and each case was settled out of court on behalf of the plaintiffs (for undisclosed amounts and terms).

The realization (epiphany if you will) even during my first case, was how *incredibly* easy it was to find fault with the employers. Philosophical mission statements were only rhetoric, there were poorly executed affirmative action programs, there were clearly biased (if not bigoted) supervisors, many poor judgments made in support of supervisors by governing officers (including elected ones), there was a clear lack of reasonable treatment and decision-making vs. following policies to the letter of the law, and many key staffers simply did not know the law! These were all examples of bad people-decisions.

The organizations paid dearly in defense attorneys, time spent on the issue by staff, plaintiffs' attorney fees, expert witness fees, and (of course) the settlements to the plaintiffs. It would not surprise me if there were no significant changes made in the way business was being done in these organizations even after experiencing these expensive lessons.

EPIPHANY #4: ARTIFICIAL QUALIFICATIONS

When asked to teach the graduate class mentioned in epiphany #1, I was impressed on one hand, because in the dean's assessment, my experience and background *overrode* the fact that I did not have a master's degree. I had presented several seminars through the business school, spoken at several classes, and had an excellent reputation in my field *notwithstanding* the absence of traditional "terminal" degrees. The class went exceptionally well, as reflected in student reviews. The university did not have professorial staff available to teach the course, and fortunately I was available to help out and fill in.

This teaching experience occurred over twenty years ago, before I knew half of what I know now in the business environment. In approaching colleges/universities recently, still without advanced "education," since I was too busy *doing* vs. being *educated*, I wasn't given the time of day. Over the years I had started the advanced degree process on two occasions, and found the professors to be so detached from reality I couldn't stand it. This realization, together with my recent experiences, showed me just how shallow and narrow-minded educational administrators and institutions of higher learning can be in the area of effective people-decisions.

Compromising demonstrated ability, knowledge, skills, diversified skill-mix, unquestionable real-world achievements, and loads of experience for a degree just seems absurd. Anyone attending a college would welcome interaction with a proven business leader and advocate vs. a pedantic academician. In other words, someone needs to look at the validity of academic credentials vs. experience for purposes of providing students with usable, practical knowledge. There seems to be a huge missed opportunity here. Moreover, this type of people-related decision-making directly contradicts the EEOC's Uniform

Selection Guidelines that require validation of qualifications for any job. In academia, it is assumed that degrees equal competence, and ignoring validation is the standard practice. This is all in spite of a historical lack of significant correlation between academic achievement and occupational success!

"MANAGERS" CREATE LOTS OF PROBLEMS

Here are a few more instances where decisions affecting people can create liabilities and/or missed opportunities in organizations:

- Too many relatives in an organization often create too many chiefs, and that can result in emotional squabbles, and even serious rifts. Organizations laden with relatives seem to have relatively short life cycles: one generation, maybe two.

- Managers may intend to motivate staff with suggestions of promotions and wonderful bonuses or salary increases if the staff works hard; but when conditions change and promotions aren't possible and layoffs or cutbacks occur instead, a legal theory called *promissory estoppel* encourages lawsuits by those allegedly misled by management. Be *really* careful here, there are many areas where this concept can be, and is, applied. Mission statements, values, and other sales-y organizational propaganda can have the same effect.

- Excessive cloning: surrounding yourself with staff just like you may give you a few more friends, but it gives no depth in terms of skills and opinions.

- Poor union-management relations can grind your organization to a halt in a hurry (or possibly into a slow, agonizing, debt-ridden death with slowdowns, sick-outs, and competence malaise). Maintain constructive employee relations at all costs.

- Having too many yes-men around you may make you feel important, but you again lose potentially valuable perspectives (unless you are infallible).

- Ineffective executive level staff can be especially detrimental to the health of an organization. This issue is important enough to devote an entire chapter to it: *see "Why Do They Keep Getting Hired?"*

- Staffing for peak activity levels costs lots of money. Staffing somewhere in between peak and low activity makes more sense. If you have fewer, multiskilled, higher-paid people, you'll usually tend to fare better when business shoots up in a hurry.

- There are too many laws affecting the work relationship these days to entrust sensitive decisions to supervisors or managers who do not work in that area all the time. Don't overdelegate in this area, there's too much risk, and supervisors need to be attending to business, sales, and operations matters vs. being excessively trained in HR practices. Instead, find *exceptional* HR/labor relations staffers and make them responsible for partnering with operations staff.

- Managers who have amorous relationships with subordinate staff are a problem: separate them or get rid of them. There's no way they can remain discreet, and their effectiveness is compromised.

- Not hiring the best possible talent, not insisting on multiple capabilities, not insisting on high output and quality, and not compensating staff well (and treating them fairly) are *all* formulas for failure.

- Operations managers can become inundated with cumbersome administrative forms and processes that make it all but impossible to be effective where they are most competent: critically assess potential business distractions and eliminate or at least minimize them.

- Discipline is an often mismanaged area. Problems include: lack of consistency, poor authorship of documents, lack of facts, emotional name-calling, and often a serious lack of good judgment. The burden of responsibility to perform as expected must be placed onto each employee through effective communication: it's often difficult and it takes experience. This is where top-notch employee relations staffers become invaluable.

CONFLICTS OF INTEREST

Loyalty to a supplier, partner, or colleague in the business environment can be a powerful alliance, as long as the performance and reciprocity is there. If performance is not at an acceptable level or if business terms begin favoring one party or the other, that *relationship* can easily become a conflict of interest and a liability. Conflicts of interest can take many forms, but the ones discussed here can have a very profound impact on the whole organization.

Undying loyalty to a supplier, for instance, based on history, tacit agreements, and/or common interests between the leaders of the respective organizations (personal friendships) is a dubious foundation for effective business decisions, and may be in direct contradiction to the interests of investors or the mission of the organization. It's important to understand how much those kinds of relationships cost the organization. Continuing board-level vigilance is the key.

Along the same lines, it is important not to confuse friendships with business relationships, especially in the context of customer appreciation events, business entertaining, business lunches, and dinners. These situations are exceptionally prevalent and serve to intentionally blur the line between business and personal relationships (which purportedly benefits the entertaining party from a marketing perspective, ostensibly facilitating communications when pricing changes, with the intention of keeping customers loyal).

Many organizations strongly discourage this behavior, if only because some people in key decision-making roles enjoy the extra attention a little too much, and indeed give the entertaining/giving party the benefit of a doubt when it comes to business arrangements over competing entities. This concept applies to giving gifts, providing various favors or opulent meals.

Many other organizations (particularly private ones, global companies, and public ones at the executive level) tacitly encourage this activity notwithstanding the potential risks. And granted, in international business matters, various gratuities are expected in the course of developing business relationships. Reasonableness and minimal expense for maximum impact are probably the answers, provided the activities are ethical.

There have been enough abuses of this relationship building by both sides to warrant serious review of these practices in public and private organizations. In its simplest terms, it's an extravagant overhead cost; and in its sleaziest terms, it's a way to buy business using shallow recipients (payoffs). In health care matters, for instance, physicians often expect to be wined, dined, spa'd, and golf'd by pharmaceutical sales reps, and often see the extra attention as a required perk to consider using the company's product(s): ultimately at the patient's expense. Call it real-world marketing, a mainstay in international business relations, an effective communications tool, or whatever. In reality it is a manipulation of people in the business realm, it is often a distraction from efficient business arrangements (restraint of trade issues and price-fixing schemes can evolve), and it can get either of the parties into trouble when it comes to explaining why a decision came down the way it did.

Whether or not this marketing tool is used, and to what extent, is an important decision. It unquestionably defines the character and culture of an organization, and determines just how political activities will be (the more gifts and entertainment, the more political the organization).

Note: For more on employee-based conflicts of interest, see chapters on "Ethics and Integrity" and "Trust."

REASONABLENESS STANDARDS

The reasonableness standard should, of course, be the governing consideration in the matter of entertainment and gifts in the business setting. As long as the nice gesture is such that a reasonable person would not believe it would influence a future business decision, then it's probably innocuous enough.

OTHER TOUGH PEOPLE-RELATED ISSUES

A little tougher, however, are intercultural standards, where officials in other countries expect "honorariums" or "contributions" before they act on an important, regulated matter. Again, act carefully, reasonably, and do as the customs dictate (provided you're not being duped).

More sensitive yet is the matter of buying a birthday gift for the boss. This should be a simple matter, with the good *empowered* boss making it clear to staff that no gifts will be exchanged—other than perhaps having a little birthday cake and a card signed by staff. The boss who expects a gift should be given a gag gift at most.

A rare problem, but of concern to many people, is workplace violence and related security. Briefly, a secure facility provides a high degree of comfort and ease to the entire staff and anyone visiting it: including night lighting, parking areas, limited access, security of documents and work areas and restrooms: everything. Having a small but spunky security staff can be invaluable in making people feel secure.

By far the most difficult people-situation is dealing with a kidnapping, especially in a foreign country. It is not unusual these days to have an American held hostage for ransom. In that case the individual must be made whole by the company, protected, and negotiated demands paid. This should be followed by aggressively pursuing the culprits.

CLEANLINESS

There can be no shortcuts, compromises, or tolerance of anything short of immaculately clean and neat physical facilities: throughout! People do not tolerate filthy surroundings in the workplace for very long.

DECOR

Avoid the institutional look in any way possible: include color, tasteful artwork, fabrics, plants, and be sure cubicles are of a comfortable size. Performance will be enhanced.

LEGAL ACTIONS

Whether or not an organization takes legal action against any internal or external party trying to victimize it, definitely defines its standards and expectations. As a general rule, if anyone illegally takes advantage of the organization, that party should be addressed legally and aggressively. If they settle and make the organization whole, then it makes an important statement to staff and to others in the business community. Be sure not to put all of your reliance on the legal/judicial system if a criminal issue is involved, because there may or may not be any follow through. If the legal system does follow through, it may not perform to your satisfaction. Pursue civil and criminal actions as mutually exclusive remedies where warranted. This is where your *empowered* instincts need to kick into high gear.

Similarly, don't make unnecessary compromises if you have been harmed; don't settle a case if you have the facts in your favor; and *do* countersue anyone trying to frivolously cajole you out of nuisance or settlement money. The same concepts are applicable in cases involving labor disputes, wage and hour, discrimination, unemployment, worker's compensation, safety, environmental, investor relations, industrial espionage, and any administrative process/hearing.

IN SUMMARY

This chapter has provided a small sampling of probably the most important aspect of organizational management: decisions involving people. Subsequent subjects all touch on this area in one manner or another: either individually or organizationally. An important consideration to be alert to is that many people tend to insulate themselves from controversial issues, and no issues are more controversial than those involving people.

All people-decisions mandate immediate and effective attention and prompt resolution of problems is critical. Nothing can impact organizational efforts or effective results more than the nature of human relationships. As you will see in later discussions, effective results come from effective interactions; and effective interactions require a high degree of insights and objective, strategic thinking.

3

Who's Doing the Real Work?

(Or, How to Really Mess Up an Acquisition)

THIS CHAPTER DESCRIBES a corporate structure that is relatively common, and is the antithesis of an *empowered* entrepreneurial organization. In a later chapter, bureaucrats are described as the antithesis of *empowered* individuals.

TYPICAL SCENARIO

A big corporation buys a small, attractive, lean, efficient, entrepreneurial company. The lean little company has minimal overhead, staff members are multiskilled, and most understand the interrelationships of the company's operating components. The acquiring corporation, for whatever reasons, has a huge management reporting system that needs to be fed (presumably to keep tabs on its divisions, make accurate forecasts, and meet federal requirements).

The little company dutifully hires additional staff to handle the bureaucracy, and multiple administratively based integration distractions dominate activities, keeping the staff from attending to the business of making money (something they had been very good at). Within the first year of the takeover, financial projections slip, key turnovers occur, and the honeymoon is over. The once spry, nimble, profitable company is drifting, as the corporate analysts descend on the new acquisition (in lockstep) with visions of a career-enhancing turnaround, armed with lots of second-guessing, ready to purge key old-timers who are purportedly out of sync with corporate goals, and with every intention of reorganizing something.

WHO NEEDS (OR READS) ALL THAT DATA?

Extensive reporting requirements within any organization should be a warning sign to a potential investor, the corporate board, and to anyone buying into or becoming a part of that type of culture. The fact is, no one is really capable of assimilating and making usable sense out of massive amounts of data that mega corporations with varied industries can generate if they want to. And it isn't likely that anyone has confirmed the real value of, need for, and impact of extensive/continuous operational reporting and forecasting (other than financial information). The assumption is: the more information, the better. Having an abundance of data and armies of analysts poring over reports certainly gives an illusion of knowledge and control, but at what real costs?

Back at the lean little company, the first reaction to collection and preparation of copious amounts of data is interpreted as a lack of faith in previous methods of managing the organization. The data requirements (and especially emphasis on less-than-significant indicators) become a burdensome demoralizer. Enthusiasm at the formerly efficient little organization goes away, replaced with confusion regarding what matters for generating profits, and a demanding attitude by the new "parent." Logic and common sense in business transactions and quick decision-making as it had been known in the little company falls by the wayside. Formerly simple matters and decisions become cumbersome, with many corporate players and corporate advisers who have their fingers in the pie.

From the corporation's point of view, the data gathering isn't seen as excessive. How else can you understand such a large conglomerate? It is also probably an effort to convince Wall Street that the corporate governance has its act together. After all, how can anyone manage without data? Data is considered synonymous with *power*. Except the reality is that Wall Street doesn't really care. To investors, good management is growth, increasing earnings, and profitability: *however* it's done. Operational and quality statistics are nice, but who really cares?

Somewhere along the line, the corporation bought into the notion that if you measure, report, and know about every detail of each operational component (quality is a popular one), the investors will be impressed and profitability will somehow morph and evolve. Popular notion, but a little too self-serving for its proponents (usually the academics/consultants/systems vendors who *do* end up profiting).

Corporate information needs tend to develop a life of their own. The overhead costs associated with the support staff required (usually several layers) to make elaborate reporting and forecasting systems work are enormous. VPs at the higher levels can't (or won't) do the work. They, after all, give the orders. So, they need a few worker bees to keep the flow of information going. But first, the VPs need assistant VPs who have specialty knowledge and focus, who in turn see themselves at an executive level. Accordingly, they need more-specialized "Directors," who in turn need "managers," who eventually need staff specialists who will complete the real work. Never mind the cost. The staff costs can always be pushed down to the once efficient little company that is expected to dutifully provide corporate information. The corporate machine isn't about to blow the whistle on itself (even though common sense screams for a need to lose some fat).

An excellent, practical argument can be made for not standardizing systems, *except* financial ones, especially in a corporation with diverse operations. The value of making a single system fit many diverse businesses successfully is beyond reasonable comprehension, too many exceptions and footnotes are needed to "qualify" unique operating and business characteristics. The cost/benefit of feeding big systems is marginal at best.

Message: *Collecting financial data is the essential informational component. Be careful not to overemphasize other extraneous data, and exalting unneeded uniformity and form over substance.*

WHAT DO THEY REALLY DO?

So, what do corporate managers really do? They seem to travel quite a bit. They grace the small divisions with their presence (after requesting elaborate reports in advance their arrival). They theorize, generalize, and pontificate, beat up division heads for not being more profitable, encourage and presumably motivate them with a few clichés at the end of a whirlwind meeting, pretend like they understand the divisional business needs, indicate that they are there to "help," and predictably declare that the division must be more profitable and lean. Then they fly off to the next division and do the same thing. So then, where is the value to this sort of claptrap? The right hand speaks of austerity while the left hand builds up a monolithic corporate support staff. The corporate managers try to *look* and speak like *empowered* people, but they don't really impact much.

Within a couple of months the newly acquired company has been totally distracted from taking care of business. The corporate types have denigrated the competency of the staff and admonished them for not being profitable (in spite of the fact they had been for quite some time). And if the division heads don't jump when asked for information, they are considered loose cannons, naysayers, and baggage from the former, obsolete management. Scapegoats are identified, and staff members are fired to make a point.

Making matters worse, corporate layering is often compounded with more than one "corporate" group, each with its own information needs and agenda: corporate headquarters, *divisional* corporate headquarters, and then the *corporate* portion of the operating units, who eventually oversee the *plant-level* staff.

DENYING AND OVERLOOKING THE OBVIOUS?

It never ceases to amaze how the same pattern of inefficiency repeats itself. Perhaps it's due to the same corporate managers being recycled from one organization to another. Or perhaps it's underlings emulating their bosses (with the subordinate staff assuming that their boss's activities are the correct way to function). It's probably a little of each, *plus* a cumbersome corporate culture encouraged by its leadership. It's the consummate *un-empowered* organization: political, philosophically disjointed, lots of fiefdoms, and lots of lost potential earnings for its investors.

One possible root cause for this runaway corporate train is an inordinately heavy reliance on outside management advisers, who tend to be very academic and system-based, and for whom all possible sources of business information aren't enough. Once these soft types of analysis-based individuals start influencing and controlling decision-making, watch out! If this is the case, lack of solid top-level leadership is the likely root cause.

By now the intuitive, bottom-lined, no-nonsense entrepreneurs who built the acquired company and made it successful have been demoted, left in frustration, or have been pushed out for by the good old boys.

But wait, we're not done yet. When sensitive, high-stakes, and/or politically charged issues are presented to our new corporate managers (perhaps at one of their visits), they assert that they are too busy with their management activities to sort out the details. So, they hire more consultants to do their analysis and charge all related costs to the formerly efficient little company!

Interestingly, the consultants have their own hierarchy. The principles do the marketing, and the real work is delegated to the recently hired MBA grad who is often overworked, but has to produce billable hours in order to become a "principal." For the corporate types, if the resulting decision-making and outcomes are somehow hosed up, consultants provide a built-in hedge (and perhaps someone to sue). Politically, for at least the time being, responsibility and accountability has been shifted away from the corporate bosses. They may actually feel they've exhibited "leadership" in this scenario.

Rule of thumb: *If you have a large staff (in any area) and you are still using consultants, there is something definitely wrong: inappropriate skill-mix, missing abilities, questionable competency, laziness, no inclination to risk making a recommendation, and lots of wasted money. What's the point of having a large staff if the work is even partially farmed out?*

Zero-sum Game

Feeding these corporate animals quickly becomes a no-win, zero-sum game for the corporately inexperienced new division. If the division performs, the new bosses take the credit. If the division doesn't perform, the corporate types swarm the company, demand more information, and start "managing" it. If the division doesn't come around with more profitability, then they restructure, change its management, and the cycle repeats. In this circular process (and logic), the corporate types have perpetuated the illusion that they have done something useful.

Concurrently, the corporate honchos continue the integration process with unrelenting training sessions, division head and manager meetings (often prolonged, offsite, expensive, and often conducted by consultants). The training sessions and meetings tend to be generic, philosophical, and only peripherally (if at all) related to making money. They typically deal with the softer, administrative issues such as information systems, financial reporting, environmental, health, safety, human resources, analysis, legal, ethical, and sometimes even marketing (still very conceptual). The acquired little company is now being ruled by the soft, administrative underbelly of the various levels of the corporate structure: the non-value-added types.

NOW THEN, WHO IS LEFT TO DO THE REAL WORK?

A corporate labor relations executive was once heard at a national conference declaring: why should he stick his neck out in a controversial impasse when he can have an arbitrator take the heat for a few thousand dollars. That sums it up: delegation of thinking and responsibility, and begging the question: *"Who's doing the real work?"* This example personifies what can go wrong with corporate thinking.

With this type of mind-set, the spiraling down effect quickly amplifies at the acquired little company, complete with the political infighting, positioning, backbiting, and credit-taking. The multiple layers of management all need more and more information to pass on to their superiors to give the illusion of knowledge. And, we see many forms of political creatures evolving: passive obstructionists, flat-out (not so passive) obstructionists, information hoarders, snitches, whistle-blowers, finger-pointers, etc. Plus, we see lots of superfluous memos, e-mails, reports, policy interpretations, and new policy declarations clogging the arteries of the organization.

MORE STAFF, LESS REAL WORK, LOWER PROFITS

The final outcome is that much less real work gets done with much more staff. And the real work is repeatedly delegated down to the lowest possible level, often to an individual least equipped to perform at an acceptable level (through no fault of their own). After all, the managers and would-be mentors are off theorizing and doing important, mysterious corporate things. They're too busy to be absorbed by lower-level details.

And where does this put that *formerly* neat, tidy, efficient, and profitable little company? It just isn't quite the same anymore. Everyone is learning a new game, and a new way of doing business.

4

Acquiring or Acquired?
A Few Practical Truths

AFTER BEING ACQUIRED twice by larger organizations, acquiring several smaller ones, and having been a business owner, a few valuable observations are worth sharing. The purpose of this chapter is to provide a few insights on how to be a little more *empowered* in the mergers and acquisitions arena through a few practical "truths." In the flurry of consummating a deal, obvious considerations may be overlooked or compromised, resulting in less than optimum outcomes; so consider this chapter a refresher and primer. A good follow-up chapter is the one on "*Negotiating.*"

TRUTH #1: IF YOU HAVE JUST MADE SOMEONE WEALTHY IN AN ACQUISITION, GET THEM OUT FAST!

The natural tendency for the nouveau riche is to count their money, over and over. Then they learn to invest it, on your time. Most will overtly or inadvertently become conspicuous consumers: car, clothes, jewelry, and houses, in any number of combinations. Employees close to the former owners see this, and there's more than enough envy to go around. Usually it's in the form of: "*I made them rich, and what did I get for it?*"

In other words, the previous owners will lose interest in the business in a hurry, regardless of what they say. If they stick around, they'll be a reminder to those less fortunate that they *are* less fortunate. Also, ship them off with a solid noncompete agreement.

In spite of the foregoing message, many acquirers end up keeping the former owners around on some type of run-out/transition agreement, probably because they don't have managers to put into their positions, or they may not understand the business well enough. You'll need to take over the business sooner or later, and the former owners may not be as valuable as you think. You could always keep them on a consulting retainer if needed, but for the most part, assuming full control *sooner rather than later* is much better! If you plan to keep the former owners around, contract their services (for specific functions, performance, time, and salary).

TRUTH #2: IF YOU'VE BEEN AN ENTREPRENEUR AND YOU'VE SOLD TO A LARGE CORPORATION, DO YOURSELF (AND EVERYONE ELSE) A FAVOR AND GET OUT OF THE PICTURE QUICKLY.

You aren't going to fit in, and it won't take you long to get totally frustrated. You'll always be thinking the big company is ruining your creation.

And, if you stick around, you'll try to control the business as you had before, but you won't be allowed the flexibility you once enjoyed. An entrepreneurial mind-set is wonderful for starting and growing a business, but entrepreneurs are very resourceful and bottom-lined, so be aware that you probably won't fare well in the political and structured corporate environment.

TRUTH #3: IF YOU PLAN TO KEEP THE PREVIOUS OWNERS AROUND, AT LEAST STRUCTURE THE PAYOUT SO THERE'S ENOUGH INCENTIVE TO KEEP THEM ENGAGED AND INTERESTED.

If you're purchasing the company based on an enterprise value with a higher than average multiple (usually because of projected earnings), then hold the owners to the projections and back-end load the deal. If you need them around to keep the business going, to keep them from competing, and/or because you don't have the in-house management to take over, then this is a good way to hedge your investment. The purchase price of the company becomes performance-based, over a one to three-year period (plus all of the other contingent liability escrows of course). If you must pay cash, with most of it up front, then be ready to introduce your own management the day after closing.

Truth #4: Even If the Former Owners Remain Involved, Get Them Out of the Financial Side of the Business Immediately and Make Sure the Compensation/Perk's Package Is Wholly Under Your Control.

Small company owners can do very interesting/creative/deceptive things with the balance sheet. Also, their previously enjoyed perk's (highly compensated relatives, household costs run through the business, four-hour workdays, lavish parties, etc.) can be a problem if controls aren't put in place immediately (preferably negotiated in the deal-making process).

The CFO (or counterpart) and/or the controller must be replaced forthwith, and must report to someone in the acquiring company unless you have full and complete trust (but let's not be naïve). Redefining the board of directors is self-evident; and don't forget to change the trustees of any welfare (benefit) plans immediately.

Truth #5: Be Careful Not to Impose Too Many New Information Systems and Reporting Requirements on a Company That Is Not Accustomed to Extensive Data Gathering.

If you do so, you risk changing the business sufficiently to ruin it. Cost of extra staff, costs of new systems, and confusion in making business decisions (pricing, purchasing, etc.): these types of sudden changes can shock an organization and keep it from performing. Ask yourself: Will the system you're about to impose be more effective than the current one? And, what is the true use/value/effectiveness of the information the system will generate? Is there a less intrusive way of getting the information you *really* need?

Truth #6: Plan Changes in the Acquired Company Before the Deal Is Done, Then Act Quickly to Implement Them.

Easier said than done, but it must be part of the due diligence and the assessment of what purpose, short and/or long-term, the acquisition will serve. Then after the deal, don't dilly-dally around and don't lie to the staff about anticipated changes (paying close attention to the "WARN" act: and if you don't know about this law, find out!). If you want the best of both worlds, try an asset purchase, and leave the staff issues to the seller.

TRUTH #7: HOW MUCH INTEGRATION IS REALLY NECESSARY?

If you aren't thorough and quick about it, then best not to do it at all, *except* for the financials. The staff you've acquired has probably been pretty busy working, so don't saddle them with a bunch of new/additional projects and expect them to give you the expected profitability. Revenue projections associated with the sale of a company tend to be notoriously optimistic. If the staff is unsettled in any manner, their output will diminish and the projections will most assuredly tank. There's something to be said about leaving a successful arrangement intact, reassuring the staff, and collecting the profits. The acquired company may even have operational methods that are more effective than your own.

TRUTH #8: IF YOU DON'T DO ANYTHING ELSE, GET *FULL* CONTROL OF THE FINANCIALS!

Assess and determine what needs to be done during due diligence and gain full control the day after the deal.

TRUTH #9: THE MOST IMPORTANT THING TO THE STAFF OF AN ACQUIRED COMPANY IS WHAT WILL HAPPEN TO THEM AND/OR THEIR BENEFITS AND COMPENSATION.

Don't underestimate the importance of this one, unless you are cocky enough to risk losing the best players. Quick, definitive, accurate communication on this front is critical.

TRUTH #10: IF YOU FAST TRACK A DEAL WITHOUT PAYING SUFFICIENT ATTENTION TO DUE DILIGENCE, THEN EXPECT TO PAY THE PRICE.

If you try to make up for oversights later, you'll likely end up in any number of lawsuits. Fast tracking usually occurs when the high-level poohbahs in the acquiring company omnipotently let it be known that "this deal must happen," or there will be a price to be paid by staff. Never mind that a price (usually bigger) will be paid later if important aspects of the business aren't inspected thoroughly.

If you are being acquired, watch the seemingly insignificant details, or *you* will pay a price you didn't expect. Pay attention to transitioning insurance coverages (w/c, liability, responsibility for carryover cases, etc.), obligations in and assignment of leases, and contractual matters of all types; and compliance with all legal issues must not be taken for granted: know exactly what's going on and what will be expected (especially if the purchaser is a government contractor)!

TRUTH #11: IT'S THE EXECUTION OF THE MERGER, NOT NECESSARILY THE CONCEPT, THAT RESULTS IN LESS THAN OPTIMUM RESULTS.

Consider carefully who you allow to be involved in the transition/ integration. Individuals assigned to this important task may very well be lower-level individuals who aren't good at very many aspects of the integration process. This is probably the cause for so many failures. Protecting customer relations, for example, is critical. If HR, legal, or the accounting department is leading the charge, they may inadvertently minimize or simply not understand the importance of customer reassurance and supplier contact.

TRUTH #12: FIND OUT QUICKLY WHO THE REAL PERFORMERS AND CONTRIBUTORS ARE, AND SECURE THEIR COMMITMENT.

This means *before* the deal is done. Include transition bonuses, in increments spanning a year. Be careful not to take the word of the previous owners too literally regarding the value of certain staff members: the needs (and staff skills) going forward may be very different than those used in the past.

TRUTH #13: DEALMAKERS (INCLUDING ATTORNEYS) CAN SCREW UP AN OTHERWISE POTENTIALLY GOOD ARRANGEMENT WITH SEEMINGLY SMALL BUT OFTEN CRITICAL NUANCES IN THE TERMS.

Compromises are bound to occur in any deal. However, if the deal is being fast tracked and the seller knows it, you lose!

Also, don't allow your henchmen to nitpick a deal to death on inconsequential (albeit important to the legal folks) points, unless you're intentionally softening up or wearing out the other side before attacking the really important points. Be careful not to be misled by models, formulas, projected returns on assets, and similar assumption-ridden data in structuring the deal. Stick with what you know for sure!

TRUTH #14: MAKE SURE YOUR CUSTOMERS AND SUPPLIERS AREN'T NERVOUS.

Little can be more devastating than inadvertently losing an unattended-to customer; or being unable to produce because your key supplier dumps you, presuming that you'll change pricing and terms (but no one has talked to them). Protecting the business is critical to the success of the transaction.

TRUTH #15: BEWARE OF THE DREAM ACQUISITION.

Acquiring a company on the upswing that doesn't need an overhaul in a developing industry (at a reasonable price) is every M&A staffer's dream. But remember that there is often an unidentified underlying reason for someone selling when you have a seemingly favorable set of circumstances facing the company. The reason for many M&A failures: too many undiscovered variables, too many assumptions, and too many unnecessary changes.

TRUTH #16: PREPARE DILIGENTLY AND THOROUGHLY FOR THE NEXT STEP OF YOUR COMPANY'S DEVELOPMENT AND TAKE NOTHING FOR GRANTED!

The owners of a mature organization (well established, reputable, profitable) eventually get the urge to move on, do something else, and capitalize on their work.

The options include: going public through an IPO, selling to a competitor, selling to your employees, selling to a large conglomerate (foreign or domestic), selling to a "roll-up" entity that eventually takes the consortium public, hiring someone to run the company and keeping it as a cash cow, selling a majority interest to investment bankers who can do what they want with it and you go along for the investment ride, or any number of variations thereof.

If you're going to cash out in some manner, there are a few important things to do in tidying up:

- Make sure there are competent (management) successors for key positions;
- Take your relatives off the payroll and out of the organization;
- Eliminate all or most of the personal perks charged to the company;
- Be sure your financials are audited, inventories are under control, assets are all accounted for (valued), and your profitability can be verified for several years;
- Secure your key players with big incentives to help you through the "sell";
- Protect those players from whomever takes over the company;
- Plan how and when to make disclosures to staff;
- Have a business plan for at least two subsequent years;
- Understand and describe how your markets are trending and your market share, along with your competitor's strengths and weaknesses;
- Cut out unnecessary costs and staff and show just how profitable you can be, for at least one year;
- Thoroughly explain your company's technology edge, unique skill-set, focus, and distinguishing features;
- Don't overestimate your company's worth—you may be embarrassed; get several opinions;
- Be careful about using and/or choosing a broker to sell the business: they are expensive, and they may not do a better job of sell-

ing than you could on your own (unless you're a poor negotiator or if you have a big ego).

And then proceed to test-market your company to determine its salability and enterprise value. Ideally, if you can get a bidding war going, especially between unlike parties (such as a corporate buyer vs. a roll-up where the terms of the sale could be very different), then you'll stand a better chance of getting the best price or deal. If you proceed with an actual sale, there'll be much, much more to do.

TRUTH #17: FULLY UNDERSTAND THE WORKINGS OF THE FINANCIAL COMMUNITY, AND KNOW HOW TO MANAGE IT!

Your connections and networking throughout the financial arena is critical to your success. There are many pretenders and wannabes, so the first order of business is to identify the real players and get to know them and all the ways they can help (or hurt) you. This includes your accounting firm, bankers, developers, real estate specialists, brokers, investment bankers/houses, pension systems, analysts, some consulting firms, and even reputable academics.

Learn their vernacular, their computer models, and their hot buttons. Understand that all individuals in this community need to justify their recommendations to a committee, and they thrive on unpublished/inside information (company and industrywide): they must look like they're really connected. Accurate data with a blue-sky spin is what they want to hear, as long as you don't oversell. Always be on the lookout for more favorable financial restructurings: it keeps your current bankers on their toes and you in control. Fully understand the terms of any financial transaction (make sure your attorney knows the game plan, the nuances are critical!)

Financial types like relationships, name-dropping, and being entertained. Give them lots of data, communicate continuously, control who has access to them, and give them lots of TLC. If you change institutions don't burn any bridges, these people are very mobile.

5

Why Do They Keep Getting Hired?!

ILLUSION OF LEADERSHIP

MANY YEARS AGO there was an inconspicuous film starring Peter Sellers entitled *Being There*. In the movie, a displaced, affable, low-intelligence gentleman inadvertently assumes the role of a corporate advisor and leader. He looks the part, but never really makes a decision. He utters sounds or misplaced clichés in response to questions, and mumbles. Many interpret his responses and misplaced metaphors as brilliant. The fact that he held an influential position provided a presumption of competence. A few people saw through the guise and understood him for what he really was: an idiot. Eventually he was discovered and his supporters ran for cover.

Many who fancy themselves "leaders" are also *illusionists*, not to the extent noted in the film, but in terms of overall effectiveness, often not too far off. The term *leader* for our purposes is used generically, including board chairs and CEOs down through VPs, CFOs, directors, managers, and even supervisors: anyone overseeing the activities of others.

Often, just because someone has held, or now holds an impressive title, many characteristics are automatically bestowed, deserved or otherwise: intelligent, charismatic, a *leader*, a politician, a competitor, a winner, technically astute, industrious, demanding, accomplished, etc. The bottom line is: *don't bet on it!* A few reasonably good indicators of someone who *doesn't* belong in a position of leadership include:

- Being too busy to consider or address little issues; or the converse, being obsessive/compulsive/anal;

- Acting like a bully or a snob: aloof, condescending, strutting their stuff, being overly demanding; only their priorities count, no excuses are valid, "my way is the only way," and naysayers are disloyal types to be discarded;

- Acting "tough": glaring without responding, using vulgarities, intimidating subordinates, degrading others openly, bragging about alleged achievements, touting the body count resulting from other experiences, and/or being boisterous;

- Taking credit for the work of others, including situations like: a coach doing the needed recruiting and other preparations to make a winning team, but being fired before having a chance to follow through; and the new coach accepting accolades for the positive outcomes;

- Assuming and expecting the organization to respond favorably to dictates, fiats, policy statements, new values, directives, initiatives, and similar declarations on face value, and not questioning the new administration;

- Demanding inordinate amounts of data, reports, and analyses; constantly insisting on being informed (vs. knowing what's up);

- Doing all the talking in most forums, including interviews (belittling or warning applicants about who's in charge and how things must be done);

- Being a figurehead and a titular leader: overly active in charities, civic activities, fundraisers, being socially visible, promoting own image, overly active in partisan political campaigns, pursuing pet projects (art collection is typical) and/or junketing all over the world.

- Lacking diplomacy, multicultural sensitivity, interest and tact; or unable to represent the company effectively to the media and the financial community.

These are fairly clear indicators of future problems. Many ineffective leaders *demand* and *expect* respect without even attempting to *earn* it. Actions like these are fairly transparent to the most capable staff, and those are the ones who will move on when faced with an annoying or ineffective leader. Unfortunately for an organization that is making money, it may take a while for higher management or the governing board to identify a problem (it would be admitting they made a mistake, and top management doesn't like to make those kinds of confessions).

Message: *Someone in control needs to really know what the leader is truly doing and/or contributing vs. just "being there."*

MUSICAL CHAIRS

Thousands of CEOs and other company executives play musical chairs every year, at what appears to be a higher rate of attrition than ever before. Never mind that many of them have either failed, just barely got by, or may be getting out before they get bounced. Someone will hire them into key positions again, over and over. The dot-com shake-out is almost complete, health care has been at it for over a decade, school superintendents last less than three years (at what cost to the kids?!), and the same story repeats itself in all industries from sports to the megacorporation. At last count, top-level tenure was averaging less than five years: not even a complete economic cycle.

The fact is that organizations have a major failing when it comes to recycling marginally capable individuals through high positions. Hiring parties often seem to stress attributes of a candidate that make the *hiring* party look good (or committee, which may be replete with political compromising) instead of making the effort to find the right candidate and then making sure that this person performs and sticks with it instead of bailing out on that all too often ridiculously generous golden parachute.

ASSUMPTIONS GALORE

Perhaps it's easy to justify hiring a high-level individual to "the board" if the executive has a pedigree. The right number of degrees from reasonably recognizable institutions helps. If the individual is very articulate, definitive, and outspoken, it has a huge impact. Previous work with several known and reputable organizations is an easy sell. But most important, a person must have been *The CEO*, or *The CFO*, or *The VP*, or *The Superintendent*, *The City Manager*, *The Hospital Administrator*, *The Coach* and so forth. The overwhelming assumption is that if they have had "The" title, they must be good. If nothing else, it corroborates, or perhaps copies, previous decisions someone else made about the person. Maybe it's too "risky" for hiring parties to recognize *potential* in individuals who may have the achievements but not the correct titles or the prestigious degrees.

Headhunters often oversell candidates, and hiring authorities often don't know any better. CEOs are often so smug about the accuracy of their insights and opinions; they barely involve others in the decision-making process for hiring VPs and other key positions. The process of selecting a good leader, especially identifying and selecting an *empowered* individual (which you most certainly want), can break down in many ways (read on).

FIRST THINGS FIRST

Before deciding to hire a high-level leader, go through this checklist critically and honestly: "*Does the position need filling?*" "*Can the job be combined with another one?*" "*Are there already too many chiefs?*" "*Who really runs the operations?*" A marginal or bad hire can do more harm than not filling the position. And if you've had a potentially good leader lower down in the ranks who would go elsewhere if not recognized for making contributions, learn to identify that talent and how to keep/nurture the good ones, and forget about taking a chance on the unknown.

We'll assume that hiring this high-level person is necessary. What follows is a primer on all the ways the selection process can falter and ultimately fail.

NEGATIVE APPROACH

If this chapter drives only one point home, it is that any and all care must be taken not to hire a leader who may not be the best person or alternative at that point in time. It has been shown that identifying someone who will *not* succeed can be predicted at a 90 percent-plus confidence level, assuming a good assessment process is used (*see the chapter entitled "Management Development" for more on this).* Identifying someone who *will* succeed is closer to 80 percent using the right techniques. Using your "gut" and even a series of interviews will usually yield only a 50 percent predictive accuracy. So, for important positions, take your time and do it right!

STYLE AND IMPACT

Management style and compatibility with what the organization needs is probably the single most important contributor to success, or lack of it, in a high-level organizational leader.

An individual may be the right fit at one point in the organization's life cycle, but not in another. And an individual's style, credibility, and personality have an overwhelming influence in shaping the response of the organization. All too often it is assumed that a person who has held a high position is adaptable. Unfortunately that's not always true: most people have only one way of managing and leading, and it is much easier to demoralize a spunky, competent staff than it is to motivate them.

Staffs emulate their leaders. Here are a few styles/characteristics to watch out for. If you find the new leader is a poor fit because of conflicts in style, correct your error as quickly and expediently as possible:

- A political leader begets political underlings and encourages manipulation and duplicity.
- If the leader is a spinmeister, then the organization becomes more superficial.
- If the boss is loud and heavy-handed, he usually likes the same traits in subordinates, and the organization becomes less tolerant.
- If the leader is a scholar but you need lots of action, watch out, and brace yourself for lots of analysis, group buy-in, and compromises.
- If the leader is a rah-rah cheerleader, then the underbosses become jocklike coaches with only occasional diminishing impact.
- If the leader is a softie, then the organization runs itself its own way and at its own pace.

- A micromanager can choke the enthusiasm right out of an organization.
- A computer illiterate boss in a high-tech organization will demonstrate passive obstructionism when it comes to any systems-related issues.
- A leader who has a personal agenda and rigid philosophical priorities can confuse the staff and split allegiances, thereby losing control and focus . This includes the "*I'll take care of you if you do as I say*" type of leader. The problem comes when that person is no longer there to "take care of" the staff, or if the staff doesn't believe the leader.

Each of these scenarios leads to gradual organizational decay. Unfortunately, it may take months or years (as in large companies) for root causes of poor organizational performance to become understood by the board, i.e., that the leader is the problem.

Boards must be more involved in the management of organizations, or they risk being ineffective and becoming puppets of the CEO. It is, after all, often the nuances of day-to-day organizational management that results in success or failure. If much of the key decision-making is delegated to the CEO, the board may be putting too many eggs in one basket, much to the dismay of the organization's investors. For example, what would be wrong with having a CFO report directly to the board, and perhaps legal counsel?

HOW CAN YOU TELL IF LEADERSHIP'S VISION & STRATEGIC DIRECTION IS "HOSED UP"?

Most employees like to think that their leaders (especially those leaders who have VP titles +) are very knowledgeable in business matters, so they inherently trust them when they disclose a new program, new product, new vision, or a new strategic direction. It's very easy to get caught up in the moment, and certainly no one wants to play the devil's advocate at such a momentous, sometimes inspiring, and perhaps even motivating time.

Here are a few points to consider in the context of deciding if an existing or new strategy has merit (assuming you have some control over the situation, or if *you* and *your* vision could use a reality check). The important point is to know when to fold a program or initiative, to minimize the damage.

- The financial aspect is most telling. If cost overruns are high, start watching closely. If the business forecast keeps getting pushed back and amended, or a start-up is sluggish in terms of consumer interest, it's time to reassess and probably back off.

- There are many places for a new program to falter: intro, ads, lack of interest by the target market, distribution, dealer initiatives, sales briefings, nonperforming suppliers, and design/quality glitches. A problem with any one of these should be a reason to stop and think it over.

- When key staffers are giving diplomatic but very clear messages that the initiative has flaws, it's time to reassess.

- Use industry trend indicators (from government analysts, not consultants who get their "inside" information from biased analysts), speak directly with competitors if possible, but mostly, listen to the consumers as directly as possible. If reports are inconclusive, stop.

- When it comes to form and function, if informed, independent individuals with good taste and a sense of style give you marginal feedback, it's time to back off.

- If base-level employees are critical of the program, and if it doesn't pass the common sense/reasonableness sniff test, it's time to listen.

- If, in spite of any of the foregoing, the leadership continues to blue sky the matter with optimistic hype, it's definitely time to reassess (there may be just a little too much ego involved).

- The same principles hold for implementing new quality initiatives, starting up new ERP (or similar) data systems, organizational restructurings, and any similar changes. Sometimes it makes sense to stop, regroup, and rethink the approach if there are even hints of resistance and skepticism. The correct groundwork may have been carelessly abbreviated in the groundswell of enthusiasm.

- If you are a supplier, potential times to abort programs include: when your customer starts controlling your floor operations, when price pressures result in losses, when program requirements keep getting tighter and margins are being squeezed, and when the product life cycle is nearing its end. High-level managers often don't have a clue until matters are out of control.

- If you're a customer, it's time for a change when a supplier isn't performing and only a relationship is holding it together, or when the supplier jacks up the price unilaterally or outside the terms of the contract. Beware of the high-level manager whose friendship protects the poor supplier.

- Underestimating global issues (such as regulatory agencies in other countries that oversee mergers and acquisitions) can be a sign of a smug CEO who overestimates influence.

All of these (and similar) leadership-related matters must be monitored and addressed assertively. Similarly, if you are looking for a new leader, investigating and determining what that leader may or may not have done in these types of situations will provide invaluable insights. Always remember that leadership is easy when all is going well. It's how those *unforeseen* issues are handled that really demonstrates a leader's philosophy, and whether he has the instincts to do well in a critical or crisis situation.

THE REAL QUESTIONS TO ASK AND AREAS TO PROBE

Now let's get right down to finding out whether or not a potential leader might fit in with the needs of the organization. The following questions could easily and efficiently be reviewed in a preliminary video interview, allowing you to not waste time interviewing/recruiting someone who doesn't have the expected presence or who doesn't have anything of substance to offer.

WHAT DID THE POTENTIAL CANDIDATE ACTUALLY DO IN HIS OR HER OWN RIGHT?

Or, is the person taking overactive credit for the work of other(s) on their staff? This is especially true if the candidate uses the "*I did this and that*" approach. Also, if the word "*We did this and that*" comes up repetitively, there's a good chance the person was a tagalong, going along for the ride vs. directly influencing events. The overwhelming assumption all too often is that if something good happened, the CEO did it, and if it weren't for this leader, it wouldn't have happened at all. BAD assumption! Never mind that a hefty bonus was granted, the success may have been in spite of the candidate. Determine *how* the candidate actually made things happen, and what the results were: don't accept general answers with a wink and a nod.

Also, don't hesitate to ask whether or not the candidate ever fired a key staff member, face-to-face, without delegating the task. The answer may surprise you more often than not.

WHAT DOES THE ALLEGED LEADER REALLY KNOW HOW TO DO?

A heavy reliance on consultants in past positions should be an immediate red flag. If something went wrong, consultants can be the excuse or scapegoats; or they can be the politically correct buffer. At the very least, they are very expensive insurance.

If a company is preparing to go public or be sold, can the leader personally develop an enterprise value for the organization, or must someone else do it? Has the leader handled balance sheet issues or simply budgets and P&Ls. If the organization is sales driven, has the leader been largely in an operations role? These are just a few examples of areas where overlooking lack of direct and hands-on knowledge, skills, and abilities will only lead to trouble. What is the person a true *expert* in? If the answer is being a generalist, then it's only an acceptable answer if the person is *also* an expert in something more specific.

IF THESE PEOPLE ARE SO GOOD, WHY ARE THEY NO LONGER THERE?

Here we are faced with sorting out the spin. Standard explanations often land in the realm of soft and difficult-to-confirm assertions:

"Philosophical differences with the board."

"Lack of support by new board members."

"Personality clash with the chairman."

"The CEO wouldn't relinquish any authority."

"The owner personally spent the company into the ground."

"The owner had a drug and gambling habit."

"I was sexually harassed."

"The chairman made me hire his relatives."

"They didn't follow through with bonuses [or other] promises."

"The new CEO wanted to hire his own staff."

The problem is, there is usually no viable source to affirm or deny such contentions; and character references are always stacked in favor of the candidate. In reality, it really doesn't matter; these types of responses should alarm the hiring authority and force a much deeper look (however it's done) before the viability of the candidate is established.

HOW HAS THE LEADER SPENT TIME AT WORK?

This issue is more important than many people think. Many assume that the leader spends every minute of every day on official business. Somehow, many company executives manage to work on developing their own wealth and on honing their pet hobbies while on the job. Some look for art, others are active in charitable matters and events, other travel excessively and too opulently. Remember, executives are not supermen: far from it. Corporate execs can easily create the illusion of spending all their time on company-based activity, with armies of staff and advisers doing endless analysis. But what does the executive *really* do all day? This is a legitimate area to probe and it may illustrate one major difference between corporate execs and entrepreneurs.

HOW HAS LEADERSHIP BEEN EXERCISED ON THE JOB?

Leadership is a very intangible and elusive property, and the perception of a leader varies by industry and even by organization and department. The power aspect of leadership is often a function of title. A CEO has the ability to influence your career, for example, where others may not have that power. Beware of executives who have *exercised their power in superficial ways*, especially if it was/is to establish themselves as decisive or tough. They may have been sacrificing scapegoats to take the heat off their own shortcomings. High-level execs who are (or have in the past been) on a power trip can be devastating to an organization. They tend to oversell their perspectives and decisions, and if you disagree, you are disloyal.

UNTAPPED RESOURCE

Although often maligned by executives in large organizations, successful entrepreneurs have paid their dues with long hours on the job doing meaningful work. They've developed many diverse practical/ analytical skills that corporate execs usually delegate, they have built something significant *themselves,* and they've experienced the stress of tackling true financial issues in a manner that corporate execs often haven't a clue. The suggestion here is that there is a huge untapped wealth of executive-plus ability, largely ignored by corporate boards when they need a solid leader/achiever.

USING SEARCH FIRMS

Another assumption/fallacy is that a search firm will help make the process more professional. Nothing is further from the truth. Search firms are primarily sales organizations and they will strictly follow the profile given by the hiring authority. They will abide by hiring authority biases to a fault (otherwise they won't be hired again). So, search firms, besides taking an unnecessarily long time and being very expensive, simply cater to the whims of the hiring authority.

Search firms lend nothing in terms of insights, but they do take away some responsibility from the hiring party if a failure occurs. Conversely, the search firm can assert they found "*just what the board ordered*" if the board can't make a decision (or accept the panel of candidates) to justify the search firm's fees. The political compromises inherent in a board decision do not go away when a search firm is involved; there is simply another layer of opinions and sometimes even meddling added to the mix.

Just because search firms conduct many recruitments doesn't mean they are good at discovering salient facts about the candidates. Most reference checks tend to be positive and superficial, and background investigations are usually inadequate and certainly not revealing. If a candidate doesn't work out, the search firm often blames the hiring authority for not being clear in its requirements, for not managing the person well, or for having unreasonable expectations.

Search firms are paid handsomely if the search succeeds or fails; and they are notoriously poor at identifying high-potential individuals who might be exceptional leaders but who are outside the formal specifications for the job. This is too risky and too discretionary for the search firms, and they simply aren't capable even when given this kind of latitude. Remember that "success" to a search firm is often +/- six months on the job. Preliminary aspects of a search are often delegated to lower-level staff in the search firm, so don't expect to have experienced staff working on all aspects of the assignment (regardless of what you're told/sold).

The use of search firms also begs the question of why the organization has a high-level HR person. If that individual can't be counted on (or trusted) to perform much of this type of search, then the question should be asked, "*Why are they there?*" If, for whatever reasons, the VP/HR is out of the picture, then a specific board member should be in charge of the search. There is usually too much at stake to delegate a high-level search to an outside party. The standard logic used by search firms is that they can dig out candidates without concern for corporate raiding. Once again we have bad logic and an inaccurate assertion. Immunity from raiding is highly oversold by search firms: raiding is raiding regardless of who does it. It's the end result that counts.

MANY WAYS TO FAIL

The hiring process for high-level individuals can fall apart or be remarkably incomplete in many ways:

- The *good old boy network* is as assumption-ridden as they come. Just because a board member knows someone doesn't mean that the person will be capable in the new position or environment! Success in a previous situation doesn't guarantee success in another with a different set of circumstances.

- With the seeming scarcity of experienced leadership in the marketplace, there is often an *overemphasis on recruiting* and selling an individual on a position vs. finding out what they're really capable of doing.

- Physical size and/or appearance often have an undue influence. The *"presidential look"* and physical presence often bias the hiring party.

- Executive interviewees can easily fool interviewers with a seemingly great but *superficial command of the vernacular* used in their industry. Be aware that dropping terms, names, and knowing definitions doesn't mean that they know the mechanics of the business processes, or whether they really know how the business components come together and influence one another. Interviewers often simply don't know any better and can't tell the difference.

- *Strong articulation and diction can create an illusion of leadership.* It can also be a sign of a bully who intimidates, rants, diatribes, and doesn't care about the position of others. A quiet, soft demeanor can be more effective than a boisterous one. Also, beware of the "likability" factor: it usually doesn't matter and it certainly isn't a predictor of anything (unless the candidate is simply obnoxious).

- Political entanglements, while often real, should also be a huge red flag. *Philosophical differences* can mean that the candidate was so headstrong that compromise wasn't possible and/or so taken back by someone questioning their position that they began pouting and decided to cash in on their severance package (a significant negotiating trap and an area in which to be very careful). A highly aware and tuned-in CEO or VP will usually not become embroiled in trite political issues if they are halfway diplomatic and not overly enamored with themselves.

- *Interviewers are often reluctant to ask sensitive questions* or probe to substantiate a candidate's basic skills, either because they are intimidated or afraid they'll scare away a candidate who may have other options. Or they may not want to find out the person is computer illiterate, a lush, old-fashioned, or otherwise inadequate. All too often the interviewer is awed or flattered to be in the presence of a person they may admire. If that is the case, the interview will be biased and incomplete in its findings, the prognosis will be positive and glowing, and if there is anything negative, it will be minimized as being insignificant.

- Be especially cautious when a candidate stresses the *superficial trappings of success.* Another red flag must flip up when there is an overemphasis on office furnishings, redecorating, luxury automobiles and/or chauffeurs, traveling first-class or use of private jets, building their own team, specific authority and/or control over board composition or board overview, ability to make independent donations, and ability to unilaterally influence policy (to name just a few areas).

- *Political assumptions and compromises* are always a problem. "*We need to hire a minority to keep the feds off our back.*" "*The largest legal firm will yield the best corporate counsel.*" "*We need a CFO from our accounting/auditing firm.*" It is very easy to hire a marginal performer based on off-the-cuff, spurious presumptions and then rationalize the new hire's need to be there; while watching but not recognizing that the organization has been carelessly maligned.

- Another red flag is a *long tenure with a large corporation,* followed by one or more short stints in key positions with smaller organizations where there is more visibility. In other words, they didn't work out, they probably aren't adaptable, and they learned all they probably will ever learn by virtue of their work in the large corporation.

- When hiring a CEO, it is difficult to think of an effective CEO who *hasn't been deeply involved with the investment, banking, and financial community.* But this is the case in many high-level placements: CEOs can rely on the CFO to handle all financial matters, sometimes to a fault. Check it out; this can be a critical deficiency.

INCREASING THE ODDS

After all is said and done, hiring a high-level individual is often a 50-50 coin toss. There are, however, several ways to mitigate the crapshoot (literally and figuratively).

Promoting from within is a good policy. Be careful that an out going CEO or leader hasn't unduly denigrated good internal candidates because of philosophical differences, loyalty issues, or flat out personal biases.

Designating a board member as interim chief and placing someone in a CEO-in-training role to assess what they're really made of may have merit. At any executive level, naming an interim individual is always a good idea; then, see if that person has the required abilities. Basically, anytime a chief executive or board member can *create a situation where a new executive can be observed* in an important but not totally committed role, the company has more control over the situation. Buying some time will allow the board to see if a particular executive position is even needed at this point in time. Turning assumed capabilities loose on an organization without close scrutiny is truly a gamble.

Definitively assessing essential skills is extremely important, albeit a little tricky. You must find out if the person who you will be entrusting with at least part of the organization's success can read, write, represent, advocate, truly understand financials, and make reasonably sound judgments (quickly). If a candidate resists being assessed (either on the job in a lower position or through simulated exercises), then think twice about pursuing that candidate. The usual excuse is they don't have time, or they may be indignant to perform in lieu of expecting to be recruited. Auditions for high-paying positions are nothing new!

SO WHY DO MARGINAL EXEC'S KEEP GETTING HIRED AND RECIRCULATED?

Largely because they can sell themselves and fool many people. Be a conscientious "leadership" consumer; you owe it to your organization.

6

Notes on Bureaucrats

WHAT ARE BUREAUCRATS?

BUREAUCRATS ARE THE antithesis of the *empowered* mind-set. It is important to be able to recognize them and deal with them. Their perspectives may be useful but shouldn't be allowed to dominate. They are rarely standout performers, they rarely if ever experience *the Zone*, and there are lots of them.

They cannot conceptualize, develop, or organize a new program. They might be able to *help* implement it, given a detailed map to follow. And they certainly *can* maintain it once it's in place; but once they've learned it, don't count on many changes or improvements. They can put out lots of work and they'll often put in lots of hours, but it won't be innovative, resourceful, or novel. They may be able to describe and analyze, but cause-effect relationships and solutions tend to elude them.

They can be friendly and even delightful, but when in a super-visory role they will demoralize a group and keep the creative staff on a short leash. They aren't inherently motivated, *empowered* individuals threaten them, and they will bring staff down to the lowest common denominator—their own, where it's safe and secure and under their control. Or, they can be *overly* friendly with their staff, trying to make them allies. Either way, optimum results won't typically occur without close control by someone above them.

Keepers of the status quo, preservers of process, not stirring things up, exalting form over substance, and sticking with what they learned and know from once upon a time: that's what they like. Then they go home and fall into rut #2, a safe haven of more routine, steadfastly familiar stuff, and probably a good dose of tedium. In all likelihood they can't figure out a different way of "being," and if they could figure it out, they probably couldn't bring themselves to doing something about it.

BUREAUCRATS AT WORK: CASE IN POINT

A classic example of bureaucrats at work occurred during the years 2000-2001 in Arizona's state government. Poorly written, although ostensibly well-intended environmental legislation encouraged the use of alternative fuels for personal and commercial vehicles. The legislation provided substantial personal property tax breaks, offered credits for the purchase of such an alternative fuel vehicle, *and* paid for the conversion/retrofitting of vehicles to enable use of cleaner-burning fuels. There was no requirement that vehicles actually use alternate fuels once the vehicle was converted.

The Motor Vehicle Division went on its merry way administering the program, following the *letter* of the legislation dutifully. Once the hundreds of millions of dollars in program cost *overruns* created a scandal, nullifying a projected tax decrease for Arizonans, it became clear that no one was really minding the ship. If they were, they didn't care, and if someone brought up the issue somewhere in the ranks, it was probably quashed. This is a perfect example of bureaucrats *correctly* doing their job. The bureaucrats didn't *really understand* what was going on: misappropriation of the likely intent of the legislation. It took the media to point it out. The bureaucrats couldn't bring themselves to correct the problem they were perpetuating.

MORE BUREAUCRATS AT WORK

My own experience with state government involved a semiconsultative assignment to change the health insurance funding mechanism for current and retired state staffers. During the second week on the job I discovered that a clerk had a drawer in her desk dedicated to (and full of) unprocessed retirees' checks for health insurance coverage, dating back over a year. After tallying the checks, they amounted to well over one million dollars. No one had ever taken the time to figure out what to do with the money. At least the clerk had the initiative to open the drawer and show me. She *thought* that something wasn't quite right.

In the same project I arranged for the daily electronic transfer of funds to an insurer, to complete a new minimum-premium funding arrangement which fundamentally saved hundreds of thousands of dollars in state monies. I had repeatedly asked the state financial types to become involved, but to no avail. Once they understood the positive impact, the merits, and the safety of this approach, the comptroller indignantly demanded control over the money movement, since that was clearly his jurisdiction, and I was legally out of bounds, over-stepping my authority in performing the task.

ONE MORE STORY

A few years earlier, working on a contract with a municipal government, I had completed a similar assignment, of reviewing bids for alternate insurance products and more cost-effective ways of funding insurance coverage. The comptroller, for whatever reasons and motivations (probably political and maybe personal), found two obscure state laws that prohibited implementation of the new funding process. One law described the duties of a comptroller, including a limited list of places public money could be placed (although not directly restrictive), and a second state law stated that public money could not be transferred outside the state. He was pretty smug about his apparent victory.

My first response was to tell the comptroller that if this project went down, I would be sure to advise the media accordingly, and I would emphasize that it was he who didn't want to save public money. His response was to call an emergency meeting with the elected body to which I reported, citing that I was threatening him and that my intended actions were illegal. My response was, *Yes* indeed I intended to follow through with what I told him, and if he perceived my comments as a threat, then I couldn't do anything about that. I stated, I was right, and if the comptroller didn't like it, he could explain himself to the newspaper, TV, and radio stations.

My second response was to immediately draw up amendments to the obscure laws and to lobby the appropriate legislative committees.

The laws were changed and the new programs were implemented. The savings to the public were not trivial, and the insurance coverage was improved. It apparently didn't matter to the comptroller that he might have an inherent civic duty as a public official to deal efficiently with public monies. Instead, he acted as a not-so-passive obstructionist. This person defined the term *bureaucrat*.

BUREAUCRATIC TRAITS, SYMPTOMS, AND INDICATORS

The examples cited above occurred in the public sector, but bureaucrats exist in all industries, occupations, and positions. They seem to gravitate to areas where they are welcomed: local, state, and federal government; academia/education; health care, especially hospitals; sales/account management; power generation and distribution; and, unquestionably, large corporations, especially those with government contracts.

Bureaucrats love administrative activities. One good indicator of whether or not bureaucrats are having an undue influence on the organization is the sheer number of staff (the more specialized, the worse it is) in finance/accounting, human resources, information systems, and any other function/department that supports operational areas.

Bureaucrats can be accountants, lawyers, public servants, administrators, academics/scholars/educators, and/or legislators as well as clerks and professionals of almost any type.

A FEW MORE INDICATORS OF THE BUREAUCRATIC MENTALITY:

- Bureaucrats know their procedures inside out and can usually quote chapter and verse of applicable codes and laws. They need specific rules to function, and if it isn't clearly enabled, it's probably illegal as far as they are concerned. Similarly, if it's not in their job description, too bad.

- There is a clear 8 am to 5 pm mentality, no matter the urgency of a project. It's not unusual to see public employees lining up at the door at ten minutes before 5 pm.

- Paralysis by analysis, concomitant risk aversion, and not taking initiative or responsibility for actions (especially for inaction). The most apparent initiative a bureaucrat will demonstrate may very well be focused on figuring out how to avoid taking on more responsibility and dodging exercising independent decision-making.

- If found to have made a mistake, they immediately attempt to shift the burden or declare some type of distracting defense. "*It wasn't my fault, the supervisor failed to train and supervise me.*" And, "*You put me in a job I didn't know or want, and then you kept me in it after I told you I didn't like it.*" Bureaucrats who are marginal performers seem to be better at keeping their jobs than doing them.

- Bureaucrats will seldom consider it their responsibility to use discretion, good judgment, reasonableness, and/or facts applicable to a particular case to determine their actions: it must be written and allowed, there must be precedent, everyone must be treated in the same manner, or a supervisor must approve it.

Note: The classic case in this area is Monel vs. NYC board of Education. In summary, school administrators discharged a pregnant teacher three months into her pregnancy. It was their policy and rule, they were the rule makers, and it didn't matter that she was physically quite able to continue earning a living. The board of education lost, at the federal Supreme Court level and a huge precedent was set, enabling the questioning of the exercise of power by public bodies (shaking up their "sovereign immunity") and allowing inflexible rules to be questioned, especially if the rules didn't pass a reasonableness test.

- Bureaucrats often do not understand that the manner of execution of a policy or procedure is often more important than the policy. Their response to a challenge of their authority can easily be indignation, legal citations (accurate or not), bluntness, coarseness, or incomplete exchange of information: "*Here's a copy of the rules, read them,*" and "*I can't do anything about it, the rules say.*"

- Innovation and novel solutions are not part of a bureaucrat's bag of tricks. Perhaps a good psychological description for a bureaucrat is (at least in part) the classic authoritarian personality, i.e., the good, obedient, unquestioning soldier who submits wholly to the directives of a superior officer, sometimes to a fault.

- Complete commitment to *process* vs. substance *and* process combined.

EFFECT ON THE CRIMINAL JUSTICE SYSTEM

It seems as though the best players in this arena are the judges who can and do exercise their judgment and discretion. However, below this elite level, discretion and independent judgment falls off quickly, replaced by self-imposed constraints and the inability to interpret and apply the law *around* real constraints, probably for fear of being sued.

Moreover, with the criminal justice system being heavily populated by bureaucrats and authoritarian personalities, it's no wonder that clever criminals mock the system with such regularity and effectiveness. Bureaucrats are no match for cleverness. Some of the more effective police administrators have admitted, off-the-record of course, that from law enforcement's perspective, the only true justice is street justice. A sad commentary.

EFFECT ON THE BOTTOM LINE

In any organization, the care and feeding of a bloated administrative structure is much more expensive than most organizations realize. It seems as though the larger a superstructure gets, the more specialized it becomes, and the more it takes on a self-serving life of its own: never mind the mission of the organization. Suddenly there are people stepping on each other's turf and all manner of political squabbles ensue.

In one small case in point, an insufferable bureaucrat managing a worker's compensation program provides an excellent example. Following the acquisition of a competitor, an investigation was conducted on why there was such a disproportionately high number of on-the-job injury claims, costing much more annually than would be expected. The administrator of the program was an in-law of the former owner. He split his time equally between two plants (one was one-eighth the size of the other, but it was in a nice part of the country where he had a second home). His manner of managing the program was to complete the paperwork and send it to the insurance company, which in turn and in its own bureaucratic way, simply accepted and processed alleged injury claims. Everyone blamed the high costs on the liberal system (a very convenient but inaccurate assumption).

Within one month, the management of the program was taken away from this individual, each case was questioned, thoroughly investigated and reviewed, and the number of valid cases went from hundreds per year to one in the subsequent two years. Costs were reduced dramatically.

Another *clear* example of how effective execution vs. "correct" process can make a significant difference in cost and outcomes.

IN A NUTSHELL

Bureaucrats are not the people you want for role models, and they should be avoided just as much as the loose cannons found in most organizations. Although they may be well educated, they aren't the bright, resourceful types who will help improve the organization. Given the opportunity, they will "wag the dog" and dominate/distract the operations areas.

Certain jobs require routine and infinite detail to complete the work, and bureaucrats can, if managed, usually perform adequately in this situation. They do, however, require supervision, or they may inadvertently create a problem by not understanding/identifying a situation as a developing issue until it becomes a *big* problem.

Message: *The best way to counteract the bureaucratic mind-set is to replace these underachievers with the best and brightest talent you can find, especially for administrative functions. Pay them well, allow them to perform many different tasks, give them room to innovate and improve processes, and don't have too many of them.*

7

Integrity and Ethics

WHAT IS YOUR WORD WORTH?

IF YOU DON'T get anything else out of this chapter, understand this potent little fact:

The cornerstones of your credibility, reputation, and the trust/confidence others will have in you are: following through with what you say you'll do, your truthfulness, your ethics, and the integrity of your actions.

This fact hasn't changed and probably never will. People remember your commitments to them and your actions, especially if you are in a position of power/authority. In a prominent role, you are watched, you are a celebrity, and people know more about you than you think. Even if you are not in a top-level position, if you do something deemed inappropriate, someone will know: that is the stuff of gossip. Following through impresses staff, and lack of follow-through confirms that you cannot be depended upon. If you don't follow through with something important, or if you do something unethical, see what happens to your reputation.

Wiggling with the truth, playing on words, suggesting that you said *you may* do something (but don't), or any and all variations thereof, all serve to confirm that your *word* isn't worth much. This is true in your personal life as well. Do yourself a big favor, and don't mess around with your credibility, or the trust and confidence others may have in you. This discussion ties in closely with the following chapter on *"Trust."*

WHAT GOES "ON-THE-ROAD," STAYS "ON-THE-ROAD"

That is a well known, rarely stated, often practiced, and closely held precept of virtually anyone in the sales/marketing, account management, executive, and management world who does a lot of traveling, entertaining, and interacting. The term typically refers to any number of activities, usually associated with entertaining business associates and usually involves activities you don't call home about. For those who know what this is all about, you'll find these examples interesting, and you'll have a little contempt for someone (me) letting the cat out of the bag. For those who don't or haven't had a clue, this is a reality check.

Consider these *very real* examples:

- The very-high-level New York banker who travels to check on an investment account he promoted, not showing any interest in the numbers, but expecting the hosts to "make him feel personally appreciated" when he's away from home.

- The CEO who has his VP/HR procure several escorts for the male corporate entourage visiting the division for several days (mostly golfing and partying).

- Several board members scheduling a joint venture meeting (about two hours long) in South America during "*Carnival,*" with the trip lasting four days.

- The account manager or the pilot who has a female (or male) "friend" in several ports, and perhaps even keeps score in friendly competitions with colleagues.

- Lavishly entertaining key clients in Las Vegas, the Caribbean, on chartered yachts, with only the best in food/drink/fun.

- Providing "customer appreciation" events at opulent resorts with open expense accounts.

- Maintaining exclusive memberships at faraway golf (or other) resorts, strictly for the pleasure and unwinding of stressed executives.

- The procurement manager who visits service or goods suppliers, accepts dinner invitations, and proceeds to order the most expensive meals and several hundred-dollar shots of rare brandy, at the host's expense.

- The corporate head from abroad visiting one or more subsidiaries and expecting to be "honored" with at least some (usually excessive) token of appreciation representing the part(s) of the country being visited.

- The account manager who binge drinks, hangs out in XXX-rated clubs, and indulges in escort services while away from home.

These instances are a matter of ethics and individual integrity. The extent to which these or similar activities are encouraged or discouraged defines the corporate culture; they are certainly a reflection of the actions of its individual constituents, but moreover, it says something about the company's leadership and its expectations.

In these types of situations, consider that while you're being serviced, catered to, appreciated, and enjoying it thoroughly, will someone have something on you that you may regret later and/or that could be used as insurance to keep the business?

EXTRACT THE INFECTION!

Now we enter the difficult world of privacy and potential/perceived invasion thereof by the *empowered* manager. Privacy rights are real and they must be respected, but consider also, that:

- Integrity/ethics have no boundaries, and that a personally unethical, immoral, untrustworthy, bribing, pandering, lying individual will at some point create a business liability, it's just a matter of time.

- Unethical/immoral/untrustworthy people tend to bring clutter to the workplace, and they can infect others with their mind-set, resulting in an erosion of the culture and eventually creating a culture you don't want.

- Individuals with less than excellent ethics are not likely to be focused on anyone's interests other than their own.

Accordingly, individuals must be tested for these characteristics before being hired, and they must be removed when discovered (especially if they are in visible positions).

Message: *These are situations in which "at will" discontinuation of em-*

ployment can be handy. If that doesn't work for you, call them conflicts of interest, disparate philosophies, incompatible styles, incongruent agendas, incompatible goals and interests, or whatever! It is important to get these people out: whatever they're up to, it's not optimum results!

A FEW MORE TYPICAL EXAMPLES

- Someone "on the make" will flirt anywhere and everywhere (man or woman), and they certainly aren't going to turn off their urges on the job: at a minimum wasting work-time, and at worst creating a harassment issue the organization will have to deal with.

- Raiding staff or securing proprietary information from a competitor will eventually result in a lawsuit.

- Hacking through internal or competitor's systems and violating privacy and/or confidentiality covenants will only lead to trouble.

- A bigot will find even more ways to resent and hate others in the work environment, especially if they are superiors or if one of "them" gets a promotion, raise, transfer, better assignment, etc.

- The small-time drug dealer will find an easy market on the job, and the heavy drinker will find ways to sneak drinks (or drugs) at the organization's expense.

- A petty thief will find plenty of opportunities on the job vs. on the street.

- The Holy Roller will try to convert people anywhere and any time, never mind critical time pressures for programs or projects; *their* mission is a righteous one to them.

- The lazy slug isn't likely to morph into a dynamo once he reaches work.

- The talker, storyteller, gossip, or comedian will try to garner an audience anywhere.

- The chronically, defensive, less-than-forthright person will be just like that in any environment.

- If you are a whiner at home, you will be a whiner everywhere.
- If you've cheated on exams in school, you'll cheat in other venues.

All of these examples and many more like them detract noticeably from a company's optimum performance. Realistically, a little bit of socializing and fun on the job is healthy; but when the reasonableness line is exceeded, socializing can become a liability and a risk not worth tolerating.

Conversely, the industrious person will probably be that way anywhere, provided their enthusiasm isn't quashed by a lousy boss or an incompatible assignment.

WHAT IF YOU ARE UNETHICAL?

It is not likely, but what if you come to the realization that you are an immoral, duplicitous, untrustworthy, unethical scumbag without any integrity? Is there any hope? Here are a few possibilities:

- Seek out and use (extensively) an *excellent* therapist.
- Find an organization where you fit in and can express yourself (meat-market bars and gyms come to mind).
- A little more seriously, take up some theology or philosophy, although you run the risk of perverting that as well.
- More realistically, look for an activity that requires a true effort to be successful: take it on with a passion, study it, and become a true expert. Find some real confidence and self-respect. *For a start, see the chapter entitled "How Do You Define Yourself?"*

The problem with people who tend to be even borderline unethical is they tend to fail the morality and honesty test in more than one way. They will never admit to anything, let alone being responsible for an error or anything that could cast dispersions on them. They are sneaky. They use half truths (or omissions) to get by. They can be self-righteous and sanctimonious. They are a hotbed of contradictions and non sequiturs. Many get by in their activities reasonably well, although most never really succeed (to truly succeed they would need to interact with people who would see right through them).

Shallowness (in many areas) is chronically symptomatic of these types of people: in their thinking, belief system, activities, tastes, and versatility. They love ambiguity since it serves them well, but their conceptual side leaves something to be desired.

If you are this type of person, the solution to changing your character is not at all a simple one. It would take years of effort and therapy to undo the habits of a lifetime.

Message: *For any and all of the foregoing reasons, get unethical individuals out of your organization!*

LOYALTY/INTEGRITY

Please see the section on "loyalty" in the chapter on *"Supervisor-Subordinate Relations"* for some useful insights. The discussion here, however, deals with the legal and moral side of that relationship.

What if your boss is illegally discriminating against you or harassing you (religious, sexual, ethnic, national origin, etc.)? There is, of course, harassment and discrimination that although distasteful, is not illegal: but *you* and your attorney can decide what is or isn't legal. Or, what if your boss asks you to use illegal pricing to put a competitor out of business? Or, what if you find that your boss is fudging on travel expenses? What if the boss asks you to "cook the books" and show more profitability than really exists? There could be many other scenarios. Assuming your boss is doing something illegal/unethical/immoral, do you turn him in?

The answer is unquestionably, clearly and definitively *yes!* If you know about any illegal activity and you don't bring it to the attention of someone who can deal with it, you become a party to it! Will that mess up your relationship with the boss? Count on it! Again, it's worth the risk, because the boss will implicate you (subtly or directly) as a responsible party at the drop of a hat if only to dilute the adverse attention he may receive. You may be left holding the bag if someone else discovers the issue and blows the whistle (it's only a matter of time), and the boss *will* implicate you in some way if he senses you may be a threat or a witness against him.

Anyone short on integrity, principles, and/or ethics will point the finger, shift the issue/burden, and/or divert attention given the slightest provocation and opportunity. Realize it, understand it, and deal with it in an aggressive manner. Don't allow yourself to be victimized or become a scapegoat in this type of a situation. Concurrently (and aggressively) proceed to distance yourself from that boss just as quickly as you can, in any way possible.

BE VERY CAREFUL WHO YOU "HANG" WITH

This concept is simple. It's called guilt by association. If you are new to an organization, be cautious who you become identified with, since you don't know about their reputations yet. At the risk of sounding parable-like: *empowered individuals must surround themselves with similar personalities, not their antithesis.*

THE CLEAN ORGANIZATION

Whenever there is something immoral, illegal, unethical, or otherwise questionable or inappropriate going on in an organization, it always seems to find its source in one individual or group with a very personal need and agenda. Integrity is synonymous with *incorruptibility* and, of course, *trust.*

It also seems that running a clean organization can be quite easy, if ethics and integrity are required in that organization's culture. Being clean does not mean being subservient or buckling under when faced with demands or attacks. It means, most importantly (this list is by no means all-inclusive):

- Maintaining accurate (including not overly creative, albeit legal) financials.
- Accuracy, truth, and a factual foundation in the representation of goods and/or services.
- Actively discouraging any and all unethical behavior, and inter/intraorganizational conflicts of interest.
- Living up to the general covenant of *"good faith and fair dealing"* in contracts and obligations.

- Making the customer or employees whole when errors are made or in the case of proven incidental or consequential damages.

- Living within the law (or better) wherever business is being conducted, and in one's personal life.

- Preserving market share by being better than (or buying and integrating) the competition.

- Controlling personal temptations.

- Avoiding dirty or clandestine tactics in controlling situations, spying on the competition, or deceptively negotiating agreements vs. using clean, hardball strategies.

- Politely declining suggestions for excessive entertaining.

- Making it clear that payoffs or under-the-table gratuities won't be part of the business picture (although international cultures and practices can't make this an absolute precept, it *can* be an absolute in this country).

- Taking actions consistent with the organization's purpose (goals) and strategies, for the benefit of its owners/stockholders vs. promoting personal agendas, philosophies, and priorities.

- Demanding that everyone in the organization subscribe to these (and similar) precepts.

PHILOSOPHICAL DIFFERENCES

Although it is often a nebulous concept, it can have a distinct impact on performance. The issue here is not a lack of ethics or integrity, but rather a disparate method of operating (style) and/or an incompatible personal orientation. Examples that come to mind include:

- A high-level manager who will not fire anyone for any reason because of personal or religious convictions;

- A successful marketing VP new to the industry ignores its dynamics and utilizes methods applicable to a different business (against valid suggestions to the contrary): resulting in a significant slowdown, losses, and layoffs (ironically creating situations the VP was also philosophically against);

- A loud, profane operations manager who alienates staff in a culture where politeness and mutual respect are strongly encouraged by top management, and who is unwilling or unable to adapt (change) accordingly;

- An inability to accept the validity of the nature of the business (animal rights activist working in a scientific laboratory, an environmentalist employed in a petroleum company, an extreme liberal in a for-profit corporation, etc.).

These situations, and many more like them, also result in less than optimum effort and results: but only because the person is in the wrong place or position Their personal convictions, abilities, and/or interests are simply (albeit honorably) out of sync with where they are and what's going on. In a different organization they could be quite effective.

Nonetheless, if this type of incompatibility exists, it must also be removed.

IN SUMMARY

Keeping integrity and ethics in an organization is not that difficult if *empowered* leadership expects nothing less. Simultaneously, the issues are just as convoluted, complicated, frustrating, challenging, and perplexing as any and all frailties of human nature. *BUT, if you can maintain a clean organization and you yourself are clean, it's much easier to defend yourself when needed and especially to assert yourself legally and competitively.*

It is reasonable to theorize that any individual with moral/ethical/ integrity problems will have their actions catch up with them, sooner or later, and in a manner they will find distasteful. At some point they will pay the price for their indiscretions and selfishness by way of: job loss and/or job-hopping, frustration with their own ineffectiveness, inability to grow in their career, guilt/stress buildup, mental breakdown, physical illness, personal life collapse, resentment and withdrawal, loss of friends and allies, or any combination thereof.

8

Trust

TYPICAL SCENARIO

AS A COMPANY (or any organization, public or private) grows and develops, the management of the company is faced with an interesting transition. The ones who built and grew the company can no longer do all the things they did before, there's simply too much to do. Now, the former entrepreneurs must rely on people who do not have the same drive, goals, vision, aspirations, or motivation to take care of the business. The overwhelming majority of these new people will be "average," meaning:

- Their competence, interest, and drive will not match that of the entrepreneur.

- Their range of activities will be much more narrow.

- It will take several of them to do what one entrepreneur was able to do alone.

- They can only handle well-defined roles and simple procedures.

- They can only deal with a few issues at one time.

- They can't conceptualize or innovate well, they must perform more mechanically and according to a rulebook or manual.

- Most important, they can't be told of your strategies or goals for the company. They probably don't care since they don't have an ownership stake, they probably wouldn't understand, if they knew they would tell someone who shouldn't know (like a competitor); and the result would be insecurity, demoralization, and diminished performance.

So who can you *trust* to share your vision, goals, and help you perhaps: grow the company, making it an attractive acquisition for a bigger fish and selling to the highest bidder, OR; find an acquisition to further expand markets and/or capabilities, OR; create any other strategic initiatives?

The fact is, you really can't *trust* or tell anyone except your banker (and that, too, is tenuous), your partners, spouse, and board members. Telling your staff would result in a serious damage control campaign, and you'll wish you'd kept your mouth shut.

TRUST AT THE MICRO LEVEL (ANOTHER TYPICAL SCENARIO)

Let's assume you are a first or second-level supervisor. If you are supervising former colleagues, this scenario becomes even more difficult. You give a close and trusted subordinate an assignment to prepare a portion of a presentation you will be making to senior management. The assignment involves detailed research, analysis, and the preparation of graphics. You describe the urgency and importance of the matter, and go off to prepare the remainder of the presentation, knowing full well you can trust the subordinate.

Within an hour of the presentation, the research isn't completed (someone didn't return a phone call). As a result the analysis couldn't be done, data could not be put into a graphic illustration, and the trusted subordinate didn't know enough about the project to even "wing it." Moreover, the trusted subordinate didn't tell you of problems along the way because it was embarrassing to her. The result: the *trust* you had in this person just went down the hatch in a hurry, to everyone's dismay. She inadvertently made you look like a less than capable or credible worker in a visible forum.

The moral of this story is not necessarily an endorsement for micromanagement, but something like that: especially when important projects or critical/complex issues are involved. Here are the points to consider and remember:

- Subordinates represent you, but they are NOT you!
- Checking on progress, thoroughness, details, accuracy, and logic is very important!

- Blind faith (or trust) in anyone presupposes they have your (or the company's) interests in mind as much as you do! Bad assumption.

- Ask yourself the question: who am I trusting to input financial, production, inventory, and other critical data into the system, and how detailed, thorough, attentive, interested, and qualified are they?

- Have you just delegated something you should be doing yourself because of lack of time, lack of knowledge, lack of ability, or similar reasons?

- If the last point is true, remember that subordinates have the ability and often the inclination to make you look bad, often with impunity. If you "dump" on them, they'll look for ways to make you look bad.

Case in point: *In a personal experience where I had just completed negotiating several labor contracts with trades groups for a large hospital, I presented the documents to the CEO for review prior to being finally signed and implemented. Her question to me was: "Can we live with these contracts?" My response was affirmative, and she said: "Excellent, go ahead, sign and implement them!" and she didn't review any aspect of the agreements.*

On one hand I was flattered and felt I was highly *trusted*. On the other hand, I felt there might have been some political "distancing" and "insulation" as a hedge for the CEO if something were to become controversial at a later date.

Message: *Regardless of how motivating it may be, don't do it that way! In an important matter, forget politics. If I were that CEO, irrespective of how much confidence I had in my negotiator, I would have insisted on being thoroughly briefed on the terms the organization had just been obligated to honor. Not so much to second-guess, but to simply know!*

ANOTHER SCENARIO

An inventory management supervisor was astute enough to set up a second mailing address for customers to send payments. He created bogus invoices and accounted for missing inventory with logical explanations (primarily quality problems, and customer rejections). He arranged for a bank account in a different city under his company's name, and he was the authorized agent on the account. He managed to divert tens of thousands of dollars into his private (embezzled) account. He had been a trusted, long-term employee who was well liked by the owner. A coworker blew the whistle when the company was bought out and the new owners took over.

Variations of this situation occur on a daily basis in all industries and occupations (receivables clerks altering checks, nurses sneaking unused drugs, office supplies finding their way to workers homes, kitchen workers dipping into the food stores, staff selling and/or using drugs on the job, employees surfing the web or checking out porno sites during work hours, the lists go on and on).

Message: *An empowered manager will deal decisively and affirmatively with this type of behavior. Company action (dismissal) must be followed up with criminal prosecution and if necessary civil lawsuits to recover whatever possible, and to make a statement to the organization that this kind of behavior will not be tolerated under any circumstances.*

INDUSTRIAL ESPIONAGE

It is real, it is prevalent, and it takes many forms. It may be outright theft and transfer of proprietary information; or it can be subtle, such as a job interview with a competitor. Important basic things to consider include:

- Your most trusted, capable, and reputable staff will often be targeted or involved.
- Trusted individuals who don't share their work with others on the staff should be suspected.
- Staff who rarely take vacations and/or who have been in the same job (usually handling money) for an extended period need to be watched a little closer.
- Supervisors should know about staff who moonlight or consult,

with whom and doing what.

- Jobs should be rotated periodically.
- Controls should be put in place to audit for conflicts of interest and outright theft.

A DELICATE BALANCING ACT

It can be very difficult to honor employee expectations for a reasonable level of privacy and at the same time protect the business from being picked apart through time, information, and/or material theft. A meager argument can be made that losses in these areas do not amount to very much when considered in the totality of the organization. A better argument can be made that any level of deception, illicit behavior, or theft chips away at the ethical fabric of an organization if it isn't addressed affirmatively.

WORKPLACE INVESTIGATIONS

Only one word of caution here: if an employee is caught doing something illegal, *do not* make the mistake of dismissing them for a criminal act. Dismiss them for violating company policies, jeopardizing the company's reputation, or simply "at will." This is a very important but subtle distinction. Try not to even use legal criminal terminology in the company's action. First fire them, and if indicated and you want to, pursue criminal charges as a second remedy.

If the company accuses an employee of a criminal act, the company may be setting itself up for having to prove that the employee committed the act beyond a reasonable doubt. Usually you won't be able to do that. If the authorities arrest the individual, the prosecutor may not pursue the case for any number of reasons (including not being interested in it or having enough staff to deal with it). The case could be thrown out of court on a technicality. If you leave the matter to the criminal justice system, you may end up with a criminal back on the job, smiling like the proverbial Cheshire cat after suing you for false arrest and other privacy infractions.

DUPLICITY

Politicians do it all the time. Nicholas Machiavelli was great at it, and he was considered a consummate diplomat. We expect duplicity from politicians and we can depend on getting it from them. Corporate memos and position statements are similarly vague when the state of the business is discussed; and senior management seems to dodge sensitive issues rather than give a straight answer more often than not. There are conflicting signals, mixed messages, and spins everywhere we turn.

There are omissions in fact and truth, there is deception, there is vagueness and obliqueness, and we are often *led to believe* in circumstances based on half truths. Explanations are often slanted to favor one party or the other, and what seemed to be important facts at one point could become insignificant later.

Trying to remain positive *(see "Positive or Negative" chapter)* in the face of what seems to be overwhelming duplicity all around us can be very perplexing. On the other hand, being negative seems to just breed more and more contempt, and eventually total psychological and/or physical withdrawal.

The reality is that truth is indeed elusive and duplicity will always be around. Sorting out the real vs. less-than-real is inherent in the nature (and limitations) of language and in the different intents people have. The classic situation is in "hearing what you want to hear" vs. what is really being communicated through evasive words, obtuse meanings, and/or body language.

The *empowered* mind-set will consider all possible implications of communication, organize the available facts, and make reasonable judgments based on the preponderance of the evidence, behaviors and indicators. That's about as well as you can do.

TRUST IS A RARE AND SELECTIVE COMMODITY

Trust is really a reliance on truthfulness and accuracy ("facts" if you will) and having confidence in any relationship (work or personal) to the point where you believe the other party will go, stay, or do something without you fearing the worst. The reality is that trust is earned over time, it needs to be reinforced continually, and it should be selective (i.e., any individual can be trusted to do certain things, but perhaps not others, especially in the workplace). Unfortunately trust can be broken with a simple action in a matter of seconds (such as getting caught opening your boss's appointment book to snoop around), and it can be lost for a long time thereafter.

When trust is broken, there is usually resentment and anger: someone is usually devastated and the other is trying to explain/minimize their actions. Repairing a broken trust is usually expedited if it is handled head-on, quickly and in as truthful a manner as possible. Stonewalling, denying, shifting blame, and all other contortions only add confusion, suspicion, and more allegations to sort out. Other options are to run away from the problem (ignore issues and work with the person as best you can), or fire them.

In summary, the concepts of "trust" and "truth" in any setting are more of an abstraction than people realize. You have to sort out fact from fiction, and you have to weigh the evidence and what it really means (to you, in the short and long run). Trust and truth are inseparable and are often confused in the *tangled webs we weave*.

THE "STRETCH" AND CONSTRUCTIVE TRUST

This is a perfect example of where a well-intended action (or inaction) by management could inadvertently create a problem with trust.

The boss has an invaluable staff member whom he wants to motivate and perhaps help develop by giving him/her a stretch assignment. Usually the good staff person won't reject the assignment, feeling they must accept it to remain in good graces with the boss. They really may not want to take it on but they do anyway.

Problems occur when the assignment is *well* outside the comfort zone of the individual. Here are a few examples:

- Asking someone to be creative when they aren't;
- Asking someone to write (like a newsletter article) when they struggle with writing;
- Requesting a cost-benefit or a statistical analysis when the person doesn't have a clue where to start;
- Assigning a person to supervise colleagues on a special project to

help overcome their introversion;

- Giving the person a job to conceptualize and develop a new program when their core competency is to implement them;
- And so it goes.

The result can be frustration on the part of the employee, disappointment by the boss, a mutual lowering of the *trust* level, and a situation that both parties will need to recover from.

Message: *If you choose to "stretch" someone, get their total buy-in, be sure they're comfortable with it, and keep it within their demonstrated skill-set and competency zone. Don't trust them to do something they aren't very familiar with, especially if it's an important assignment.*

The converse can occur as well. I can recall a personal situation, wherein:

In a particular organization, I was motivated and wanted to take on more responsibilities. I had the "band-width" and time to do much more. I had performed additional duties elsewhere successfully, but I wasn't given the chance in the new organization even after several overtures to my boss. The answer was that I was very good at what I was doing, I was needed there badly, and for the good of the organization the boss didn't want to dilute my attention. Perhaps sometime in the future additional responsibilities may be a possibility (provided I found or developed someone equally capable to take my place).

I think I was being complimented, but at the same time I felt stalemated and not given mutually acceptable assurance. My response was to look for a bigger job, commensurate with what I could and wanted to do. I won, and the organization lost.

Message: *DON'T EVER lose a good staffer in these circumstances, they're too hard to find. Do whatever you must to keep the good ones! If someone tells you they want more responsibility, LISTEN! Trust them!*

9

Notes on Quality and Compromise

BAD MOVIES

HAVE YOU EVER wondered why there are so many bad movies? Some that have been produced were so poorly acted and/or written, they were embarrassing to watch. One probable reason is that movies, like many or most other products and services, are a balance of quality and cost. Even though the film is crummy, a calculated portion of the population will pay to see it, and the film will likely return a profit if a proven formula is used (forget artistic merits).

In filmmaking, quality lapses in the same ways as in anything else. There are time pressures, deadlines to meet, and not enough time for retakes. Money constraints dictate the use of less than the best actors, supporting actors, locations, and special effects. And even exceptional acting can't offset a bad script, bland story, and poor writing. Given all of the specialists needed to bring the production together, there are many opportunities for making a mess of it. But then good marketing can still make it *financially viable*.

Industries may differ, but the dynamics and results are similar. It may be a sports team that never seems to get its act together (but the team still makes money for someone, notwithstanding losses shown in the accounting/tax records). It may be a product that everyone wants, but there are always failures and/or design flaws that eventually surface. It may be a lower caliber of service received from a proven mainstream consulting company: new, inexperienced players (consultants) are hired, and often aren't as capable, thorough, or talented as the once-hungry principals. The company still makes money. It's always a matter of balance: costs vis-à-vis quality. But quality can be materially enhanced if excellence is *built into* individuals performing the work and into the organizations. It's like the adage: *"If you don't expect and demand excellence, your expectations will always be met."* At the same time, having a high quality product or service in and of itself won't assure success. Even *good stuff* needs the convergence of good marketing, good distribution, and a receptive market.

ALLEGED QUALITY OF STUFF

Enter the world of marketing, sales, and spin. Everything is "the best," or at least as good as the best (if it costs less). The product may be intended only for certain discerning people who deserve it, ostensibly making all of us want to be in *that* class (above those who are unable to comprehend good taste). Wouldn't it be better if only good stuff were made, as marketers assert (but then trick you)?

If the final outcome of whatever you make or do is crummy (and it's usually because the design or ingredients weren't the best, or not assembled in the best manner), all of the quality systems, procedures, processes, training, or analyses in the world you may have used won't matter. It will remain a crummy outcome.

Conversely, if your final product is class-leading and "the best" and you haven't used much in the way of quality mechanics, how much do you really need in the way of quality systems? If your quality (outcome) is excellent and your price is competitive, no one will particularly care how things got that way (systems or no systems). If you have minimal scrap, no warranty activity, and it's profitable, whatever you've done is just fine!

In most situations, the question facing top management is, how much *quality* can you afford? Therein lies the compromise. The numbers will always favor a quality compromise. If the 80% solution solves 99% of the problems at 50% of the cost of the 100% solution, with less time, energy, staff, and distraction from the business, guess which solution will be used! A small percentage (contingency) can then be budgeted for failures, returns, and lawsuits. That's a no-brainer.

QUALITY CONTROLS

Many quality theorists assert and advocate that if you have a quality culture, you may not need oppressive controls (inspection and containment); and that people innately want to see quality come from their work and efforts.

Those assertions are theoretically compelling, but logically a stretch and not really practical. Just watch any person perform any repetitive task for any length of time, or a nurse who's worked two consecutive shifts. It won't be long before those individuals could care less about quality systems and what they're doing. They're just *doing,* and hoping they won't make a mistake (like lop off a finger or overdose someone).

The adage: "quality must be built in" (meaning people are designed out of and eliminated from the process) is the only *theoretical* way consistent quality *may someday* occur. But even a machine will malfunction, if only from wear and tear; and it will occur at inopportune times because someone didn't effectively execute predictive and preventive maintenance.

QUALITY CULTURE

Quality culture is a very vague and elusive concept. In practical terms it rarely exists beyond an individual or small group. Many organizations have mission statements built around it, and they play up the attributes and use measurements, often to a fault. Quality glitches will invariably occur regardless of how much emphasis and awareness is placed on the need to produce quality outcomes.

The *theoretical* aspects of quality are still compelling enough to keep thousands of quality staff and consultants not just fully, but overly and excessively employed. Training, lectures, consults, and initiatives in vogue today may help a little in the short term and on specific projects; but in and of themselves these types of efforts aren't going to create much of a long-term change, except for lots of costs for the initiatives and reduced efficiencies while key staff are in training. Here are a few realities from the quality front:

- Very few people understand correlations let alone statistical projections, but few will admit it, and fewer yet can assess the accuracy/validity of statistical analysis or interpret what the statistics really indicate.

- Notwithstanding good statistical information, if it's critical, the goal of any quality committee (in it's normally timid fashion) will be to discredit the value/meaning of the indicators or methodology used, and the emphasis will be to reconsider or reprove the conclusions vs. dealing with the often-obvious solutions that may provide the needed results.

- Prior to a quality audit (ISO/QS/Baldridge/JCAHO/etc.) the same pattern occurs: panic, staff cramming to review policies and procedures, training is documented, a bunch of other missing documents are generated, explanations are developed for missing components, and the auditor(s) are wined and dined.

- After the audit, obligatory warnings are issued about what *could* have been cited, everyone's cooperation is applauded, and the *passing* certificate is issued (along with the hefty check for the auditor's services). At worst (usually), follow-up visits (for more fees) will be scheduled to be sure committed improvements have been made.

- On a day-to-day basis, few if any of the staff (including supervision, and certainly not management) ever read quality manuals unless they are forced to. Some can't or won't read, others are too busy or too lazy, but most just prefer to wing it.

- Quality inspectors and auditors are often very political types who like to exploit their power and strut their stuff. Very few have the diplomacy to make constructive changes, and almost none have the authority or inclination to shut down production or work based on discretionary, interpretive calls.

- Most staffers in the quality department don't have the technical skills to perform their work credibly or accurately. They complete the "mechanics" of the job, but can't deduce or induce trends, find causal relationships, or determine root causes. Forget about fixing the problem even if the root cause is accidentally stumbled upon: that's another department's responsibility. Sound familiar?

- Statistics/data are fudged more often than most managers realize.

- For quality systems to work, they must be simple and easy to update, understand, and implement.

- Built-in quality (engineered to minimize human involvement/ error) is unquestionably the best approach.

- Problems very often result from a failure in *execution* rather than a failure in the concept, design, or formula/algorithm. The culprit is often inappropriate delegation to lower level staff who may not care as much about results or processes, they may not have the requisite skills, and they may not know enough to incorporate *poke yoke* and similar, frequent controls on key quality aspects. Excessive, inappropriate delegation of important programs is truly a formula for failure (or at best, mediocrity).

No Substitute for Good Management

There is *no substitute*, if you want a quality culture, for *senior* management being on the front lines frequently, looking at meaningful details, being truly interested, discussing issues with all staff, giving guidance and implementing solutions *on the spot. If you as a manager and leader don't know enough about the details of the business to do this, then you probably don't belong in that position.*

Using various frameworks (Kaizen, SPC, Fishbone, Shainin, Six Sigma, 10x, etc.) for solving problems may be useful for the disorganized, if you want plenty of staff exposed to and spending a lot of effort on little projects, and if time is not of essence. True root causes and causal relationships often surface through trial and error on the floor, not in a drawing or meeting room. Quality must be expected and demanded right where the action takes place, with the people who do the real work heavily involved!

Peter Drucker's classic adage is very applicable here: *"It's better to take the wrong solution to the right problem, than the right solution to the wrong problem."*

A Sense of Urgency

Probably the single most important characteristic that weaves quality into the fabric (culture if you will) of the organization is the *sense of urgency* to fix problems as quickly and affirmatively as possible. If there is a problem that needs to be addressed, *time* will always work against you. The problem will not go away on its own, it will continue to create more havoc, waste, and risks until you finally do something. This is true in any organization, situation, problem, and environment. In customer service matters, this precept is even more crucial. The longer a dissatisfied customer has to wait for some satisfaction (or even attention), the more friends that customer will tell about how badly you treated them.

The *sense of urgency* is also an individual, personal trait that is often absent from many managers and employees. If that trait is absent from staff in the quality department, it's time to replace the quality staff! The same people may know quality systems, procedures, and assessment methods inside out, but concurrently lack an innate sense to do something *quickly*. Rapid response is a huge opportunity. If an individual staff member is frustrated with continuing problems, with staff inaction, and has viable ideas and solutions, *promote that person now!* That's the *empowered* mind-set you must have to instill quality at all levels.

The analytical approach (paralysis by analysis): forming a committee, gathering the facts, reassembling the committee, may have its limited place in some situations, but you lose lots of time. Wouldn't it be a better use of a committee's time if the group were to consider a variety of efforts tried and/or completed that either failed or solved the problem, enabling everyone to learn from those efforts?

Message: *Hire people at all levels who are willing, interested, and responsible enough to take an occasional, reasonably calculated risk to solve a problem forthwith, stat, at their own initiative; even if it requires replacing current staff. Your quality efforts and results will be enhanced immeasurably.*

DOING NOTHING DIFFERENTLY...

...and expecting better results is to suffer a fool! You've heard it before, and it's absolutely true. *"Time and staff experience with the technique will solve the issue"* is a common solution. Ignoring problems and simply hoping they'll disappear without any impetus or without a catalyst ("*the machine just needs break-in time*") is another easy solution. Unfortunately, doing nothing (or doing very little to fix a problem) is a pervasive natural tendency. It is a defense mechanism and a head-in-the-sand reaction to change, which is (at least perceived to be) a destructive process to many people. Someone's work and efforts (maybe even reputation and competence) could be on the line as peers and managers critique processes, designs, setups, programming, and examine how *well* the work was done. Did someone screw up through omissions, oversight, incomplete thinking, or being rushed to complete the job? Or was it a bad design or process to begin with? And, who designed it and implemented the process? It is critical that the *leadership/management* does not tolerate the "*doing nothing and expecting better results*" mentality under any circumstances!

The tendency (as an offshoot of this "do nothing" thinking) is to deal with symptoms and functionally beat around the bush so that blame is diplomatically ameliorated. Unfortunately, using problem-solving frameworks for softening impact on whoever messed up, and/or for discovering and solving issues, can easily result in becoming caught up in the framework's own structure, limitations and procedures (i.e., you *must* follow the Kaizen, or similar, rules if you expect to succeed). If the Kaizen approach doesn't work, the tendency is to start over with another theoretical approach, consuming yet more time. A more effective approach is *attacking the problem, especially when a simple fix may conceivably be the answer. Don't worry about stepping on someone's ego or offending someone (as long as you don't do it overtly and rudely); take action NOW to solve the problem!*

SOME ADVANTAGES OF THE QUALITY "PROCESS"

Visibility resulting from collaborative meetings, the ability to express one's self to others in management, improved awareness of certain problems, all help to create a quality theme to rally around. If the *theme* is continually seeking better ways of doing things, and the time/money spent on discovering and exploring better practices doesn't offset the benefits gained, then it's worth the time. Also, if a serious problem or condition requires multidisciplinary review, a committee concurrently reviewing problems may help. But often the committee review *process* becomes an end in itself, and the charge/responsibility/obligation for committees to produce results/outcomes is not typically emphasized as much as it should be. Keep in mind that meetings require preparations and follow-up, and committee members are drawn away from completing presumably productive work in the meantime. The people closest to the problem (especially the managers) must be held primarily responsible for developing remedies.

"EMPOWERED" IS WHERE YOUR QUALITY THINKING NEEDS TO BE

Nothing beats attacking a serious issue from several angles if needed. But the keys are: *act quickly and act decisively*. Determining root causes and solutions is essentially, if done well, a *search-and-destroy mission*. It is fast, decisive, includes several contingencies, may or may not be clean (some *collateral damage* can be expected and tolerated if within reasonable parameters), it is swarmed with a purpose, and some level of success usually results from it. Plus it can be fun. But it requires a *true, determined leader who has enthusiasm and high expectations*. Adopt this form of action-oriented thinking (through assertive, engaged staff who really think that way), and you will have the foundation for a quality culture. Anything else is slow motion, if not just "going through the motions."

THE POWER OF EMPOWERED THINKING

On the "quality of business results" front, an empowered attitude (taking the initiative to solve problems) helps in areas often considered untouchable. It gives you the confidence to:

- Dump the unprofitable, and maybe even the marginally profitable customer(s). Why not replace them with better margins ? But find the better ones first!
- Replace customers who eat up margins by demanding excessive attention and staff time on useless progress and quality reports.
- Raise your prices if the margins arc being squeezed.

- Renegotiate pricing with *your* suppliers. If you feel the price pressures, there's no reason they shouldn't share your misery.

- Take out unneeded staff costs before a huge precipitating event such as a business loss (leading to a layoff): preempt it proactively! Ask yourself the question, even with staff at the VP (or even higher) level: *"What would happen if any particular staff member weren't there?" "What is this person truly contributing?"*

- Quickly phase out unprofitable programs or products.

- Find better banking/credit arrangements.

- Find some way to buy out or merge with that good but annoying competitor who's obstructing your progress.

You get the idea....

QUALITY TRAINING

Of all of the reputable (expensive and long) quality training programs I have attended, I can confidently say that I have come away with very little that I found useful for the day-to-day fire fighting most of us are involved with. I can also assert that I came away with very little useful conceptual/theoretical knowledge. TQM-type training is astonishingly and irritatingly obvious, inadequate, and incomplete. Quality training programs are more like infomercials. They are overly generic, they provide academic labels and descriptions, and they seem to be intended to sell more training and/or consultations. Their basic messages are: if you don't *really* understand their concepts, then you need more training; and, if you really want to learn how to improve quality, you'll need *much* more training: where they still don't address how to resolve real, specific problems (they only provide problem-solving frameworks).

Message: *Quality improvement, when examined beyond the engineering aspects, is dependent on individual mind-sets and is very much a long-term behavior modification process: no amount of conceptual preaching will change that fact. Change and control unacceptable behaviors (however you choose to do it) and quality will be better. More important, if* *you hire people who have better abilities and quality mind-sets, replacing current staff as needed, quality will be <u>much</u> better, <u>much</u> faster, even without doing anything else.*

QUALITY IN YOUR LIFE

This is a somewhat different idea than the standard "quality of life" idea, which addresses concerns such as being stressed, living in crime-ridden areas, breathing polluted air, being packed into tiny quarters, and so forth. This concept is also a little different from "quality time," which speaks to spending enough time doing things that make you happy.

Ask yourself the questions: *"Does my taste in everything I have and do raise my self-esteem?" "Do I have good taste?" "Do I look for excellence in all aspects of my life that are important to me?"* Or, *"Is the preponderance of my life a compromise?"* On balance, if there is too much compromise, it's time to reassess yourself, your position in your life, your relationships, and if motivated enough, to do something *differently.*

Here are a few good precepts to try and follow:

- Surround yourself with quality on all fronts (especially your appearance, demeanor, and presence).

- Diversify your activities, interests, abilities, knowledge, and skills (in hobbies, work, socially and culturally).

- Buy the best quality things you can afford, and hold off on buying if you can afford to wait so you *can* get "the best." This includes anything from hobbies, appliances, cars, vacations, etc.: try not to compromise on your prime interests and the tools that would enable you to perform at your peak.

- Surround yourself with people of quality. Remember, "birds of a feather…" and if your friends are losers, you will be (at least) guilty by association. Quality friends and associates are ambitious, ethical, intelligent, multitalented, and interesting.

- Find work that leads to something. If you can't find that kind of work, go back to school!

- When it comes to elements of style, good taste, and excellence, there aren't very many trendsetters (but lots of copycats and wan-nabes). Try to be, a trendsetter or at least associate with them.

ARE YOU "THERE" BECAUSE YOU DESERVE IT?

A very difficult possibility one must consider is: *are you where you are in your life because you deserve to be there?* Assume you just got laid off (for example). Maybe there's a good reason for your employer to have taken that action. This is where soul-searching, religion, personality, and motivation (positive or negative) all converge. If you're not a fatalist, then take control of your personal "continuous improvement." But you must think of it with the *empowered* attitude discussed earlier. Perhaps it's time for a personal "makeover" and "debugging" (so to speak). If you happen to be in a nice, cushy situation (and perhaps don't deserve it) enjoy it while you can, because things will change.

PERSONALLY SPEAKING...

The *"doing nothing differently yet expecting improvements"* concept is even truer in the personal realm, especially in the minefield of relationships, where one party or the other is somehow dissatisfied. The other party knows it, but hopes it will go away by ignoring it and/or letting *time* purportedly defuse any issues. Openly dealing with issues, finding solutions, and resolving matters can be a difficult proposition in emotionally charged situations. The language and approach used (execution) is the most critical factor. Unfortunately, someone may feel wounded, and attempts at improvement may encounter significant highs and lows. Even a little affirmative communication, however, usually makes things better. The *communicating/taking action* risk is a necessary one, because the truth is, in this area, unresolved problems fester and dissolve the fabric of any relationship.

PERSONAL EMPOWERED ATTITUDE

The way you carry yourself and the image you project will determine how people react to you and the impact you will have.

If you think of yourself at the top of the food chain (even if you're not), and you follow through with the self-improvements discussed in other chapters, you may just learn how to change, continuously improve yourself, and the results will probably amaze you.

10

Clarifying & Correcting Institutionalized HR Habits

THE PURPOSE OF this chapter is to illustrate how the bureaucratic attitude (the antithesis of *empowered* mind-set) can be operationalized, institutionalized, and allowed to continue unabated. While the human resources function illustrates this dilemma very clearly, the same precepts can be applied to all administrative functions.

Interestingly, a close facsimile of this chapter was offered to several professional human resource publications in the late 1980s and all were rejected. The minority opinion of several editorial boards was *"This needs to be said!"* (operations-oriented reviewers). The majority opinions, however, were *"Your positive and constructive support is needed, this type of critique is not productive"* (HR practitioners: sounds like them doesn't it?). Unfortunately, this occupation has indeed become a less than productive institution. Anytime any field or discipline can't face reasonable criticism (and even quashes efforts at disclosing flaws) it underscores the need to do exactly that.

FORM VS. FUNCTION, FUNCTION VS. DEPARTMENT

Managing the various areas typically associated with human resources (recruiting, benefits, records, compensation, employee relations, payroll, training, quality, safety/security, employee communications) is indeed important, if not critical, to the success of any organization.

When Human Resources, as a department, operates effectively, an excellent example is set for current staff and for new employees. They experience a professional, efficient, organized, and responsive operation truly interested in servicing its customers (current and potential workers). Often, HR is the only exposure the general public has to the company, and HR inadvertently assumes an internal/external-marketing role, providing a glimpse of the company culture.

When HR functions well, the impact resounds positively throughout the organization. Well-qualified individuals are hired, supervisors are informed/trained, policies are clear, paychecks are accurate, staff problems are quickly solved, and all forms of disputes are mediated. HR staffers are simultaneously company and employee advocates. A knowledgeable HR staff that fully understands the business and its needs demonstrates good judgment and reasonable discretion, provides logical solutions, and is flexible when needed.

This is where form (the "department") and function separate. Without a full and complete understanding of the intricate workings of the organization, the credibility and/or applicability of any actions HR staff might suggest are only hesitatingly accepted. Without this business ingredient, the spiraling down can occur quickly. HR becomes viewed as obstructionist, a bureaucracy to work around and/or avoid. Job descriptions are out of date, recruitments don't generate qualified candidates, HR staffers can't identify a good candidate from a bad one, and resulting operational needs are perceived as not being met. HR begins to view the managers as arrogant and noncompliant. Calls aren't returned (in either direction), training sessions aren't attended, supervisors take serious actions against employees without consulting HR, safety audits are considered witch-hunts; and an adversarial, wasteful attitude develops.

Most HR operations are somewhere in between these extremes.

BUREAUCRATS AT HEART

Individuals who gravitate toward the HR function tend to lean toward the bureaucratic side rather heavily. Many of the practices we'll discuss have evolved and continued over many years through ingrained, repeated, imitated procedures and assumptions about their need. Legal counsels have helped promulgate less than efficient processes, in many cases to offset inconsistent management, by insisting on excessive documentation. The root problems, of course, are inconsistent management and an inability to use good judgment (let alone document it). Since HR types depend on documentation to somehow instill better judgment, we have a circular, self-defeating, perpetual motion bureaucracy that doesn't quite satisfy anyone.

MYTH #1: HR DEPARTMENTS ARE CONTINUALLY DEALING WITH DIFFICULT/COMPLEX ISSUES IN THIS EVER-CHANGING MINEFIELD (OR, WHO IS REALLY PERFORMING THE KEY HR FUNCTIONS?).

Typical scenario: A well-qualified (experienced, certified, educated, and purportedly accomplished) HR executive is hired to shape up the department. A new organizational chart includes directors of employee relations, benefits, compensation, HR systems, recruitment, training, safety, quality, communications, organizational development, and maybe a couple of others. The "directors" also need support staff, perhaps "managers" in each area, followed by "technicians" and administrative support staff. Once the superstructure and specialists are in place, the work is about to begin, *or so we think.*

Let's examine where the important work is being done:

- Significant legal activities involving labor/employee relations (labor negotiations, EEO complaints, grievances, and unemployment challenges) are often farmed out to labor attorneys.

- Benefits costs are a province of the accounting department.

- Benefit cost projections, actuarial and benefit design work are typically performed by benefit consulting firms.

- Recruitment (particularly for key or higher level positions) is commonly given to search firms, and lower level positions are often filled through temporary agencies. Some internal "recruiters" collect applications and then dump them all on the hiring party (delegating work to someone who should be taking care of other business).

- Communications (newsletters, benefit updates, etc.) are often given to outside firms.

- Policy manual revisions go right back to the outside attorneys.

- Implementation of HR systems is almost always contracted with the firm selling the software.

- Training is almost always purchased from outside the organization, especially for management development.
- Consultants abound on the safety/environmental front.
- From the financial aspect, HR practitioners (at most levels) can't tell an EBIT from their elbow: *see Epiphany #1 in the chapter on "People Decisions."* This list goes on and on.

The company has the expense of a department of specialists, yet important work is often contracted out to yet more expensive *external* specialists. Other functions that either go undone or are contracted out include: assessing management potential, validating selection methods, updating/interpreting plan documents, assessing benefit costs and cost controls, new benefit plan designs, introducing "cultural" changes, and simplifying historically cumbersome HR forms and processes.

Paradoxically, HR execs and related specialists are generating higher salaries, for passing through difficult issues to outside parties who formulate the solutions; but the illusion is that since they are somehow involved, they are worth it.

MYTH #2: JOB DESCRIPTIONS ARE AN ESSENTIAL COMPONENT FOR RECRUITING, TRAINING, AND COMPENSATION.

REALITY: Job descriptions are notoriously woefully inaccurate, with no one very interested (or often knowledgeable enough) in keeping them updated. If they are inaccurate, they are useless.

A BETTER WAY: A few years ago I experimented with eliminating job descriptions altogether. The result was that no one missed them. Instead I developed occupational task lists. As a job opened up, the applicable tasks were listed and served as the foundation for the recruiting process, performance reviews, and for establishing training needs: simple, up-to-date, useful, multifaceted, job related, and very efficient.

MYTH #3: STANDARDIZED PERFORMANCE EVALUATIONS AND FORMS ARE NEEDED FOR CONSISTENCY, ASSURING NONDISCRIMINATORY REVIEWS, AND ACCURATELY DOCUMENTING AN INDIVIDUAL'S WORK.

REALITY: Most performance reviews are dreaded by everyone and are generally inaccurate. If they are inaccurate, they can be harmful in dismissal lawsuits. Many are behaviorally based (one or two steps removed from the actual work) and fundamentally invalid; and even those with goals (which often change during a rating period) have marginal impact and value.

A BETTER WAY: In another successful experiment, I boiled down performance reviews to their essential elements. This involved a short, concise *factual* narrative about the person's contributions (initially prepared by the employee), *facts* about how well the person completed the essential elements of the job (task lists), and a schedule for strengthening certain tasks. Supervisors learned what "facts" are vs. opinions or conjecture, the approach served several purposes, and accuracy improved immeasurably. Schedules for completing "reviews" became more flexible as well (often as-needed).

MYTH #4: ALL JOBS REQUIRE A SALARY RANGE AND COMPENSATION RULES TO REMAIN FAIR AND BE COMPETITIVE IN THE JOB MARKET.

REALITY: Each *person* and their respective knowledge, skills, abilities, and impact has a value, vs. lumping seemingly like-individuals into salary cubbyholes and artificially topping off their perceived earning potential. Operations managers will find some way to work around pay policy restrictions when they need to anyway.

A BETTER WAY: If you must have salary ranges, at least broadband them. Flexibility here is essential. Include incentives for completed education and acquired skills, use special bonuses (not just annually) for successful and timely completion of projects, give raises for assuming additional responsibilities, and adjust "ranges" (and even benefits) as the market changes (providing across-the-board adjustments selectively where needed). Static compensation plans, especially for key employee groups, are a problem. Better yet, enabling a blending of benefits and salaries has enormous positive impact.

Case in point: *Several years ago I implemented a phase-in of "flexible benefits," allowing individuals who were topped-out in their pay range (and anyone else as well) to eventually add as much as 10 percent of their compensation in additional nontaxable, flexible benefits (more time off, additional life insurance, additional contribution to health coverage, disability coverage, etc.). Once elected, the dollar value would have to stay in the benefit arena. Individuals could opt to put all or some of their annual salary increase (assuming there was one for the person) into this program. The positive impact was tremendous, tailored to individual needs, and easy to administer.*

MYTH #5: AUTOMATED AND STANDARDIZED RECRUITMENT/ SELECTION PROCESSES ARE NEEDED TO PROTECT AGAINST DISPARATE TREATMENT AND TO EXPEDITE THE PROCESSING OF LARGE NUMBERS OF APPLICATIONS.

REALITY: Good applicants/candidates for jobs (especially in a hot economy) usually have options, and they will simply go to a welcoming employer who recruits them, makes them feel wanted, and doesn't make employees jump through unnecessary hoops. Requiring standardized applications, for example, for technical or high-level positions, or screening out applicants by using rigid criteria (such as those often found in the infamous job description) or artificial deadlines, are self-defeating exercises that hurt the organization.

A BETTER WAY: This is where HR marketing and company advocacy have an important role. A good recruiter will convince the good applicant that they really want to work for this organization before compensation is even discussed. Also, something is lost if a recruiter doesn't review a resume and determine if the person's skills may be applicable somewhere else in the organization at perhaps a different time. Screening applicants for only one vacancy, or automating the process to pick up on key words, or not recognizing applicable (albeit not exact) experience and/or education, or eliminating candidates by imposing artificial deadlines, or just not knowing who the promotables are in the organization, may be easier for the recruiter, but there is no logical reason to allow these types of practices to continue (it's often a problem of the HR staff not being effective enough and trying to make life easier for themselves).

MYTH#6: TURNOVER IS EXPENSIVE, BAD FOR BUSINESS, AND IT MUST BE REDUCED AT ALL LEVELS AND AT ALL COSTS.

REALITY: For jobs that can be controlled (in terms of quality, speed, and output) with processes, strict adherence to procedures, and which can be learned quickly, turnover keeps production/labor costs lower (examples: production in Mexico, and producing fast food).

A BETTER WAY: Key contributors in the organization must certainly be retained as long as they are key contributors (things change), and individuals with potential should be promoted. But let's not agonize excessively over entry-level turnover in many noncritical jobs (with notable high-impact exceptions such as health care and others, which require lots of training and/or ability, with lots of potential consequences). In basic, repetitive jobs, high turnover keeps labor costs down and profitability up.

MYTH #7: SPECIALISTS ARE NEEDED IN THE HR FIELD TO KEEP UP WITH THE CHANGES AND COMPLEXITIES.

REALITY: Specialists have difficulty understanding the business in depth and they even have difficulty integrating all aspects of the HR program. Specialists never seem to have enough staff, systems or data to analyze assignments to their satisfaction, often resulting in the proverbial *paralysis by analysis* (attempting to compensate for not understanding the business).

A BETTER WAY: The effective HR operation sees the interplay and actually integrates all of the components in HR. A good operation also sees how HR impacts the entire organization. In other words, generalists are much more effective and responsive.

Myth #8: Certification Programs Have Established HR as a Viable Profession.

REALITY: Indeed, certain areas of HR have become increasingly complex and are ever changing. Unfortunately, many HR practitioners feel overwhelmed, and many key services have been contracted out, as discussed earlier. This has, perhaps inadvertently, relegated HR to a procurement role (i.e., not what it purports to be). Data gatherers and data input staff now seem most important in HR, with increasingly less decision-making taking place. Certification programs don't seem to have improved the occupation very much.

A BETTER WAY: If all of that knowledge gained from being certified isn't being exercised, for whatever reasons, then it's time for the organization to rethink what it would take to make HR useful and effective. See "Summary" for key ingredients in an effective HR operation.

Myth #9: Company Rules Should Be Issued to Staff in a Simple, Abbreviated Form, or They Won't Be Read; and Policies That Resemble Those in "Contracts" Will Only Encourage Unionization.

REALITY: Let's not be patronizing to our employees. All staff members must, and usually want to know, all the rules and expectations that apply to them.

A BETTER WAY: Give the staff details and eliminate arguments such as: "No one told me."

Case in Point: *In yet another successful experiment, I allowed nonunion staff to take grievances up to and through arbitration. Potential unions lost a major organizing weapon, nonunion staff felt like their grievance process had substance (vs. managers rubber-stamping each other's decisions), and managers became better at taking care of staff concerns.*

MYTH #10: FORMS ARE ESSENTIAL FOR DISCIPLINARY AND OTHER ACTIONS TO ENSURE CONSISTENCY IN ADMINISTRATION.

REALITY: Disciplinary actions are usually more stressing to the recipient on a "degrading" checklist type of form than they need to be. The essential element is the documentation of facts; and not the form.

A BETTER WAY: Use a memo format for documenting performance deficiencies or "disciplinary" situations, there's no good reason not to.

MYTH #11: STANDARDIZATION OF HR DECISIONS IS NEEDED WHEREVER POSSIBLE TO ENSURE FAIR AND LEGAL TREATMENT OF STAFF.

REALITY: It would be nice (and easy) to look up a similar (previous) problem with its documentation and prescribe the same remedy, but with most HR related areas that can't be done. Labor court decisions have been consistent in establishing that management decisions and actions must stand the test of *reasonableness*, and *good faith and fair dealing*. The mandate is that each case be considered on its own facts and merits, using good, prudent judgment and discretion. This is a good thing, and that is why so many adjudications are sui generis. There is no template: you have to think! Simply following the letter of the law, even using a precedent, and overlooking the nuances (which could be critical) of the immediate case is a common failing. This discretionary aspect to HR decision-making frustrates and stresses out many HR practitioners. Discretionary thinking (if it isn't there) is difficult to learn and be educated in, but many HR practitioners can't accept that fact. If a solution could be looked up in a procedures book, a clerk could be in charge.

A BETTER WAY: Using good judgment and taking a stand in a sensitive issue is very difficult for many people, and some just aren't good at it. In today's world, HR staff MUST be good at it, or they're in the wrong occupation.

MYTH #12: THERE CAN NEVER BE ENOUGH STAFF AND MANAGEMENT TRAINING TO ASSURE OPTIMUM RESULTS.

REALITY: Ensuring compliance with methods, policies, and procedures on the job (however it is done) is important. Training sessions (particularly classroom type) in and of themselves are often inefficient and wasteful. Retention of information from classes is often in the 10–20 percent range, time spent away from productive work often cannot be made up, and mistakes occur when good employees are away from their assignments. Management training is usually at the forefront of useless efforts. It is naïve to think that training will effectively change ineffective behaviors of managers in a few short sessions.

A BETTER WAY: If classroom training is absolutely essential, then be sure it is conducted by someone who knows the subject inside out, and keep the sessions short! On-the-job, on-site training is always best for jobs that don't require a great deal of discretion. Hiring capable managers who have the requisite personality traits is much better than trying to shape, mold, and/or work around individual behavioral attributes incompatible with management (it may take years if it works at all).

Note: see chapter on "Management Development" for much more on this subject.

MYTH #13: HEAVILY REGULATED AREAS SUCH AS UNEMPLOYMENT COMPENSATION, WAGE AND HOUR, LABOR BOARD ISSUES, WORKER'S COMPENSATION, SAFETY, AND ENVIRONMENTAL AREAS LEAVE LITTLE ROOM FOR MANAGEMENT, GIVEN THE PLETHORA OF LAWS, JUDICIAL CLARIFICATIONS, AND PRECEDENTS; AND IN THE CASE OF SAFETY/ENVIRONMENTAL ISSUES, SCIENTIFIC STANDARDS.

REALITY: Heavy regulation is all the more reason to manage in an *empowered* manner. The alternative is to be managed by those who would take full advantage of the situation and interpret laws to their benefit (see chapter on "*Bureaucrats*" for specific examples). Remember that courts require the use of discretion, the use of reasonableness in executing policies, legal decisions are very narrow (and should not be generalized), and each case must be considered on its own merits. Safety/environmental areas, which appear very scientific and precise, are in reality open to broad interpretation, speculation, opinions and varied solutions: a prime example of when even *science* can be something considerably less than *exact*.

A BETTER WAY: Heavily regulated areas MUST be managed assertively if not aggressively, with an empowered mind-set and approach.

In Summary

The bottom line: If you are going to have an HR department, the leader and the staff must have a broad base in law, accounting, statistics, psychology, business, safety, marketing/advocacy, and communications, and they must be technically able generalists. Most of all, they must know the industry and the specific business they work in, inside out: operationally and administratively. To be worth their salt, they must be multifaceted thinkers, not just personable/affable/likable people. If much of their work is to be contracted out, and outside parties are better at it, then HR doesn't need much staff, just a few clerks.

HR needs to take a good look at itself. Are its operations and procedures self-serving, bureaucratic, and cumbersome or do they genuinely and efficiently help improve the organization? Is HR solving problems important to the organization? Does the HR department know why it's there? Hopefully the answer is something like *"to enable all staff to complete their work as effectively and efficiently as possible and to improve the quality of human services throughout the organization."*

If flexibility, superb judgment, sound discretion, reasonable/defensible actions and decisions, responsiveness, practicality, innovation, accuracy, thoroughness, and being fully informed aren't in HR's bag of tricks; and/or if an HR superstructure relies heavily on expensive outside parties for key activities, then it's time for a change.

A likely argument from large organizations is that the foregoing suggestions may be workable in small settings, but not large ones. That assertion (and institutionalized Myth #14) falls under the weight of its own lack of logic, and indulgent need for expensive, monolithic control systems: *decentralize!*

Since HR should be the fabric of the organization, able to shape and/or change the culture as business needs change, integrating the function more completely than most companies do is a useful exercise. Rotating operations staff through HR and visa versa on a regular basis may be helpful. Most importantly, staffing HR with quality individuals is vital.

11

Why Management Development Programs Don't Work

LET'S REFLECT ON WHAT YOU HAVE TO WORK WITH

AT CONCEPTION, GENETICS have created a personality. Parents, relatives, friends, school, church, and television then socialize the person. Extracurricular activities, for which the person has affinities, further shape attributes, interests, skills, knowledge, and abilities. The person is motivated by any number of unknown factors: socioeconomic and personal. Behaviors and habits are learned over the course of (and ingrained for) many, many years.

The person may go to college or trade school, where specific subject matter of interest is learned, but little if any time is spent on learning leadership or management. Perhaps one reason is that teachers, professors, and scholars typically aren't themselves standout leaders or managers. They are knowledgeable and good at other things.

Now our brand-new career person goes into the world of work as an underling and observes supervisors, managers, and people with titles controlling their activities. Our underling learns (mainly through observation) how supervision and management happens. The person doesn't really know if it works well or not, only that management may be a pressure pot for whomever is in the role; or, the person may experience a lousy boss who is intolerable; or, if lucky, our new employee may be a recipient of good management, and it may be a reassuring (almost parental) encounter.

Our novice performs well and now it's time to be promoted. Bingo, a common assumption and error: a good worker is often presumed to be good supervisor/manager/leader material on the strength of their previous work and compliant personality. When the anticipated supervisory attributes and skills aren't demonstrated quite as quickly as expected, our aspiring supervisor is sent to a seminar to learn to be a leader.

Note: Other chapters in this book address the concept of effective empowered leadership, and serve to define the term from a variety of perspectives, all of which involve elements of: confidence, a sense of urgency, an action-orientation, common sense, sense of reason/discretion, comfort with challenging issues, being technically prepared, having a purpose, being motivated, and taking control of situations. This chapter stresses the development and assessment process vs. the elements essential for good leadership.

TYPICAL SCENARIO

So, for a few days and a few thousand dollars, our aspiring leader is off to a management development program where there will be 360-degree feedback, personality inventories, group interactions and lectures. The self-discovery process is underway.

The expectation by superiors is that a metamorphosis will start taking place, with the training providing needed insights, skills and confidence. Our new leader gives great feedback to the seminar instructors: the program was extremely interesting, enjoyable, new contacts were made, some personal soul-searching took place, and the seminar teachers were very knowledgeable and enlightening.

Upon return to work, our new leader quickly realizes that not much has changed. Our leadership graduate may be aware of more things, or so it seems, but someone didn't explain what to do on an issue-by-issue, interaction-by-interaction, day-by-day basis; and mentoring is hard to come by because everyone is too busy.

So, another follow-up training program is attended with about the same result. Frustration, disillusionment about management, and stress set in. Eventually our former underling fades into mediocrity as a manager, changes to a non-supervisory job, leaves the organization, or gets fired.

BORN OR MADE?

Message: *If you don't have "it" (the personality attributes to be an effective, successful supervisor or manager), you will not "get it" in a few hours of training.*

Changing the fundamental makeup of an individual is a many years process of *relearning*. Learning to compensate for weak management skills also takes time and lots of effort. Some individuals find management comes easily and naturally: they have an affinity for it, they handle and even enjoy the pressures and stresses, and the results are good. But many more don't perform very well. The answer to the age-old question of "Are leaders born or made?" is, if we don't try to complicate it: leaders are both born and made: it takes both. A naturally *empowered* mind-set is probably largely wired in from birth, but it requires refinement (diplomacy), preparation (technical and tactical) and practice (experience) to be effective vs. being brash, distracting, and even annoying (and thereby largely ignored).

Some are born/made for management, but those who are not shouldn't think twice about it (unless they're prepared to tackle loads of excess stress). In many cases, training someone for management when they don't have a "tough skin" (for example) is much like putting data into a poorly written or nondebugged applications program: the results won't always quite make sense.

Before you jump into management (for whatever reasons may possess you), put yourself through an assessment program: see a reputable industrial psychologist if your company doesn't have one, and determine if you fit into management. A common mistake occurs when someone with an aggressive personality honestly feels that he can effectively manage people. The result/impact from that kind of personality is often intimidation of staff, impatience, harshness, and an inability to find compromises or workable solutions. Honing aggressiveness into an effective management form can be as difficult as lifting a timid or introverted person into that role.

Regardless of how badly someone wants to be a manager (perhaps for the money and status that goes with it), if the personality attributes aren't there (regardless of how much training, education, and development takes place), it will probably be a marginal success at best.

Studies have shown that failures in management rarely result from technical inabilities in the person's occupation, but due to various style incompatibilities with the staff, with their boss, and/or with expected performance/results. Remember that it takes years to offset inbred and learned traits/habits, and you really can't change your personality. So, before you jump into management, make a genuine effort to find out if you should (or really want to) be there!

ELUSIVE TRAINING OUTCOMES

Management training and development programs (especially generic canned ones) suffer from a lack of ability to correlate with increased effectiveness and improved results on the job. Most such programs cite plenty of disclaimers (if you pay attention to them) about what the program will or won't accomplish, probably for legal protection.

On the other hand, if a person has an affinity for management work, providing the technical knowledge/tools of management is a viable exercise. Effective tools would include detailed how-to's, case studies, simulated exercises, and theories in fundamentally all administrative functions (supervisory issues, management expectations, legal issues, HR matters, financial/costing aspects, communications, data collection and assimilation, sales and marketing, strategic planning, analysis, etc.).

MANY WAYS TRAINING PROGRAMS FAIL

- Reputable programs are usually expensive. Add to that the cost of transportation, lodging, food, and time away from the job. High costs result in management having high expectations for results. When results are marginal, stresses begin to build.

- Most management development programs are very general, descriptive, academic, theoretical and/or behaviorally based. In other words, their applicability to any given business environment may require some real stretching (assuming *any* tangible new skills are offered, attained and retained).

- A training program can be well over the participant's head due to: minimal or no basic understanding of management, overly advanced concepts/design of the program, or due to the participant not having sufficient reading/writing/thinking abilities to follow what's going on. Not many (if any) expensive development programs turn away participants.

- As stated earlier, changing a person's behaviors or personality isn't going to occur after one or two programs, and maybe not even after many of them. Changing those overbearing or introverted personalities, for instance, would likely take years of therapy, if it occurs at all.

- There are too many technical pieces to management to have a new participant in a general program really understand how all the complex and often contradictory and confusing elements come together.

- The program may be too specialized to have much, if any, on-the-job significance. Or, the program, although interesting, may be well out of reasonable reach for the person for years to come (e.g., learning about legal theories in adjudicating acquisitions and divestitures is hardly applicable to someone who only manages a small department and budget).

- There may be too much of a junket atmosphere. A new manager may be sent to say, San Francisco, where he has never been. All the sights, sounds, and smells of this unique town overwhelm the person. A party atmosphere can develop quickly, especially among new acquaintances, even to the point of not paying much attention in class vs. planning the next day's explorations.

- The program can turn out to be just plain crummy. My own experiences recount a legal seminar in Denver, accredited for sixteen CEUs, and touting nationally known speakers. The class notebook was passed out during registration, and the speakers proceeded to read directly from the book. I left midway through the first day along with half the class and in a few weeks received my CEU certificate. I guess no one really wanted to be there.

- A training course can be very interesting, entertaining, receive high marks from its attendees, but not have any applied value:

such as with motivational speakers. The upbeat effect and/or inspirational message wears off quickly.

ASSESSMENT TECHNIQUES: THE WAY TO DO IT RIGHT!

Job-related assessment techniques are probably the best predictors of determining: who *cannot* perform *any* job (including management); to a slightly lesser extent who *can* perform *any* job well; and with exceptional accuracy, indicate areas needing attention, development, training, coaching, and/or improvement.

Assessment techniques, when administered correctly, are especially good at discovering the depth of some very important traits essential to leadership such as: discretionary use of power, judgment, reasoning ability, ethics, and integrity as well as any and all technical abilities.

The *very* best way to determine ability to perform is to put the person into the job and see what happens. That is probably any manager's (and risk manager's) worst nightmare, especially if it involves an important position. Short of that, the next best method involves simulating the most important and/or difficult aspects of the job, and having a "jury" (several people already successful in that job) rate the results. This process is called *assessment,* and some companies call them *assessment centers.*

For supervisory and management positions, traditional selection processes yield results similar to a coin toss. Then, once someone is selected for a supervisory+ position, the one(s) choosing the person often overlook small deficiencies, to (they think) protect management *integrity.* Unfortunately it doesn't work that way. A poor supervisor will make all of management above look bad, and the damage done to good employees may be irreversible (i.e., they'll leave). Assessment techniques, when executed well, can predict poor performance with 90–95% accuracy, and excellent performance in the 80–85% range, as contrasted with the traditional 50% prediction rate resulting from even multiple interviews. It is well worth taking the time and effort to choose well.

Moreover, encouraging individuals to participate in exercises designed for the position they are trying to eventually achieve (even though they're not quite ready) provides one of the best reality checks possible and some of the best training available in the management development area. It's time-consuming, but it's worth it.

Assessment techniques involve a series of exercises, all taken directly from actual experiences of those performing the work, and mimicking actual work performed and decisions made. The candidate may have to: make several written responses to complex or difficult (discretionary) issues; role-play an interaction with a colleague or employee (with a prestated, desired outcome); make a presentation; chair a group problem-solving session; complete a financial analysis; develop a plan or recommendation on a sensitive matter; determine how to address an issue; make important decisions and then defend the action(s); perhaps complete a psychological profile; and there are many more possibilities. The jury of experts each has their ratings assessed for reliability vis-à-vis the other raters, to ensure consistency in observed behaviors and responses. The process works remarkably well when done correctly.

ATTRIBUTES OF A MEANINGFUL MANAGEMENT DEVELOPMENT PROGRAM

Assuming you choose not to embark on a full-scale (or even an abbreviated) *assessment* program, the following suggestions will be an improvement over traditional efforts, and it would be an efficient way to follow up on performance deficiencies you have discovered.

Beware of canned or prepackaged programs, their usefulness is extremely limited. Unfortunately many in-house trainers often don't have the curriculum development skills, or the experience or expertise to pull together a credible high-impact program.

Message: *It is well worth the extra money to find an excellent assessment-capable individual to run any of your training programs. The difference in approach (total job-relatedness) and the difference in impact will be significant. Standard "trainers" tend to use canned/purchased formulas and structures that can be very general and often ineffective.*

Let's examine the elements of a good *macro* approach (for several participants in a continuing program) and a good *micro* program (for individuals and their specific development needs). Using both approaches, preferably as a supplement to your *assessment program,* will result in surprisingly good (and measurable) outcomes.

IN SUMMARY, AN EFFECTIVE MACRO (GROUP) PROGRAM LOOKS LIKE THIS:

- It must have 10% (or less) theory, and 90+% specific how-to's, do's, don'ts, whys, and why-nots.

- Most important, real-life case studies and problems must be actively practiced, role-played, solved, and critiqued (by the group and the instructor). Written and verbal exercises must be utilized, including some requiring research by the participants.

- Programs must be brief (1–2 hours maximum).

- Sessions should be conducted in the organization's on-site facilities, bringing together a broad range of supervisors with similar amounts of experience.

- There should be no more than twelve participants at each session.

- Subject matter must focus on a maximum of two to four messages per session.

- Sessions should be held once every two to four weeks (allowing time for absorption), with the entire program being completed in three to six months.

- There should be one moderator for the entire sequence of sessions, with a variety of presenters, consistent with their expertise.

- Local college accreditation (and/or CEUs) and a certification of completion should be provided (if all sessions are attended).

- Providing several levels of training would be appropriate, consistent with the experience and level of the participants.

A PRACTICAL MICRO (INDIVIDUAL) PROGRAM WOULD INCLUDE:

- Completing a list of the important TASKS the individual *must* perform well to be effective.

- Completing an inventory of the person's knowledge, skills, abilities, and proficiencies in executing each of those tasks.
- The resulting list of weak areas will identify the development needs.
- Then, focus on addressing not more than two (2) needs per year, and assessing on-the-job progress in the weak areas continuously. This could involve any combination of: seminars, one-on-one coaching/mentoring, temporary or special assignments, college classes, on-the-job training, or even self-study. The key is to give weak areas a lot of attention.
- Insist on execution of the plan during the year, no excuses.
- Repeat the cycle, usually after a year, or immediately upon a promotion or reassignment.

Using this approach, task lists can replace job descriptions, that are notoriously out of date. And a proactive, constructive development approach partially replaces the dreaded and often useless performance reviews: often effectively shifting the burden of performance and improvement onto the staff member.

EXECUTION

The remaining issue is: *Who should pull all of the aspects of the programs together?* The *macro* sessions should be moderated and/or conducted by a manager who has a good reputation and lots of experience dealing with practical issues, along with the administrative help of a training staffer.

The *micro* approach is strictly between participant and supervisor. The champion for making sure there is continuing momentum should be the VP/HR or even the CEO. A word of caution: delegating aspects of the program to an outside consultant risks losing the critical perception of a close job-relationship. Training consultants all too often tout customized programs, but most really aren't.

These formulas for improving the effectiveness of management training and development are simple and effective. It is very important that the programs are conducted by and carry the credibility of someone who has been successful in your organization. The role of training specialists should be to help organize material for these in-house experts, and not to conduct the sessions (they simply don't know enough).

COACHING: ONE OF THE BEST DEVELOPMENT TOOLS

Case in point: *A very effective way to develop an upcoming management understudy is to give that person an opportunity to make a significant decision, on their own. Give them options with the upsides and downsides, provide general parameters (with maximum dollars if needed), and then tell them: "You decide, follow through, and keep me informed of any problems!"*

You've shown trust, given them responsibility, and now you'll see if they can handle the pressure. If they're good, they'll appreciate the opportunity, be flattered, feel good, perhaps even be motivated, and will probably perform quite well.

12

Organizational Development and "Training"

WHAT ORGANIZATIONAL DEVELOPMENT SHOULD BE

IF YOU ENVISION *organizational development* as anything other than being totally synchronized and integrated with the strategic business plan, then you're missing an excellent opportunity.

In many organizations, this term, where it's still used, has become a euphemism for succession planning, job expansion, and training. However, to be truly useful and effective, "organizational development" must include *any* method that serves to constructively change, improve, and upgrade the effectiveness of the organization; and to fundamentally prepare it for its next phase of evolution (it may be growth, sale of the business, purchase of and combination with other operations, vertical or horizontal integration, taking it public, downsizing for cash-cow profitability, or other possibilities). And, of course, the direction the company chooses to go will determine what needs to be done. The point to know in this context is that there is no single course of action that fits all possibilities.

So first you must know what you want to do with the organization in the one-to-three-year time frame. Without that framework, anything you do in this area is flailing around without purpose and direction. The next ingredient of effective *organizational development* must be a full and complete knowledge of how the business operates, and what it takes to be successful and improve upon any success within the context of your strategic goals.

Extensive knowledge of where current business/organizational deficiencies exist and how long the organization can tolerate those

114

deficiencies is the next key component. Knowledge of the industry as a whole, including competitive activities, best practices, but more important the markets you hope to secure and what it will take to do it are all critical. Qualitative and quantitative benchmarks are certainly helpful for measuring progress, but let's be very careful here; it's very easy to get caught up in seemingly important but truly peripheral activities and efforts.

Message: *The element common to any direction the organization will take and the single most important point of reference will always be financial, and all the ingredients that lead to profitability.*

The next critical ingredient is having a broad repertoire of methods to achieve projected plans, fix deficiencies, and fundamentally continuously improve various aspects of the organization. The list of methods to consider in addition to the ones mentioned earlier should include any and/or all of: mergers, acquisitions, divestitures, company restructuring, joint venturing, departmental/divisional reorganization, outsourcing/contracting, removal of extraneous costs, making operations as lean and streamlined as possible, introducing automation wherever feasible, and of course financial restructuring in any number of variations.

Note that "training" pales in importance when compared to any- and all of the strategic possibilities. From the business perspective, except for reducing liabilities or waste in technical and/or medical areas, training is the least efficient way in terms of time and impact, to achieve big-picture, strategic success.

Nonetheless, all organizations have to work with the aggregate staff competence available to them, and the balance of this chapter will describe how to kick off an effective internal people-development program, totally integrated with the workings of the business.

IMPLEMENTING PEOPLE-DEVELOPMENT

The following outline illustrates how the simple and logical integration of several systems can provide immensely improved usefulness, reduce bureaucracy, and improve impact when it comes to improving staff resources. This approach is especially attractive in that, if it is executed well, it meets/exceeds ISO/QS requirements.

- Start with a list of departments in your organization.
- Fill the list in with all of the essential tasks and functions for that department (you may expand it to include all of the knowledge, skills, and abilities needed, but be careful not to clutter the list with behavioral characteristics and "qualifications").
- Add to that list, all of the utilized titles and check which tasks/ functions apply to each title. Now you have a grid with Departmental Tasks in a column, and Titles across the top, with checkmarks noting which tasks apply to each title.

IMPORTANT: Now you have the guts of effective, easy to update job descriptions, elements you may want to include in performance reviews, a checklist for job applicants to complete (very valid), and the components for an advertisement to attract those applicants. This exercise provides a factual, cross-functional, job-related foundation for many applications.

Now for the implementation:

- Have current employees check the list and indicate which tasks they are fully capable of completing without supervision. Have the supervisor review each list. This provides an individual _development needs_ list, and a basis for setting up improvement schedules with finite timelines. This exercise also tells you who may be in the wrong position(s) and help you place the individual commensurate with their knowledge, skills, and abilities.
- Next, take the matter up a level and have management look at the task lists per department and indicate where problems have occurred in terms of day-to-day errors and execution problems. This exercise provides a list of _performance deficiencies_ and a way to prioritize areas that need immediate attention.
- This in turn prompts any one or more remedies: department-wide training, individual training, reorganization, recruiting individuals with better credentials and/or experience, realigning responsibilities, combining with another department, providing individuals a deadline to raise their skills or be reassigned, to name a few options.
- The decision on how emphatic and rapid the solution should be

will be dictated, as mentioned earlier, by how much tolerance there is for allowing the deficiencies to continue. Then it's just a matter of implementing the best solution(s).

So, now in one meaningful exercise, you've addressed: job descriptions, advertisements, performance evaluations, individual training needs, aggregate development needs, departmental quality issues, helped identify the most needed and expedient remedies, and *all are job related* (not a trivial consideration in today's litigious environment). But it gets better.

You've also created a mechanism to determine whether or not the initiatives have any impact. Correlations can be made with the initiative (training, reorganization, etc.) vis-à-vis any performance or business indicators you choose, preferably financial ones. Again, this too is not trivial, since it is always expected, rarely done, and it provides an empirical base for measuring meaningful improvements. This quantifiable aspect plays well with quality audits of any type and level.

YET MORE POSITIVE IMPACT

Other multifunctional benefits to this approach include:

- *Pay programs* can be tailored to individual improvements, providing incentives for timely completion/attainment of key skills. Also, individuals can be frozen in pay until they meet certain expectations: correctly and effectively shifting the burden.

- *Succession/promotion* planning programs spin out of this approach very easily and effectively. Staff will know the skills they need to develop to progress in their current (or other) career, and individual plans can be tailored to meet their interests. If combined with *assessment* processes mentioned in earlier chapters, identifying promotable individuals becomes immeasurably more effective.

There is every reason to try this streamlined approach. In practice it is very efficient and it works! The biggest problem will probably be finding the "champion" capable of understanding, integrating, implementing and managing all of the components. Although intuitively simple and obvious, the concept may be perplexing to many traditionalists.

NOTES ON ADULT LEARNERS

For anyone conducting training sessions within an organization, here are a few points to consider as you develop programs and make presentations.

I have found that with today's adult learners, relevance, applicability to the everyday work environment, specific solutions/remedies to problems, and enthusiasm in delivery are essential to providing the job-related and useful experience they expect. Personal diatribes, soapbox oratories, heavy reliance on history/theory, and monotone reading from prepared text are typically met with indifference, yawns, and inattention.

Message: *When developing/administering training programs, don't assume that reading/comprehension, writing, and math abilities will be anywhere close to that of a high school graduate (even for management-level sessions). Few (if any) instructional programs check the level of proficiency adult participants may have in these areas. If there are deficiencies, and there will be, the effectiveness of the program will be substantially compromised and results simply won't be there. Consider offering remedial reading, writing, and math programs as a practical, continuing need. Most adult learners will not admit deficiencies in these areas, so you will probably have an unexpected prerequisite program to deal with, and/or an unexpected challenge.*

When it comes to actually making presentations to adult learners, an effective teaching philosophy would challenge the instructor:

- To be excited about the material to the point of being infectious, to be affable, and to be fully prepared for each session.
- To draw out/generate/provide real or realistic case studies, anecdotes, situations that need some action taken by management.
- To explore solutions, assess risks factors associated with different actions, and try to find the most appropriate remedy and reasonable closure to the issue(s).
- To explore and experiment with novel concepts and multidisciplinary approaches.

- To interact, participate, and guide learners vs. dominating and dictating.
- To use active oral interactions (role-plays) and critique written responses (memos and reports) openly with the learners to simulate on-the-job feedback.
- To expect effort, accuracy, thoroughness, neatness, attention to detail, logic, research, involvement, and active participation from each learner (fundamentally, a high quality level).
- To inject some fun, lightheartedness, levity, and creativity into classroom activities.

Example: *For a graduate class in labor relations, I had the students choose a side: one negotiating team was the faculty and the other was the students. The two groups had to negotiate the standards by which the students would be graded (papers, tests, etc.). I told them if their negotiated settlement was reasonable (I reserved a veto, like a governing body), I would accept it. They played their roles well and they learned the dynamics of negotiating in a team environment. Since they had something real at stake, they paid lots of attention to the details.*

Section 2

Individual Realities

13

Are You Competent
...and Successful?

VIRTUAL COMPETENCE?

THE *WEBSTER'S COLLEGIATE Dictionary* definition for *competence* that applies most closely to our discussion is: "*having requisite or adequate abilities or qualities.*" The notion of being adequate certainly seems flat, very average, and smacks of getting by. Even the sages view competence, in and of itself, a little cautiously, to wit:

> "Work is achieved by those employees who have not yet reached their level of incompetence." *Laurence J. Peter*

> "Even if you're on the right track, you'll get run over if you just sit there." *Will Rogers*

The elusiveness in operationalizing and assessing anyone's *competence* occurs when one starts asking: *"At what? In whose opinion? By what standards? At what point in time? Under what circumstances?"* and so forth.

And then there is the matter of being truly competent vs. giving the impression of being competent. There are those who are verbose and very articulate, but are they really competent? See chapter entitled *"They Speak with Such Power and Conviction"* for more on that subject. Making matters a little more confusing, if a person holds a title such as "professor," "CEO," or "manager," there is a built-in assumption of competence by virtue of having attained a powerful or influential perch. Then there are the people who can't help but embellish (or slightly exaggerate) their achievements (ostensibly competent at what they claim, but more certainly competent at overstatement; and there's usually no one interested enough to call a bluff). Truth-stretchers are discovered and understood as such by most people quite readily.

An interesting question for your intellectual curiosity: Is there the same proportion of competent and less-competent people in each occupation (from laborers through scientists)? The number of superstars in any area can usually be counted on one hand per activity or occupation. So, is it a skill alone, or are there other elements that allow one person to really excel and become successful, while the bulk of people in an occupation or pursuit are average, denizens of the hump on the bell-shaped curve? If the answer is *yes*, which is the likely case, then there are lots of *diversely* competent people out there (a broad range: from barely to exceptionally competent) in every occupation and pursuit. That notion can be unsettling when applied to your medical practitioners, lawyers, and others you tend to depend on. In the organizational setting, controlling and channeling various degrees of competence is probably the foremost management challenge.

WHAT IS COMPETENCE?

Most people would say that being competent is simply being good at doing something, at least as good and perhaps better than others doing the same thing.

Competence is a combination of a well-practiced/disciplined set of technical knowledge, skills, and abilities demonstrated through a package of personality traits (social skills) that enable, or deter, the person from a desired outcome. In the case of an athlete, or a creative type, having the requisite physical structure and/or mental makeup adds another dimension. Two of the aforementioned three categories are usually good enough for establishing competence (the technical skills and the enabling mind-set).

Without *competence*, your *success* is likely to be relegated to occurring (if it does) in spite of yourself or by accident: not very good odds.

WHAT IS SUCCESS?

"Success" for the purpose of our discussion does not necessarily mean fortune and fame, just *achieving what you want*. But as we will soon see, you really have to want whatever it is, make sure it is realistically attainable and then go for it with an *empowered* attitude. *Webster's Collegiate* defines success as: *"favorable or desired outcome"* and *"the attainment of wealth, favor, or eminence."* Our sages give us a few more succinct insights:

"Success is simply a matter of luck. Ask any failure." *Earl Wilson*

"The secret of success is constancy of purpose." *Benjamin Disraeli*

"Do your work with your whole heart and you will succeed—there is so little competition." *Elbert Hubbard*

"The chief factor in any man's success or failure must be his own character." *Theodore Roosevelt*

"Success usually comes to those who are too busy to be looking for it." *Henry David Thoreau*

"The road to success is usually off the beaten path." *Frank Tyger*

So there we have it, *competence* is the beginning, and *success* requires a few more ingredients. The most important ingredients for *success* appear to be having a purpose and the *empowered* attitude to go for it.

HOW DOES ONE BECOME COMPETENT?

The basic elements of competence are: *technical skill, personal attributes,* and *physical abilities.*

For most people, two out of three of these elements is all they get, and often that's all they need, along with the right mind-set, to be successful. Luckily, most people end up being competent in *something,* whether they like that something or not; and many people are quite good at several things.

A disciplined athlete with the right physical attributes can probably get along fine without social skills. An accountant with lots of technical knowledge and the ability to pay close attention to details, but without superb physical abilities will also fare well. However, a knowledgeable professor who is intolerant of lesser mortals, talking down to them, will probably fail as a teacher. Similarly, the aspiring musician who has superb technical execution but no soul will never break though, and drift in mediocrity.

Lets examine each of these areas in a little more detail.

TECHNICAL SKILLS

Acquiring technical knowledge, skills, and abilities is pretty straight-forward. People will gravitate toward an activity, occupation, pastime, hobby or whatever it may be because they are interested in it, or they tend to have easy early success at it, because they're competitive and want to show up their friends, or any combination of this or other factors. Sometimes their parents just make them do it!

They are interested enough to persevere, study, learn, and practice; eventually becoming good at the nuances, and *that* sets them apart from others (essentially giving them an identity, purpose, and acclaim through early successes, *and successes become addictive*). They'll usually gravitate to others performing the same activity to learn more; and the circle of friends begins to revolve around the area of *competence*. Growing up is certainly in part a quest for recognition, fulfillment, and identity through competence in something.

Now it gets a little more complicated. How that *technically* competent and physically able person exercises his acquired skills is controlled/governed by his personal attributes (personality). Most professional people (up to and including executives) fail because of an unacceptable style of executing their assignments (inappropriate interpersonal skills is a common failing) and poor fit with the organization (not so much for their lack of technical competence). This is especially true for athletes participating in team sports.

PERSONAL ATTRIBUTES

That elusive *personal attributes* side of the equation also has three vital components: *timing, politics,* and *credibility*; and while two out of three will probably *also* get you by, all three will be needed to become viewed as *very* competent *and* successful.

TIMING

The subcategory of timing has two primary components: *personality traits* and the prevailing set of *circumstances*.

Personality traits are fairly obvious and critical to success. Here we're dealing with a set of traits that people seem to have or not, like *taste* or *alertness*. It's that intuitiveness that makes a person alert to what's important, and when to act or not act. It's recognizing an opportunity and seizing on it in a timely way (i.e., having the confidence to make things happen vs. being influenced by events; the guts to make a move before it's too late). It's also being able to focus and be *in the Zone* at the right time and as much as possible (key events, meetings, presentations, big plays, speeches, debates, competitions).

Circumstances means constantly, actively looking for the right activities to be involved in, creating an environment that might lead to competence and success (i.e., controlling your destiny and *making your own luck)*. It involves being prepared, persevering, and not being obsolete. It is essentially being in a perpetual state of learning and readiness to seize on an opportunity when it's in reach and/or presents itself.

The following chart is an illustration of how a typical career person in one position might fare over time. In this example the *physical* part is the organization, the *personality* is one that prefers the security of the status quo (thereby allowing obsolescence), and the *circumstances* are "change."

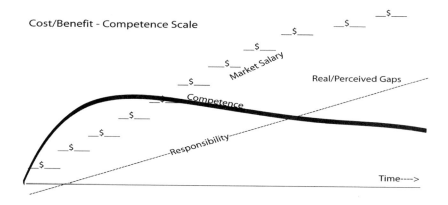

The individual characterized in the chart is not unusual: many people experience this dynamic. To take charge of the situation (intervene), the person must assess whether the organization is the right fit personally. Are the circumstances (environment) such that the person is out of date or hasn't grown through expanded duties and responsibilities, or has perhaps become overspecialized? Or maybe the work the person was doing is replaced with a new technology or eliminated altogether. Has the person been aware of what has been going on? The person represented in the chart is a prime candidate for being restructured right out of the organization.

POLITICS

Regardless of how one feels about politics, it will be in any activity where more than one person is involved. How one deals with politics often determines how the person is perceived:

- *Team player* or an independent *gnome*,
- Individual contributor or a leader,
- Enabler or a naysayer,
- Motivator or a high-maintenance type,
- Loose cannon or someone to depend on,
- Doer or a tagalong,
- Copy-cat or a trendsetter, and so forth.

Ultimately you have control over which role you play and how you are perceived. If you are on the wrong side of acceptable in the prevailing corporate culture, you won't ultimately be considered all that competent, you won't quite fit in, and you won't be successful in that organization.

Changing a reputation is difficult, as tough as overcoming an established role (such as a secretary trying to become an operations professional: most will continue to see and even treat that person like a secretary, regardless of the new assignment). Changing the environment (finding another organization) in these cases may be advisable.

CREDIBILITY

Credibility is also straightforward, but certainly worth mentioning. Credibility starts with having an excellent set of knowledge, skills and abilities, and being able to exercise them *consistently* and accurately in your chosen field (good performance). These characteristics are then coupled with excellent *communication* in a factual/nonhysterical manner, and *reliability* (delivering quality work as committed and on schedule). Credibility also includes: demonstrating high ethics and integrity, the absence of being involved with petty work issues, giving credit where it's due, taking responsibility, and being affable/approachable. Establish credibility in the right corporate culture for you, and you will be successful!

PHYSICAL ABILITIES

If you want to be competent at some things, such as being an athlete, you'll have to find which physical activities match your genetic makeup and/or physical structure. Most people find out through trial and error, and that's usually good enough. But if you are built like a jockey and think like a football lineman, something will literally break. A subset of physical abilities might be dubbed *physical coordination*: good rhythm is needed for musicians; athletes must coordinate their speed, strength, and agility; dancers are better off if they're extremely flexible, etc.

We would be remiss in not including mental abilities under the physical attribute category, since some people are mentally incapable of doing certain things. For example, a person who can't carry a tune isn't likely to be a competent singer (at least not to others); and different types of mental capacity/ability need to coordinate with what a person can or can't understand to enable competence in any given field. For example, if you can't conceptualize, you won't be effective in quantum physics, in creative writing, or in other artistic pursuits, but you may be superb in many noncreative areas where creative types get frustrated.

TYING IT ALL TOGETHER

Hopefully these notes on competence and success have helped with a little *soul searching,* and maybe even provided a "wake-up call." Don't get too comfortable (like the Will Rogers adage about being on the track, and as the "obsolescence" chart illustrated): competition and change are perpetually nipping at your heels, in any organization.

You can control your set of skills, your environment, and to some extent how you choose to exercise your personality. Those choosing not to be *empowered* enough to be aware of and in control of those elements will eventually be relegated to some level of mediocrity and will probably feel a little incomplete (and experience all the coping that goes with it).

Message: *Only you can be held responsible for your level of competence and success: no one else can legitimately assume that burden.*

Not many people have all of the admirable characteristics described in this chapter, but many have a preponderance of them, and they are the ones who make things happen. They are the leaders, formal or informal, and they are probably secure and confident in themselves. Their colleagues look up to them and they are often role models for us. Take a lesson from those who are indeed *empowered.*

The important thing to take away from this chapter is that you have control over how others perceive you, even in spite of possibly less than perfect personality or character traits. There is always room for continuous improvement, self-discovery, and greater satisfaction (at least within yourself) if you are inclined/motivated to make things better.

14

Managing Anything and Anybody

SOLID, GENERIC FOUNDATION = ADAPTABILITY AND NEW PERSPECTIVES

A PERSON WHO has a sound technical foundation in something (and it can be anything), coupled with the ability to quickly sort out facts objectively, who can pay close attention to details, who is able to be diplomatic with plenty of common sense, who understands financials, who has an affable/flexible personality (preferably with a good sense of humor), is inherently *empowered* and can probably manage almost anything the world can throw their way.

Well-rounded individuals who are good at managing their lives, their work, and their play tend to develop an intuitive standard of reasonableness, values, and good taste, and have an innate sense of quality. If they also have a sense of logic and can empathize (an outcome of research and applied intelligence), they can (if they want to) recognize if not identify the best solutions, regardless of whether they've had industry-specific experience, and regardless of whether they are technically prepared in an area. *Good* managers can navigate through different industries surprisingly well.

Unfortunately, this theoretically appealing concept is in stark contrast to the way things really work, where someone is not considered capable (competent or successful) unless their career has been devoted to the technical aspects of a specific field. Too bad, because the locked-in perspectives and biases inherent to any field are perpetuated, with new ideas and potentially needed changes/improvements going unnoticed. This "cloning" is most evident in higher education, where instead of accepting new concepts from whatever source they may emanate, the value and validity of concepts is often measured by the degrees and prominence of a person rather than on the merits of the concept. *More on this in the chapter on "Assimilating Information."*

THE FRUSTRATION OF PLANNING

The problem with planners is that they can't quite get it right, and sometimes they just don't get it at all. Many disparaging, mocking remarks have been made about the planning function and the planners who inspire those quips. A common perspective is: *"Those who can't win, plan."* Not unlike the famous *"Those who can, do. Those who can't, teach."* Both suggest that the respective subjects are out of touch with reality, much like financial "planners."

The biggest problem "planning" suffers from is that plans are notoriously inaccurate and are constantly being changed: even critical path documents that look so official and authoritative. Timelines are seldom met, costs are always higher than predicted, alterations are frantically made to meet budgets (sometimes with ethical compromises), and unforeseen situations or conditions require reengineering or replanning. Construction jobs, which seem as thoroughly planned and structured as they come, always build in a 10–20% job cost contingency for the unexpected and unplanned. Urban planners take plenty of well-deserved heat when politically astute developers trash (often totally redefining) their visions of organized growth.

But the fact is, not much would get done if it weren't planned, even if the plan is simply in a person's head. Anything with any quality doesn't usually happen accidentally or in a random, haphazard manner. An initial plan is usually someone's vision. It could be an architect envisioning a modern edifice, a CEO considering a megamerger, a designer creating an ergonomically functional cell phone, or someone planning their dream vacation. Plans are important, but in some circumstances they can also be overused and misapplied.

When plans inadvertently become an end in themselves, without a clear vision of the final result, they can easily flounder (as in case of problem-solving frameworks). This point is worth reemphasizing.

Overemphasis on frameworks for problem-solving can: eat up too much time, digress, emphasize inappropriate actions, overemphasize minutia, involve too many "cooks" resulting in compromised solutions vs. expedited ones, and consume huge amounts of money and energy (studies, projections, reports, analyses, committee reviews, consultants, making certain all of the politically correct parties have been included, etc.). *See chapter on "Quality."*

Message: *When it comes to planning, sometimes what's actually needed are a few important, salient facts and someone with a little backbone to tell people what to do (a leader). In many instances the simplest plan can be the best plan (except perhaps in space travel, medicine, or nuclear anything).*

THE ESSENCE OF LEADERSHIP

Leadership can be pretty laid back and even easy—until you have to deal with something unexpected, something you've not encountered before, or something outside your comfort zone. Leadership is easiest in very structured organizations (military, religious, etc.) where the primary role is to make sure everyone is obediently following the rules and procedures (and they usually do). The challenges come when you *must* use discretion and judgment, when the rules and precedents don't address the subject, and you enter the realm of having to reasonably interpret, determine, and apply a solution independently.

Most subordinates expect that when they bring up a problem that they can't or shouldn't handle to their leader, the leader will be able to give guidance, stability, make a nonemotional assessment/evaluation of the issue, bring in the needed resources, make an array of independent judgments on the issue, and come up with viable solutions (including the right one) *on the spot!* The subordinate goes away from that meeting feeling that things are under control and knowing what needs to be done.

In other words, *leadership is synonymous with: discretion, judgment, lots of action, knowing what to do (or figuring it out really fast); and giving clear, concise, salient, confidence-inspiring directions.* Action is easy to rally around; *rhetoric is not* (it usually comes off poorly, even though subordinates usually indulge the boss and listen, and it tends to confuse, frustrate, and demoralize). Rhetoric (or "lip service" as subordinates call it) in this context includes: diverting the matter to a committee, *"I'll get back to you later," "Let's think about it," "You give me some options," "Check with so and so, and research this and that and get back to me,"* or *"See me later when I come back into town, in the meantime keep a lid on it,"* and variations thereof.

Message: *If you (as the ostensible leader) can perform as described in the last paragraph (nonrhetorically of course), people will respect you and have confidence in you. If you're in a leadership position and you can't do that most of the time, look for another job, career, position, opportunity, anything else!*

QUALITY IN EXECUTION IS CRITICAL

In a public presentation or even a training session, it never ceases to amaze how two people can take the same material (such as in a canned presentation) and produce such different results with such different impact. One will be effective, hold interest, and even be inspiring; and the other can be flat, dull, and lifeless. It's all in the execution (voice, feeling, inflection, emphasis, pausing, enthusiasm, etc.) and the amount of heart/soul or the lack thereof.

The same holds true for any process, procedure, policy, method, technique, measurement, etc. It isn't always *what* you do, it's how *well* you do it. Doing anything without paying attention to the details and nuances will usually result in an oversight, a mistake, or something that comes off marginally at best.

In speeches or other performances, the delivery makes all the difference. In completing a form, it's using the most accurate/responsive words. In anything discretionary, it's sorting out facts/symptoms from superfluous noise (emotions, opinions, labels, and conclusions). In taking any type of a measurement, it's *knowing* the instrument is calibrated and positioned precisely. For anyone in the business arena, it's knowing the intricacies and interrelationships of the business.

THE ACTION MIND-SET

The discussion on having a sense of urgency in the *"Quality"* chapter is certainly worth reemphasizing, since it is the essence of being successful or completing anything efficiently.

It's the difference between *"getting back to someone"* vs. solving the problem *now* and moving on to the next issue. It's the difference between *"getting everyone's buy-in"* vs. taking care of the issue and focusing on more important ones. It is the difference between *"forming a task force"* vs. taking a risk, using independent reasoning, and going for a solution *now*. The *empowered*, action-oriented mind-set takes involvement in the business to the next level. If you can deal with an issue now, why delegate or divert it elsewhere? It's the difference between influencing events vs. fishing for direction. In supervisory and management ranks it's the way to earn respect and credibility. In lower ranks, it's the road to becoming credible, effective, and eventually a good supervisor/manager.

There are, of course, issues and environments that necessitate more encumbered paths to resolution (such as influencing a group of physicians to perform differently because their rates of infection in a particular procedure are unacceptable). Tact and diplomacy are always essential, and sometimes "group-thinks" or "think-tanks" are a politically correct approach. As a rule of thumb, however, tap into your instincts and try the obvious and simplest solution *first;* it may just be the right one.

INFORMATION TECHNOLOGY

Various systems and Internet/digital communications of all types are here to stay. A word of caution, however: don't let staff conveniences or preferences replace direct person-to-person contact when it's more effective or if it may give you an edge on the competition.

When a customer has a serious problem, nothing is more irritating than voice mails or endless bouncing from one uninformed person to another. Not getting through to a real, responsive person is as bad as it gets (government agencies, cable/phone companies, utilities, educational institutions are all notorious for aggravating already wound-up customers). Human resources operations are even worse about not talking to people directly; and they're the ones who should *want* to be doing just that! In other words, don't put in expensive, automated systems if the final result frustrates or turns people away (customers, clients, applicants…).

FINANCIALS

There is a huge difference between knowing and understanding the real financial workings of any organization and managing a budget or even the P&L. Most people don't have a clue about the $ side of the business, short of someone complaining about: *overexpenditures,* needing to bring in *more revenue,* or improving *profit margins.* When one or more of those problems is brought up, often nothing changes, because most individuals just don't know what to do (and they won't admit it). Even more often (even if their face didn't glaze over and they had some idea of what to do), they may not have the *authority* to take remedial or significant actions. The result is the same: no significant change or improvement.

Message: *Don't just identify and lecture on undesirable symptoms in financial areas, and then expect improvements. Once a financial problem is evident, it must be addressed quickly and affirmatively. Include specific solutions, designate and authorize specific individuals to take specific actions, and diligently monitor progress!*

MARKETING, MULTIMEDIA

Any marketing campaign will be misdirected and ineffective if it doesn't play off what people already think they know and believe. You aren't going to change too many minds with hype. So you shouldn't insult the targeted group by telling them what they "know" is stupid and hope to sell anything. You must reinforce what people want to believe. After that, you can close the deal with the right price for the value (be careful on the value pitch, and stick with facts).

Much of the *sizzle* in PowerPoint and similar presentations is gone, now that most of us have seen all the "cool" contortions and backgrounds that can be used. Stick to the facts of your subject matter and ease up on the fluff. Besides, it takes too much time and often costs more than it's worth.

TIPS ON MANAGING DIFFERENT "TYPES"

Different occupations or groups of people have distinctively different characteristics. Here are a few clues on how to approach and/or manage them:

- *TECHNICAL* staff (engineers, medical practitioners, technicians, skilled trades, IT types, etc.) tend to have a "show me," "prove it to me" attitude and are protective of solutions they come up with (never mind the cost). Their world tends to be hot or cold, black or white, and they struggle with the tepid and the gray. In other words, nonquantitative, judgment-based, discretionary thinking is not their cup of tea, and projects with these aspects should be given to someone else.

- *CREATIVE* individuals tend to set their own agendas and priorities. Here we're talking about scientists, researchers, chefs, writers, artists, designers, photographers, and similar seemingly independent personalities. Their insecurities tend to make them introverts or overly gregarious; and their egos often need constant attention and close direction, otherwise they'll stray from the organization's priorities. They are often articulate and outspoken, but they don't always have a stream of logic others can follow. They can be very compulsive about their pet project, vs. where you want them to be. A group of bright thinkers can be awesome and successful, but they can also miss big and not know when to give it up. The important point here is to make sure the creative/bright individual has a structure to work and think within (they need controls, rules, and limits), otherwise they'll drift and/or get confused. A common mistake is to put a successful creative person, like a designer, into a project management role: *everyone* is likely to become frustrated. (More on managing creativity a little later)

- *PHYSICIANS* are the elitists of the technical world. Luckily most are smart enough to realize what they know and don't know, and often what they're good or bad at doing. While not as dominant as in past generations, doctors will find ways around impediments and constraints better than anyone, and they're pretty good at understanding $$. Choke chains don't work well here, just explanations and succinct logic: these are sharp, resourceful people, so be careful not to insult their intelligence (expect them to challenge your assertions and check your information). They most assuredly expect to be wined, dined, and entertained.

- *UNION* workers are probably the easiest to oversee. Read the contract, their job descriptions, watch the clock, and get on with it. Step outside the established boundaries and expect to see the steward with a handful of grievances. Save significant changes for the next contract talks.

- *SALES STAFF* need superficial pumping up, lots of partying, freedom from someone hanging over them, the ability to stay out of the office (preferably out of town), and lots of monetary incentives. If they produce, indulge them; if they don't, dump them. They'll often try to cover up their lack of results with their personality, and they'll rarely take responsibility for failings.

- *HOURLY CLERICAL/FACTORY* workers need structure and the ability to somehow crank through another mindless day without being "hassled." Small interpersonal issues can become a big deal if allowed to escalate. A little bit of positive, constructive personal attention, even occasionally by the supervisor, goes a long way.

- *SALARIED/PROFESSIONAL* staffs generally want attention from and to be close to the boss so they can show they are valuable, to pave their road to success, to be visible, and to secure that promotion or desirable assignment.

- *"BRILLIANT" or "GIFTED"* people may or may not be gifted in a practical way. If someone is great with remembering literature, history, proper names and places, and a host of trivia or if they're into linguistics, they may be well suited for game shows, academia and/or research. The question is whether or not the person is good at inductive and/or deductive reasoning (a la mathematicians), can they solve intricate problems, and can they find causal relationships and solutions? Actuaries and statisticians, for instance, can drive you nuts with their (often) unfounded, formulated assumptions, and their undying reliance on models. The caution here is that brilliance, while admirable, may not always be grounded in logic, common sense, or practicality. There are distinct similarities with the creative types. If the creative person is also gifted, there could be some very interesting results.

- *MULTICULTURAL/RACIAL* staff need someone of their ethnic background to supervise them, including fluency in their language. Otherwise no one will really know what's up. Don't discourage the use of other languages on the job, you won't be able to anyway. Expect clannishness within different ethnic groups, and an occasional misunderstanding on personal levels. Work processes must be foolproof.

- *MENTAL CASES* are ones to watch out for and accommodate only within reason. If an individual is on medication, know its side effects and don't jeopardize a person's well-being. Once someone isn't taking the needed medication and/or they start acting strange, get them off the job and/or away from others in a hurry! *"SPECIAL"* people need lots of attention, and they like simple routine. Other staffs are often impatient with or afraid of them. One thing that brilliant and "special" people have in common is that both should be kept far away from anything resembling supervision.

Note: also see the chapter "They Speak with Such Power & Conviction"

TECHNICAL CAREER TRACK

As a general rule, every organization should have a technical career track for those whom you want to keep in the organization. This is especially true if they are terrific individual contributors, but who really don't fit into a management capacity. Nonmanagement career tracks will keep people interested who would otherwise try management for the money and status (perhaps in another organization), but who may also be totally out of their element.

MANAGING CREATIVITY

Keep a close eye on who creates or develops what and who owns the rights. There must be no misunderstandings here! Often engineers will garner ideas and concepts from their suppliers and try to patent a variation of something they didn't fully conceptualize and/or create. Also, be leery of the technical specialist who hoards information (who may be up to something on the outside).

There are stereotypes galore about the manner in which creative individuals go about their work. The misconception is that they are loosely wired, temperamental, disorganized, undisciplined, and largely uncontrollable. While some may be like that, most aren't. They definitely become focused on one mission or purpose and seem to go after it *like killing snakes*. They may became preoccupied, leaving all and everyone else alone while they contemplate their work.

Creative people tend to be more methodical than most people realize: disciplined, structured, and organized in their thinking and analysis. If they are not this way, they are probably pretenders. You must be inherently disciplined to create a complicated mathematical proof, to develop and test a conceptual theory, to complete a symphony, or to blend shapes/perspective/colors and messages into an elegant and meaningful work of art. They work as hard as anyone, become frustrated (usually because of their often daunting and seemingly impossible challenges), and their persistence (overcoming failures or disappointments) usually leads to some level of success. So these people aren't the flaky, asocial, nonconformists they're often portrayed to be. Creative people are simply in a different *zone* of perception, and they are often channeling their time and energy into solving a problem that you or I couldn't begin to handle.

Creativity/conceptualizing flows from individuals, not groups, and it is an inherently lonely endeavor. Don't ever inadvertently preempt a potentially great, evolving idea by getting a committee (or any others) involved too early. Timing is pretty critical in this delicate area. Think of a developing idea or creation as a very personal work in progress: like practicing a new piece on an instrument. It's hard to listen, or believe it will ever sound good until they finally get it all together. If you have someone "perform" or disclose an idea too early, and everyone has an opinion or suggestion on how to improve it (jumping all over it, and perhaps embarrassing the creative person), the idea may be shelved, perhaps forever, before it has a chance. Be cautious not to inadvertently, even though you mean well, quash or discourage something potentially good.

Unfortunately, in a traditional work environment, the window of opportunity to be creative is often relatively small. Some estimates are that creative individuals do their best work within the first four to five years on the job. After that, realities such as corporate or academic cultures and their innate frustrations jade the individual. Or grant "obligations" leash their exploratory independence with political and financial realities (such as predetermined expectations from research when someone "very interested" provides the funding).

NEPOTISM

Nepotism leads to unexpected squabbles between relatives, usually about how to cash out the company and make lots of money. It can be the scourge of larger organizations, when perceived unearned promotions go to a relative vs. the one(s) who helped build the organization. Sometimes it works in smaller (ma and pa shops) or in the lower ranks of larger organizations (husbands and wives or other relatives in nonsupervising jobs), but most of the time it becomes a problem somewhere along the way.

15

Positive or Negative, Which Will It Be?

(And Other Sources of Motivation)

ARE YOU AN optimist or a pessimist? Is your glass half full or half empty? Are you a skeptic and a cynic or bubbling over with love for mankind and positive goodwill?

Do you have the required optimism of a salesman, coupled with the flattery and memorized interest (profile) for everyone you've profiled? Or do you have the pessimism of a cop who doesn't trust anyone, anytime, anywhere? Perhaps too much of either will get you into trouble.

BEING POSITIVE

On the upside, very positive people tend to be liked by lots of other people, so they'll have plenty of friends. Very positive people probably do others more favors and pay more attention to others' needs than they're attended to. There's a real risk they may be taken advantage of, and some may not even realize when it's happening. Positive/optimistic people may feel guilty about saying *no*, for fear of offending someone. And if they do say no, it will be so mild and qualified that it may sound like *maybe* or *yes* to the other person. They sure can't bring themselves to being direct and definitive. Self-criticism seems to run in this personality, often to the point of not receiving compliments well (i.e., disclaimers abound, like "I was lucky," or they'll point out all the bad stuff about themselves to offset the compliment).

This blissfully happy individual steers naturally toward giving the benefit of any doubt. Accordingly, denying the obvious when trouble starts may be an area to really be aware of. I haven't quite figured out if drug addicts are optimists or pessimists. They may actually be close kin to the born-again personality. Each seems to have a dependency on something that makes them feel good and happy. Perhaps when both are juiced up in their own way, they lean toward the positive. Optimists seem to do well in church, since they believe they are doing the things to undoubtedly land them in heaven. When the church tells them they are intrinsically bad, they believe it and end up doing even more nice things. They just seem to have a propensity for guilt, and they seem much easier to sell on spiritual and charitable causes.

BEING NEGATIVE

The negative person may be hard to live with, but they're also hard to trick or swindle. They aren't shy about telling you or others (such as service providers, and almost anyone else) where *they* screwed up. They're likely to get their money's worth in many aspects of their lives. Unfortunately, rampant suspicion can lead to paranoia, withdrawal, and some very "postal" results in extreme cases.

One big upside for being negative is that you're always questioning stuff, and that is a beneficial characteristic when you're looking for facts and truth. And if you look at cynicism as a protective process, discouraging victimization, then it certainly has some innate value. It's the *"No one's going to tell me what to think!"* attitude.

WHAT A DILEMMA

Too many compliments, and the comments become meaningless or taken for granted; too many criticisms, and you demoralize or create poor self-esteem. Almost everyone will tell you that you must be positive, with only a little healthy sprinkling of cynicism. It seems as though women tend to prefer the positive, and men tend to lean a little negative. Although men would argue that they are being practical. There are notable exceptions and there are clearly no absolutes in this discussion.

A HEALTHY MIX: THE EMPOWERED MIND-SET

If you're totally optimistic, you'll probably trust people when you shouldn't and end up being taken advantage of in some way. If you don't trust anyone, you'll probably withdraw and end up a recluse with lots of cats. Having a healthy mix of optimism and pessimism is probably the right way to think.

When channeled into action, optimism is a very potent force, especially if all of the difficulties, hard work, and downsides are ignored (and the overwhelming nature of the task isn't taken into account). Then, when an otherwise overwhelming task is completed, it's a very fulfilling achievement. A pessimist, when allowed to think unchecked, will come up with every reason something can't be done, and accordingly, nothing gets done (or maybe that's procrastination and laziness).

The *empowered* mind-set is clearly focused on action and results. That, and a few other attributes, suggests a positive inclination. When faced with obstacles, *empowered* individuals will work their way around them, ignore them, exercise options (all negative encounters), but they'll be persistent (positive), without letting the negative side dominate. The negative side is not denied, but anticipated and handled. The negative side also provides the caution and/or moderation when calculating and then taking risks, so that actions won't be catastrophic if they fail. A risk should also be considered negative, if only because there is less certainty, control, and may have unpredictable and/or unforeseen implications. *Empowered* personalities take risks. They are usually dissatisfied with something, or feel strongly something can be done better (negative). But they also have a huge *will to succeed* and a strong *"can-do"* component that gives the *"positive"* side the edge.

This is probably also a reasonably accurate operational definition of a *motivated* mind-set.

WHAT IS MOTIVATION?

The terms associated with *motivation* are: incentive, drive, stimulus, need, goad, spur, impulse, desire, and "...*something that causes a person to act"*: as described in *Webster's Collegiate Dictionary*. So, what is the genesis of an *empowered mind-set?* A fair amount is probably built-in when you're born, but it can also be developed given there's enough interest in doing so.

There have been a variety of psychosocial perspectives rendered over the years on *motivation,"* with the most quoted being *Maslow's "Hierarchy of Needs"* which now seems so obvious that it's embarrassing. Peter Drucker stated it interestingly when he said: *"We know nothing about motivation. All we can do is write books about it."* And in the cighteenth century, Claude Adrien Helvetius made an astute observation, indicating that: *"Every man without passions has within him no principle of action, nor motive to act."* Mark Twain provides a thought-provoking perspective from a 1906 essay "What Is Man": *There is no act large or small, fine or mean, which springs from any motive but one—the necessity of appeasing and contenting one's own spirit."*

Perhaps I can offer a less philosophical, more practical and up-to-date way of looking at this elusive concept:

Motivation is defined by the intensity, conviction, urgency, relevance, thoroughness, and competence of the action(s) used to achieve or gain something that one believes one must do or have. Success measures the individual's competence, and persistence/effort (or lack thereof) defines the depth of commitment.

A person can be tricked or threatened into acting, they may have a host of personal reasons to act, or they may not have any interest in any kind of action (no purpose, no motivation). The visible result of motivation is action, or lack thereof. The underlying compulsion (motivation) to act is as varied as each individual their own and inclinations.

Ascribing intent is a very tricky business, and that is what we do when we observe single actions or patterns of behavior, and then give them a label: *aggressive, driven, focused, trustworthy, untrustworthy, irresponsible, inconsiderate, disruptive, disloyal, passive, and any number of other positive or negative opinions.* In reality, many motives are fleeting and they can change from day to day. In other words, pinpointing real motives (even in criminal cases) is difficult, and most people aren't very good at it. However, ascribing intent is the stuff of gossip and melodrama, and most of us find it fascinating if not irresistible.

DISCIPLINE AND MOTIVATION

All of us agree that *discipline* is not the warmest and fuzziest of concepts. It just sounds negative. At best it suggests very hard work, and at worst it implies being thrashed with a cane. But if discipline, as a concept, is viewed primarily as an organized means to achieve something, then it starts becoming a little more positive and palatable.

Discipline is indeed required to organize yourself, your thoughts, and your actions to enable you to complete something important or participate in an activity at a proficient level. When viewed objectively, discipline (at least theoretically) results in something positive. A *lack* of discipline is thought of as a very negative condition. Would then "discipline" be a logical component of (or a foundation for) *motivation?* If it means controlling your behaviors and channeling them into something constructive, then it has possibilities. Military training advocates would certainly affirm that notion.

Military types would also argue that their tough training instills self-confidence; and they are probably right. Self-confidence definitely has a role in *motivation.*

The huge downside of military conditioning and motivating, however, is that the discipline and self-confidence created in that setting works in a structured, authoritarian organization. Once outside that highly ordered and controlled environment, a person might be like a fish out of water, wondering where everyone's motivation went, with lots of disparate agendas and seemingly no sense of direction.

Perhaps that is why many people gravitate to structured organizations that have strict rules: it's a safe haven, a comfort zone, where many others subscribe to the same concepts and way of life, it's a social order with a purpose, and it's all set up for you: making it psychosocially easy to be a part of. So, is that a motivating environment? Probably. But it seems only vicariously *empowered*: it requires a specific structure, and once outside the structure, the motivation seems to soften. Read more about this in the chapter on *"Religion."*

Another hint at what motivation embodies involves being curious and exploratory (also in a person's nature). The question is: *can someone become curious and exploratory if they aren't?* The answer: possibly, but again only if they really want to.

INSTILL MOTIVATION?

From the grand scheme, big-picture perspective, a good argument can be made that motivation is there or it's not. It's in a person's personality and character, often rooted in deeply seated psychological inclinations, and practiced for many years. Accordingly, it's almost impossible to change the sum total of a person's experiences and their way of thinking about (and dealing with) situations: to essentially *motivate* them. Changing behaviors requires using the same process that caused the behaviors to be learned initially, and that could take lots of time and even intervention.

Once one motivation has been satisfied, even temporarily, another takes over. Motivations can be short or long-term in nature. Short-term examples include: getting a drink if you're thirsty, or having sex if you're ready. Long-term examples include: getting rich, or getting married. Many motivations to act one way or another are outside an individual's control: you're the family's sole supporter and your spouse spends too much money, a gravely ill child, dysfunctional families, addictions, psychological problems, grief, etc. Privacy issues are a reality, and no one else's business; and employers are often the last to know what's going on in an employee's life (if they know at all). And all of these variables make it difficult, if not impossible, to affect very much when it comes to individual *motivation*.

If you're an employer, you may be able to scare someone into behaving better (by threatening their livelihood), but you can't change the underlying motivations. If you're a police officer, you may be able to keep someone from breaking the law, but only when you're around.

If motivation is not there, an outside party is not likely to instill it. It's a complex and multifaceted mind-set that requires the *convergence* of many stimuli to alter. Sometimes, a tragic life-altering event can jolt and cause someone to reflect on their lives, resulting in a new direction and purpose in their life. Usually it's religion-based, and it works well for many people. For less than tragic situations, see the chapter entitled *"How Do You Define Yourself?"* for a plethora of ways to snap out of it if you aren't motivated, and how to raise yourself to the next level if you are.

MOTIVATION AND PURPOSE

Much of *motivation* is centered on having a purpose, and wanting to see that purpose satisfied. Call it having goals, a mission, a calling, or whatever. It means knowing what you want to do and going for it. Constructive, positive motivation also means having enough confidence in yourself to avoid pursuing pointless superficial gratifications and temporary solutions such as: dangerous thrill-seeking (including taking drugs), crime, superfluous toys, gambling, pornography, and similar or deviant activities. "Motivation" is being able to focus on improving yourself and pursuing *real* solutions once you discover your purposes and interests.

The problem with some people is that they don't know what they are dissatisfied with. Then there are those who don't seem to comprehend that they really are (or should be) satisfied with their position in life, their partner, or their career; but feel compelled to think they deserve something better. They might compare themselves to others seemingly more fortunate, or yearn for some thing or some one, even though others admire them. Taking a good situation for granted is a formula for trouble if it becomes a motivating drive into irrational, risky, destructive behavior. The results will probably be very unsatisfying.

Some motivations stem from the need to satisfy destructive *habits*: drugs, alcoholism, gambling, overspending, overeating, and other indulgences. This is where people make conscious choices between right and wrong, and it also defines their character.

ORGANIZATIONAL MOTIVATIONS

As far as organizational motives for existing and acting are concerned, they are relatively easy to figure out. Many will simply tell you in their value and/or mission statements.

- For-profit organizations want to make money for their shareholders.
- Most want to stay alive and thrive (like people).
- Charities are motivated to "do good" for the needy.

- Religious organizations feel it is their mission to save souls, convert nonbelievers, and perpetuate their kind.
- Special interest groups want to change attitudes and practices.
- Political organizations want to control government, which in turn controls you.
- Nonprofit hospitals (at least so they say) are there to heal the needy, and make some "non-profit."

I haven't heard of a negative organizational motivation or mission, although in practice, some use hate (pretty negative) to rally supporters...unfortunately it works all too often *(see chapter on "Religion")*.

16

How Do You Define Yourself?

WE'VE ALL HEARD the comments on TV and in the movies, read them in books, and often poked fun at them because they often came from California and that cutting-edge, conceptual, and surreal lifestyle. *"I'm trying to find out who I am." "I'm undergoing a self-discovery process with my therapist." "I'm trying to connect with my inner self." "If I can learn to meditate and be centered, I can find happiness and fulfillment." "If I can discover my karma, I will be at peace." "I'm finally comfortable with my sexuality."* Those are pretty trendy concepts that give the alternate-forms-of-consciousness practitioners full-employment possibilities. Everyone likes to feel a little mysterious, to feel they are exploring new realms of mental awareness, and there's probably nothing wrong with that notion. But in reality, and in practical terms, things don't have to be (and usually aren't) that mystical, esoteric, or complicated.

People usually define themselves by: the cars they drive, the clothes they wear, their net worth, their toys, where they live (and stuff in their home); by what they do (work, play, education); what they are (culture, heritage, race); and who they associate with (partners, family, organizations, religious groups, country clubs, who they know, clubs, interest groups, etc.). If you are motivated, satisfied, feel in control, confident in yourself, and comfortable with whatever defines you, then keep up whatever you are doing. But if you feel things aren't quite right, or if you want to move to the next level, keep reading.

IN A RUT?

Are you a burned out, unmotivated shell of the person you once were? Are you so entrenched in daily habits (and what often *seem to be commitments*) that you're not sure if you're bored or not? Do you find yourself following the golden rule, "*doing for others as you would have them do for you*," but finding *they* aren't "doing" for you? If you hesitatingly say yes to any of these questions, or even aren't sure, then you're due for some reengineering, reorganization, rejuvenating, and/or reinventing (i.e., *improvement*)!

Do You Want to Be "Average"?

If asked, *"How would you assess yourself?"* many people would say, on balance, competent or average (whatever that means). "Average" could easily mean you're somewhere in the pack, non-descript, and pretty blah. Being average may be okay if that's what you want, but just remember that *you* chose to be that way.

I would suggest that it is a good, healthy thing to be an expert or success at something, not just average, and to be proud of it! It distinguishes you from everyone else; gives you a special identity, and helps define at least one of your purposes. If you were to say you're a *"Jack of all trades but master of none,"* that's pretty good too. It would be better if you were really great at lots of things, and many people are, or could be if they tried. The secret is to at least try to let your creative side come out in some manner (*any* manner) and continuously try to use both sides of your brain.

The More Roles You Play the Better

Psychologists knew long ago that the more things you do, the more complete a person you will be. You will be better adjusted, more satisfied with yourself, and you will appreciate/understand other people in other, diverse situations and be alert to their attributes.

This concept is *so* full of logic and common sense. The more roles you play in your life, and the more things you are exposed to, the more you will experience, and the more your thinking and your mind will be expanded. Learning and experimenting will become second nature, with your interests changing as you move through life. You will be better at empathizing with others (seeing things through their eyes), and having respect for their strengths while minimizing their shortcomings. The more facets you have, the more you can relate, converse, and understand. If you are seeking "truth," even as a subliminal goal in your life, this is one way to help you get there.

Conversely, the narrower your array of daily activities, the less tolerant you will become of things and thoughts outside of your contracting circle, and your perspectives will be limited. *See chapter on "Assimilating Information."* You will likely become bored (or at least become a boring person) and your feeling of self-fulfillment (or self-actualization) won't quite be there. The results? The worst-case scenario might be a gradual slide into depression. Whatever the manifestations, they will likely be undesirable. Another old adage that applies here is: *"the difference between death and being in a rut, is only a matter of degree."* We've all known people who are old well before their time.

WHAT ELSE IS IMPORTANT?

Without feelings and sensitivity it would be pretty hard to go after a purpose with any passion. This doesn't mean continually expressing/showing your feelings or *"wearing your heart on your sleeve,"* it just means you have them, you are tuned in, and you find significance and meaning in what is going on.

Knowledge is also important. It doesn't matter how you get it, as long as you know how to get it and maintain it. Schools, colleges, self-study/reading, do whatever works for you. It helps you be aware of the world if you've learned about geography, literature, philosophy, psychology and sociology, history and anthropology, current events, other languages and cultures, arts and sciences (the things a classical education is made of: it helps you think). And, make sure you can read and write well.

TIME TO GET PRACTICAL

What we're really dealing with is another component/symptom of *motivation*. If you are mired in a state of dullness, boredom, and comfortable routine, it will take some effort to *not* be that way. It's easy to tell yourself you're happy and satisfied, and this is the way it is; but indeed things can be better! Since habits are a conditioned behavior and a mental state, you may not even conceive of the notion that something different might be an improvement. You're probably just not motivated, yet.

If you look into your repertoire of friends and acquaintances, think about individuals you would label as motivated. You will probably describe them as having endless energy, they are always doing something different, they are probably very good at doing many things, they are confident, and they are interesting.

In reality, in an ideal world, day-to-day activities can and will be a mix and balance of creative and procedural (or technical), routine and exploratory, exciting and mundane. This applies to your personal life and your work life. If you don't have the balance, and particularly if it's shifted to the procedural-routine side, your brain is probably on autopilot. If you're on autopilot, you're not doing enough to exercise that most important asset (your mind). You can be very busy in your day-to-day commitments and normal activities, and it may seem impossible to change those activities, but you really should at least occasionally mix them up.

IF YOU'RE BORED, IT'S YOUR FAULT, RESPONSIBILITY, AND CHOICE

Ask yourself a few questions. Am I fundamentally bored with my life? Am I doing anything about it? Do I even realize I may be boring? Why am I bored and listless? Do I know how to start doing something differently?

Let's put it a little differently. If you are bored, it's because you made it that way: no one else, just *you*. Not your friends or spouse or circumstances, just *you*. If you are bored, you are not likely to be motivated, and you may not be able to figure out what this discussion is all about. You are probably boring in many facets of your life (work, play, recreation, sex, etc.)

Message: *Don't expect anyone or anything (employers, friends, speakers, movies, clergy, etc.) to motivate you! That is your job and your sole responsibility. You can't delegate it. If you don't have it, then work at getting it, because the alternative isn't pretty.*

Message: *Remember that motivation and action are almost synonymous: focusing efforts, thoughts, and actions on something that's meaningful is important. When it comes to actions, think of the adage "If you want something done, give it to a busy person!" They are the motivated ones.*

PRESENCE

The French have a very eloquent way of describing this phenomenon: je ne sais quoi, or something that is beyond adequate explanation. We call it *charisma*, referring to a magnetic appeal or aura of some type. Whatever you call it, *you* want to be *there*. Making efforts to achieve this state will pay dividends you never thought of. You'll have a mission, you won't be bored (since your project is yourself), and when people react to you favorably (at least better than before), the process will be a rejuvenating one that will develop a momentum of its own. Moreover, it will help you have more confidence in yourself, you'll be more effective in everything you do, and the practice and process will help you start feeling *empowered*. You'll *want* to do many more things!

Presence is when someone (like you) is in a place with lots of people, and eyes are drawn to you. Not because you look bizarre or weird, but because the "package" appears all together, and an air of confidence and security is exhibited in body language, posture, expression and movement. Call it whatever you want, but it's striking and it's important to everyone. This physical aspect is just the start. It helps if you already have many roles that you play to enable you to be informed and conversant in many things.

A "PRESENCE" FOR EVERY OCCASION

The more roles you play, the more variations of *you* there will be, and the more fun you'll have (i.e., your interests, personality, competence, and confidence in an activity will determine how "apparent" you are and/or want to be). Your *presence* can easily range from totally nondescript (like an FBI or CIA agent blending in at a rally, or politely listening to the homily at church) to a competition where you let your actions speak for themselves, to a stage presence where you are performing with everyone focused on you, to demonstrating your sexuality on a dance floor *(discussed in a separate chapter)*, to typical day-to-day communications where you simply want to be respected and understood. We'll focus our discussion on improving the latter area, since it occurs constantly and has the most overall applicability and impact. The *presence* you choose to exhibit and the impact you wish to have in any particular situation are totally up to you; and you have more control than you think.

VOICE, DICTION, AND CONTENT

First we'll address voice and diction. You must remove the clutter: no extraneous sounds, filler, or unneeded words. Your voice must project: don't whisper, don't mumble; enunciate, and don't swallow your words or squeak them out. If you have something to say, say it succinctly, clearly, and so all in your immediate vicinity can hear easily. If anyone is straining to hear you or asks you to repeat yourself, your presentation is lacking. Don't speak too quickly, and it is worse yet to speak too slowly. Direct your comments at the chair (or the dominant party with whom you're speaking and glance at others periodically, but don't let them distract you). Do not use words you don't really know or like (no off-taste jokes or vulgarities). If you must use a vulgarity, use it and say it naturally and in context, otherwise it falls flat. Stand or sit a little taller when you are speaking.

Of course, your content must have substance, followed by vocal tone variations and emphasis on important points *with a significant degree of conviction*. If you choose to qualify your comments and cite excuses for their inadequacy, you risk losing your audience very quickly. If your delivery is slow in coming to the point, few will consider your message seriously: most certainly it will not be interesting. No one cares to listen to someone who doesn't have confidence, power, conviction, or delivery (see chapter on *"They Speak With Such Power and Conviction"*).

Another key point on the discourse side of presence involves facial expressions while listening. Listening is especially important, and unless your intent is to discredit someone in a rude manner: maintain natural eye contact, don't dart your eyes around, don't stare, don't squint, and don't furrow your brow. You may be giving away your feelings, or it may suggest you're a little slow to hear or understand. Excessive smiling comes off too "blond." Don't fidget, and try not to restate what someone has just said (it's patronizing, insults the person's intelligence, it's annoying, and it's unnecessary). Nod occasionally and acknowledge points the person makes. If you disagree, do so gently and after the other person has spoken.

BE RELEVANT

When speaking, working, writing, or seeking a solution to *anything*, focus on important matters that lead to and have an impact on reaching the *best* solution and driving your point home quickly. It's very effective to have a quickly developing stream of logic. Don't digress and spend much time on symptoms, emotions, wild speculation, spurious matters, irrelevant chatter, and mundane minutia. *Knowing the difference between what is important and what is not is a very valuable attribute.* Your presence will fade quickly if you drift into the land of irrelevance, impracticality, or esoteric discourse (like the sesquipedalian who fancies himself gifted in ratiocination).

Being a good conversationalist and showing an interest in the other party's activities has an enormous positive, constructive, relationship-building impact. This is especially true if you know enough about many subjects to facilitate a real discussion and enable intelligent questions. Similarly, understated compliments and empathetic comments are usually received very enthusiastically, as long as you don't overdo it (or you risk sounding phony, contrived, and superficial...unless the recipient is receptive to and wants to hear that kind of dribble).

BODY LANGUAGE

The confident athlete stands tall, the back of the neck is straight, and the chin is down slightly so when he looks directly at you (usually right in your eyes), it looks like he can see right through you. It's called psyching out the competition. They face the person they're talking to, and they usually have a pleasant, confident aspect. They are not intimidated, and that calmness and confidence can make *them* intimidating.

In contrast, the person who lacks confidence and/or is awed to be in the presence of someone better often acts submissively, rather like a dog approaching the alpha in the pack. They almost seem to slip and sneak around, stature is low or even humped, head is down, eyes moving around with insufficient contact, and they can easily slip away without anyone even noticing (they would probably be good spies). They seem to fidget and not face the person with whom they are speaking (and not for very long if they do).

CLOTHING AND APPEARANCE

If you need a crash course in getting "GQ'd" (*Gentleman's Quarterly* magazine), do it. If you're a man (because women already know this), do a complete makeover; you may be amazed at the new you. Buy fewer but better quality clothes, make sure they fit in every respect (color, fit, style), make sure the clothes are tasteful (preppy if you can't make up your mind), and get your body in shape. If you're overweight, you'll be preoccupied and distracted with thoughts of what people think about you and how someday you'll become physically fit: until you finally do something about it.

The fact is that *everyone* has some redeeming physical characteristic (there really aren't very many truly ugly people out there). Emphasize the excellent physical feature(s) you have, and make sure the whole package is tasteful. What you don't have physically, you can offset with an affable personality, knowledge, diction, or some other attribute. You *must* be there with your best appearance whenever you need to make a statement (in any social or work environment). If you "GQ" a dork, the worst-case result is that you'll have a dork with a redeeming characteristic; and at least in one way, the dork will be better than before.

It's always better to be a little overdressed than habitually casual or grubby. This means pressed shirts and slacks, and making sure you're tidy all day.

Your self-confidence and esteem won't be evident to you or anyone else if you are unsure of your appearance. For men again, since women already know this, take a serious look at your hair and hairstyle. Take a page from the actor's books: each actor's identity tends to focus on hair first and then their body and clothes. Your hair (or lack thereof) is a very defining personal feature, and the right cut/style can compensate for other shortcomings. *Hair* includes moustaches and beards: experiment, it'll always grow back.

AFFECT

This is another important area, and there is no compromising here. If you are obnoxious in any manner, you will neutralize all of the other improvement efforts you've initiated. You won't have an effective *presence* if you have a coarse, nasty, self-indulgent, arrogant, rude, or in any way unpleasant demeanor. Table manners, ordering protocols, and conversation must all be civilized (no extreme opinions and no raunchy jokes).

If you are in the company of individuals from other cultures, take a genuine interest in their heritage. If possible, prepare ahead of time with an expression or two in their language, read a little about their history, location, customs, and especially current events. But be really careful about talking politics, and never joke about their culture. Businesspeople should take special note of these suggestions.

LOOKING GOOD AS YOU AGE

Here is where women (and many men) very often really don't get it. Many resort to excessive cosmetic surgeries, making too much out of tiny blemishes, spa treatments to take out the lumps, layers of cosmetics, vitamins, sports cars, anything and everything to give the illusion of being *younger*. Some of this activity is okay if only to make you feel better or make you function better, but sometimes vanity has no boundaries and it can easily get out of control. *The fact is, as you get older, you will look older regardless of what you do!* You also have to ask yourself, "why am I doing all this *look young* stuff?" To remain the sex symbol you once were? To attract and/or be admired by younger people? Just don't get even a little delusional here, you *are that old* and you'll only get older.

The important factors are:

- Get into or stay in the best physical shape you can be in, just so you can do more (or lots of) things;

- Get rid of excess weight and take care of your health with the best eating habits you can muster;

- Take care of physical symptoms/illnesses/injuries expediently before matters get worse;

- Cosmetically/hygienically be very neat and clean, but don't go overboard *(one of the most comical things is to see an older woman with a stretched face, after a face-lift, all pasted up with tons of makeup, thinking she doesn't look old)*;

- Having said that, if there is a physical trait that is annoying or restricts normal functions and that is easily fixable, fix it *(men with loose skin under their chin that flaps back and forth, hair transplants if you look better with than without hair, LASIK if you have Coke-bottle glasses, knee surgery if you're limping, laser surgery for that wart on your nose, fix those varicose veins, straighten and whiten your teeth, etc.)*. Just be *extremely* hesitant to take that next step into liposuction, tummy tucks, face-lifts, nose jobs, boob jobs, chin/jaw enhancements, and other supernatural alterations.

Case in point: *One of the most attractive older women I ever knew was a retired professor, still living in a college community because of the vibrant educational/cultural environment and interesting people. She was fit (but not skinny or chubby), had long, natural salt-and-pepper hair (mostly gray), wore comfortable clothing (often collegiate: preppy or sweatshirt-jeans), and was always neat and well kept. She spent the summers volunteering at archaeological digs on the Yucatán Peninsula, she was comfortable with herself, had lots of stories (articulate but not verbose), carried herself proudly without much makeup, did lots of things (including being elected to the city council), and was all-in-all an exceptionally interesting person. She had a presence seemingly without trying. She was well into her sixties when I first met her. I don't think she cared much about how old she was. She was too busy discovering things.*

INTERACTION TO AVOID BEING "ZONED OUT"

All too often we've encountered the physically well-put-together sales/account rep whose credibility plops as soon as he starts talking.

A standard repertoire includes: forced interest, personal questions about hobbies and family, crummy jokes, overly attentive reactions, and gratuitous compliments. All of the foregoing are rehearsed, patterned, memorized ways to convince you that he is your friend and you can trust him. Now you know what *not* to do in today's no-nonsense way of interacting, especially at work.

Be affable and, relaxed; listen, don't force your points on people, provide technical facts (as it makes sense or when asked), avoid excessive or unwelcome programmed hype or contrived compliments, stress accuracy, promptly research what you don't know, and be responsive without being patronizing. Getting to the real issues quickly (i.e., *prices/services*) is also very important.

REALLY LOOK AT YOURSELF

On the physical side, have someone videotape you in action at work or in any *real* situation, and then try to be objective about what you see. If you can't be objective, hire a pro to help critique, and don't expect only compliments. An interesting footnote: if you look like everyone else, there won't be much to distinguish you *from* everyone else.

Case in point: *A friend was looking for his wife (a tall, skinny, in-shape blond) at a department store in an upscale mall. It seemed that all the women in that store were tall blonds. Everywhere he looked, he thought he saw her; but he didn't find her until he called her on the cell phone!*

The same is true in any other venue; if you want to stand out, it won't happen if you look like everyone else. Being a brunette when the rest of the world thinks it wants to look blond may be an advantage.

SET THE GROUNDWORK AND BE READY FOR OPPORTUNITIES

On the personality side, you want to be in a state of mind that allows you to prepare for and create *defining* events, moments, and actions (achieving something purposeful). This is the "fate vs. free will" dilemma for some people.

The message and caution is: *if you rely on fate to guide you without taking matters into your own hands and controlling your destiny, it provides an easy excuse for not having tried hard enough.*

If you don't like your current reality, you can effectively deny it with a fatalistic attitude. It's a form of escape, and it's often easier to blame fate and run away from the issues than to put out the effort to fix things. Fatalists also rationalize that "This is my place in this, life, where I'm destined to be," "If I suffer through it, the next 'life" will be better." Unfortunately it's an attitude that, although possibly comforting, takes away responsibility.

OBSESSIVE/COMPULSIVE/ANAL?

There is a very important difference between trying to control everything *your* way vs. attending to *important* details, monitoring critical path activity, and expecting a high level of quality. Very often the obsessive/compulsive person is given more credit than they're due, especially in the workplace, since they seem to work a little on the excessive side, but sometimes focusing on less than the important matters, and even impeding other's activities.

Obsessive types tend to be less than the best listeners, since they strongly prefer their own course of action. If it isn't their idea, they'll discredit it. That's how an obsessive supervisor/manager can easily demoralize subordinates. After a few admonishments, the staff learns not to take even reasonable independent action without the boss's approval. Staff enthusiasm is neutered, and constructive input is functionally eliminated. Unfortunately, when compulsive types miscalculate on matters such as a vision for the organization, they can miss big-time (it's really a one-person, one-opinion show). They *can*, of course, be right on, too.

If you have this defining characteristic, fix it or at least tone it down. Some workaholics are obsessive to the point of getting so consumed with innocuous detail they continually rework things. It ends up taking longer to output the same amount of work (at the same quality level) as someone who is "just" a smart worker.

TAKING RISKS

There are a number of things that you should *not* take risks with, and they include quite an array of items *(see chapter on "Protecting Your Assets")*. Fundamentally, protect things that are important to you with a vengeance, or you'll have regrets. And, stay away from foolish risks (drugs, philandering, unsafe acts, etc.)

MANAGING MOTIVATION

Message: *Managing your body, your actions, your affect, your presence, and certainly your mind all eventually culminate in self-assurance and confidence. And that leads to something called motivation. Behavioral therapists argue that once you make yourself start doing something, your mind will tag along and rationalize that whatever it is, it must be good. Then it becomes a habit and after that a way of life. Motivation comes from what you do (action).*

17

In the Zone

WHEN IT HAPPENS at just the right time, you are invincible! The last time it happened to me, I was writing this book. I had completed eight chapters, and suddenly I was dry, no ideas. For a week I couldn't think of anything: stuck in the mud, lost in the fog, and augured into the ground. Then out of nowhere, on a Sunday morning it happened. For about three hours I became a veritable treasure trove of ideas, thoughts, and concepts. Within that time I had outlined the next ten chapters. What a feeling, totally focused and *in the Zone!*

THE BASIS FOR IMPROVEMENT

Each time you enter *the Zone*, you experience and achieve a higher level of performance or consciousness. Even though it's temporary, it gives you a taste of what's possible, ratcheting up your standards and expectations, and enhancing continuous improvement (challenging you to try and achieve that higher level again). If you never have this experience, realizing what you're capable of will be much more difficult, and significant improvements may not feel like they are within your grasp.

"Only a mediocre person is always at his best." *Somerset Maugham*

If you haven't experienced *the Zone*, it's probably because you haven't prepared sufficiently, perhaps you're not trying hard enough, or maybe you don't really want to excel (just going through the motions).

Once you have the momentum or euphoria of being in *the Zone*, ride it out: follow through with what you're doing while you're hot. It's an idea or action whose time has come: don't let up *or* overconcentrate, seize the moment; and once you're in, don't let anything interfere, just let it happen. If physical, the results will be superb; if conceptual, you'll be producing thoughts or ideas (abstract and practical) that you can apply now or in the future.

VERY, VERY ELUSIVE

Getting into that state of mind is rare and elusive at best, and staying there is impossible (if you could, you would probably trip a breaker, i.e. your synapses).

Initially, athletes coined the term. It's when everything you do works, and it's effortless. Musicians have felt it too, when the mechanics and soul come together perfectly. You may have felt it when giving a presentation, and all the words were clear, the thoughts just rolled off your tongue, everything made sense, and there wasn't a question you couldn't answer!

The problem is that the harder you try to concentrate and talk yourself into *the Zone*, the less likely you'll get there. It's probably tension/pressure that blocks entering this semimeditative and concurrently acutely aware state. Looking back on my last experience, it seems to have come after a physically and emotionally stressful time, and just after I relaxed.

The rage in athletic circles these days is "brain wave training." It is ostensibly a means for tracking and measuring brain responses when you are in or approaching *the Zone*. At least theoretically, since you can't feel brain wave changes, electronic monitors may give you a clue when your individual patterns are approaching peak performance. Maybe so, we'll see as more experiments are conducted. Perhaps a more natural, less exotic, more pure approach (without gimmicks, gadgets or gurus) can ultimately be shown to work just as well; it would feel less synthetic, less artificial, less staged, and much more genuine (at least you wouldn't have electronic sensors attached to you).

ENDLESS PREPARATION

Individuals who experience *the Zone* appear to be those who have prepared themselves, and are pretty good at something already. All of the long, lonely hours of practice and preparation (mechanics) converge with the complimenting rhythm, balance, coordination, confidence, and execution.

Practicing is indeed a lonely, often ugly, and even tedious process:

- With music, it's hard for others to listen to your mistakes and constant repetition of a difficult measure, until it all finally synchronizes.

- With writing, if you conceptualize and then discuss your ideas too quickly, dispassionate listeners may quash ideas; and a pure idea may get confused, convoluted, or discouraged by frivolous, whimsical, or unsympathetic comments.

- With athletics or dancing or ice skating, it can only be you (usually alone) repetitively ingraining those properly executed moves: thousands of times over, and visualizing the way it should be.

- With actors, perfectly timed and inflected lines (after endless mistakes, retakes, rehearsing, and practicing) are suddenly executed to the point of looking easy, supplemented with radiant self-confidence.

- With artists, the colors finally blend, the shapes almost proportion themselves, and the depth and perspective pulls them (and you) into the work (after gallons of oil paint have been wasted).

The preparatory stage for entering *the Zone* clearly must include discipline and programming (mind and body). After that, if you can relax *and* not be distracted, you *might* enter *the Zone*. The key elements appear to be:

- Removing the clutter, fog, and distractions, and placing *one* subject in your mind (the one you want to perform);

- Leaving nothing to chance: rehearsing/ingraining all pertinent details, technical elements, and mechanics repeatedly, then;

- Visualizing: mentally programming and imagining yourself producing perfect outcomes;

- Followed immediately with *clearing* your mind: turning your mind loose, relaxing, unleashing it, placing it on autopilot, and not forcing *anything;* (not allowing "do this," "don't do that," or any kind of thoughts in your mind), and then;

- Letting it happen!

RELAXING YOUR MIND

Relaxing your mind takes practice. It can be done quickly, and the results can come quickly as well, providing "mini-*Zone*" experiences that can generate alternative solutions to gnarly problems in an instant. Make sure you have something to write on or tape onto, because thoughts are often like dreams: you may think you'll remember them, but they can slip away quickly. Here are a few natural ways to relax your mind:

- Go for a walk, run, hike, bike ride, swim , or do a walkabout in the wilderness/desert. Be prepared to stop and make notes at any moment: forget schedules and artificial time constraints;

- Try a nap, self-hypnosis, yoga, tai-chi, meditation; or stare at an innocuous, inanimate object: whatever works for you;

- Change the environment: sit under a tree in a park, follow a butterfly, watch a sunset, wander by a river, walk to the top of a small mountain, go to a museum, anything to help you see things differently (or see different things);

- Try visual stimulation (lots of color can help): pictures, paintings, photographs, or sculptures (it's good to have these items in your home or office to keep some level of subliminal stimulation around you);

- Try audio escape: headphones, your personal surround-sound stereo (although the themes in songs can be distracting); or better yet play a musical instrument just for yourself.

Worries will detract from relaxing, unless you adopt the mind-set of not sweating the small, big, or *any* stuff. If you feel like you have even some conceptual control over a problem, it's much easier to relax and clear your mind. If it's an emotional issue, it will probably take more effort. But again, exercise as much control as possible and adopt an attitude that helps you "get over it" quickly.

Message: *Self-discipline, self-motivation, self-confidence, unforced concentration, interest, study, and work will at some point (often unex-*

pectedly) pay off with an exceptional performance/result, and you will have been in the Zone.

BEGINNER'S LUCK

There's a hint on how *the Zone* works with beginner's luck. Someone who is learning something may do very well, the first time. But the second time around, the same effort may not produce anything close to the first pass. The first time was fun, with no pressure or expectations. The second experience carried with it an expectation, perhaps a presumption of being easy, and a performance standard: that equals *stress and pressure.* The person tightens up, tries too hard, and the results aren't nearly as good.

INCREASING THE ODDS NATURALLY WITH PRESENCE

When applied to the nonathletic, interdependent, relationship-filled world we're in, it's a cliché, but it's worth repeating: *on a day-to-day, hour-by-hour basis, you tend to act the way you look!* If you can't come off eloquently in your presentation (speech), if you are overstressed/tense, if your clothing is distracting, if you can't command respect or attention, and/or if you act (or look like) a dork, you are not likely to experience peak performance and achieve optimum results.

Presence is important when you want to be effective in any situation. Your presence establishes what role you'll play in any group encounter. It's totally up to you which role you choose to play, or end up playing: submissive wimp or confident leader. For ideas on how to act to develop a constructive, effective presence, see the chapter *"How Do You Define Yourself?"* Having a presence will help you feel *empowered,* and that will help you get in *the Zone.*

EMPOWERED ATTITUDE

Once the physical package is as good as it can get, and once you realize that superficial preparation (winging it) isn't enough, then "attitude" is next on the list for giving you the self-assurance to perform at peak capacity.

The term *empowered attitude* in this context and for the purpose of helping you *zone in*, means believing enough in yourself and having enough confidence in your abilities that your enthusiasm is infectious, affecting anyone you encounter. Perhaps even to the point of intimidating those who might try to "put you down" or "put you in your place." You will have a presence, others will defer to you, they will look for your reactions/approval, they will address comments toward you, and you will have *respect*. If you can elicit those types of reactions, you're *there*.

This attitude is especially helpful in any negotiations. In other situations, people will tend to want to be around you and see what you're up to. Confidence is contagious if you are a supervisor or manager, and your job will be that much easier (in difficult situations) if your staff has *respect* for you and starts emulating your good example. If you are acquired, and the integration team is assessing what to do with your company (including who to keep), this attitude becomes invaluable. If the acquiring company still turns you loose, your *empowered* attitude will be *"It's their loss, not mine, I'm off to a better place."*

IMPORTANT WORDS OF CAUTION

The *empowered* attitude is indispensable in any competitive environment: sports, work, games, chess, debates, attracting a mate, anything, but with one very important qualifier. The assertiveness and even aggressiveness associated with this mind-set must be encased in and tempered by being a genuinely polite, diplomatic, tactful, affable, nice, pleasant (if not fun to be with) person. You cannot be overtly self-centered/indulgent, hedonistic, negative, haughty, critical, or similarly unpleasant. In Islam, there is a precept that applies here: *"True strength is being able to demonstrate it with kindness and gentleness."*

Also be aware that *empowered* mind-sets run a clear and distinct risk of being fired. It can happen simply because they may pose a political threat to someone above them or to a connected peer (who will discredit others in order to eliminate promotion competition). The *empowered* individual will be feared and avoided by the useless and marginal staff members and admired by the secure, intelligent, and ambitious ones.

A typical situation may involve a besieged CEO who prefers to surround himself with timid yes-men. If a scapegoat is needed, then a visible, confident, *empowered* personality may become a target and an overt statement to the others to be more compliant and submissive. A dismissal in this situation should be considered a compliment.

Nonetheless, developing and exercising an *empowered* attitude, and being a part of the effectiveness/achievement that usually goes with it, is a risk well worth taking and infinitely better than the alternatives.

"ARTIFICIAL" INTELLIGENCE AND STRENGTH

Many people have resorted to artificial means (drugs) to ostensibly achieve advanced states of mental awareness and attain physiological advantages. As far as the mind goes, drugs will more likely provide you with delusions that your thinking (manifested in music, lyrics, writing, creating, developing, conceptualizing, etc.) has any value. The result is probably trash, but you're in a fog and don't have the capacity or clarity of mind to realize it. Nothing can substitute for unobstructed thinking. If you're into steroids, growth hormones or similar stuff, be prepared to pay the physical price at some point in the relatively near future.

TYING IT ALL TOGETHER

Message: *If you're prepared by having put in the needed effort (to reengineer yourself if indicated), the hard work (being at the expert level in what you're doing), and if you have the confidence in yourself to take control of any situation (without feeling guilty), you can afford to be pleasant/calm (even while intensely competitive), you don't need to feel insecure, and you can also afford to relax your mind. Now you've done about as much as you can to occasionally, albeit transiently, be in the Zone, and move to the next level of competence.*

18

They Speak With Such Power and Conviction

WE HAVE ALL EXPERIENCED THEM

THE DICTION IS clear, and eloquent, and their voice seems to resound above all others. The sentence structure and syntax are complete. They know the correct vernacular, their vocabulary is endless, they drop names without hesitation, and they can opine on current events in fine detail. They seem so knowledgeable that no one dares to speak up. People seem to gravitate to them. They speak with such conviction and authority and are so definitive; who are we to know any better? They know exactly how to execute their communications skills! If you speak up to controvert or add another perspective, watch out! You've made a challenge, so get ready to be corrected. What would you give to speak with such power and conviction? *For a few tips see "How Do You Define Yourself?" and "In the Zone."*

THEY ARE ALL AROUND US

It happens in many forums and situations. It may be at a social gathering, while working on a group project meeting, listening to a motivational speaker, or being glued to someone in a pulpit. It might be a celebrity carrying on during a TV infomercial. It may be your teacher or professor on a soapbox. It could be a *talking head* expressing an opinion as if it were fact. Or, it may be in more important settings, such as a CEO (or someone else with control over your career) conducting a "participative" meeting.

Individuals who speak with such conviction tend to have their own agenda, and usually have a following. Many are quite successful in their pursuits, and many are considered leaders. It doesn't seem to matter whether or not they have actually done something (such as with politicians, and often executives), their ability to spin a situation in their favor often gets them through the toughest situations. Sometimes it's real but many times it's just smoke and mirrors *(selling)*.

ARE THEY REALLY SAYING ANYTHING?

Overly articulate (verbose) individuals often forget what they've said to whom and how often. It's common for them to get tangled up in their own comments and contradict themselves without realizing it. Politicians do this all the time. They produce so many words that most people don't really hear them much of the time, they just *sound* like they know what they're talking about.

Articulate people tend to get vague, given enough time to articulate. They run out of facts, and tend to focus on trying to make a lot out of very little, but with lots of emotion and philosophical embellishment. Their bag of tricks includes: using obscure references, tossing in a foreign phrase, being quite esoteric, and posing questions and issues (often with no closure). They can leave an issue hanging mysteriously with a smile, as if they have the secret answer, but you'll have to discover it yourself (i.e., you dummy). If you try to take the stage away from them, they will put you on the spot with a *"What do you mean?"* immediately followed by an *"I don't quite understand"* and then *"Could you explain the part about…"* They'll get a less articulate fish on the hook in a hurry, while holding the audience.

When it takes a talker a long time to get to a point, often the talker is compensating for a lack of substance. Talkers see themselves as glib, charismatic, righteous, correct, and often infallible, if only because they can garner the stage longer than others. Talkers often dominate group or team dynamics. At least they use up lots of time and energy focusing on *their* perspectives, interests, and points.

ARE THEY REALLY THAT SMART?

More often than not, they don't have much of substance to say, and they're really not that smart. But they sure can get a lot of attention from those inclined to listen. Like most people, articulate types have a finite set of knowledge, making their opinions not necessarily any more refined, informed, factual, cross-disciplinary, cross-cultural or multidimensional than anyone else's. Many are super-specialists with an extremely narrow technical focus, and many others (like political pundits) simply have a definitive opinion on everything and are very willing to express it. Either way, glibness and ability to attract attention makes articulate individuals seem broader in knowledge and wisdom than they often really are.

Case in point: *I recently noticed several highly respected legal scholars debating whether or not politically appointed judges tend to be political in their decisions. The debate attempted to distinguish between political appointment/affiliation and a judge's personal philosophy, which (of course) tended to follow the judge's political inclination. Talk about circular! And these were prominent individuals making big assertions and endless observations about something very obvious.*

What this example underscores is just how nonsubstantive and noncreative articulate people can be at times, and how much they can stretch an insignificant issue to make a seemingly significant point. To the casual observer, less versed in the subject matter and having heard their credentials, one would think there *must* be substance in what they're saying, after all they're intelligent people. But don't count on it: talk is cheap and no one knows the quality of their decision-making. Perhaps they have been so busy learning speech, diction, and advocacy they forgot to include content, logic and common sense. In the case above, the debaters spoke incredibly eloquently, at length, and with much conviction, about fundamentally nothing new.

The articulate types can (without effort) string together many polysyllabic words that just roll off their tongue. By the time we mortals catch up, they're on to the next sentence. We're not sure if they said anything significant and we haven't necessarily followed their stream of logic, but often we give them the benefit of the doubt, assuming they have deep, profound insights.

WHY ANALYZE, PROGNOSTICATE, AND PREDICT?

Other than for the self-serving interest of the speaker or pollster, or if you're into gambling and you want an edge, there is no logical reason to listen to much of the prognostication (often nonsense) that bombards us. Most analysts are capable of describing the *past* with some degree of accuracy (albeit with a slant), but most are wholly inadequate at foretelling the *future*.

With political advocates, economists, brokers (including your 401K rep.), consultants, lawyers, marketers, salespeople, sportscasters, professors, and academics, it's up to you to sort out reality. These folks can put a great deal of emphasis on minutia, circumstance, anecdotes, and assumptions.

These people can speak with impunity and they're often legally protected (not liable for recommendations). They have nothing to lose and much to gain with their assertions. If they help you fail, you still end up paying them (lawyers, brokers, consultants, tax accountants…). Often they lack: real-world experience, common sense, urgency, and knowledge of/attention to important details (any of which could substantially influence outcomes). Or, their idealistic/theoretical perspectives (liberal or conservative) can cost you lots of time and money.

Management consultants, for example, have a propensity for the 100% solution (doing it perfectly or *right* the first time, or not at all) and all it takes to get there vs. the 80% solution, which may take care of 99% of the problems at 50% of the cost in time, energy, distraction from business, and money. Of course the 100% solutions favor *many* more billable hours, so there is a winner somewhere in their formula.

THE SOCIAL OR WORK SETTING "BULLY"

The articulate *bully* might push you aside with a quip, a gesture, or a quick disclaimer belittling the validity of your comment. It might be through facial expression or through body language (either method clearly suggests you don't know what you're talking about). It may be by interrupting you and/or changing the pitch of their voice, or even making a distracting joke. They may be polite or flatly rude, depending on their position vis-à-vis yours (in the perceived pecking order of the group) and how desperately they want the attention. In any case, they will retain or regain control of the discussion at all costs, taking on any/all challengers.

It becomes apparent that your correct and expected role is to nod your head in agreement, submit to and accept what is being said, and beg forgiveness if you accidentally disagree (assuming you can get a word in edgewise). There is hope for you, however, so read on.

THE SPIRITUAL SIDE

In the case of spiritual leaders, they really don't have to do anything except assert that *"God said: if you don't believe me you'll go to hell after you die!"* Interestingly, many people believe this. Intimidating, scary, big, definitive assertions can have considerable acceptance, appeal, and impact (it's often just a matter of how effectively the message was delivered). The immediate, real message is *"God said: send money!"* If the followers (or their "flock," as they are interestingly called) buy into the message and have confidence in the prophet's ability to interpolate supreme wisdom (since he has the connection and we don't), they send money and presumably everyone is happy *("buying a stairway to heaven?").* After all, who are we to question divine revelations and tempt fate? These philosophers have the best of all worlds. If you don't like the message, you can just go away (or not contribute or tithe) and continue your quest for enlightenment elsewhere.

THE CORPORATE SETTING

If you have a boss or on-the-job colleague who tends to be elegantly (verbally and otherwise) controlling and manipulative, the situation can be tricky. Now you are entering the realm of office or workplace politics. How you should act depends on how well you understand this intangible maze, and how well you can read who has what kind of influence on whom (power) and when.

If the articulate individual is the CEO, whose efforts are successful, then there is probably nothing to say or do except to go along for the ride and learn. If the CEO's efforts and pontifications are not successful, then the board needs to act: they are probably being tricked.

MARKETERS AND ADVERTISERS

The emphasis in many companies is packaging, promoting, spinning with half-truths, selling, and closing. Maybe this and many other variations of deception are the reasons for so many lawsuits in our society. Schmoozing and cajoling someone into doing something or buying something invariably increases the risk of dissatisfaction, and even litigation for misrepresentation. Sales staffs are also good at skirting challenges after a sale. If you can even reach them, typical comments are "*I didn't say that!*" or "*It's in the fine print!*" or "*You just didn't hear me!*" or "*You didn't understand!*" Don't let them do that! Go to their boss or higher if you are ignored.

SO HOW DO THE MEEK INHERIT THE STAGE?

How do mortals deal with these (and similar) silver-tongued devils? The goal is to establish balance in dialogue and create a fair exchange of information. Bear in mind that people often gravitate to talkers because they're the only action at a party or other gathering, not because they are really interested in what is being said, so give the scenario some time to play out. An applicable transliteration of an old adage might be: "*Those who can, do; those who can't, talk a lot.*" Using an *empowered* mind-set, here are a few ideas on how to take control of a few situations.

SOCIAL OR WORK GATHERINGS

- In a social setting where there would not be much in the way of negative impact on you or inadvertent repercussions, ignore the talker, blow them off, and walk away.

- If you want to have some fun with them, look for incongruities or contradictions in what is said. Better yet, set up a talker so he contradicts himself. And don't let him off the hook; point out duplicities over and over in different ways.

- Interrupt the talker, albeit politely, and break the train of thought. The interruption must be thoughtful, provoking, funny, or it could be totally off the subject; but it must be good or a quick thinking talker might embarrass you.

- Persistence and brevity are critical. The talker can't be brief, cogent, pithy, or succinct *but you can*, and those are wonderful weapons. Others listening to the conversation may just gravitate to you, if only because they can understand what you're saying more quickly and easily. Given enough time, you can let the talkers punch themselves out; but it isn't as much fun as confusing them.

- Ask for clarification on a philosophical point, and immediately follow up with a technical question. This can create havoc and you'll enjoy the stuttering and stammering (or platitudes).

- Ask for their position on an issue or their proposed solution (and don't let them off the hook). Or, ask if they know what solutions have been attempted, which ones failed and why (due to poor concept or poor execution?). That may force them to take a stance or use judgment/reasoning. If they aren't adept at taking and defending a position, you've got them!

MOTIVATIONAL SPEAKERS

The main consideration with motivational speakers (usually general, philosophical, and often very successful) is that it is very easy to be that way after the fact, looking back on a great experience or career. The reality check for you is: what are the odds of duplicating one or more components of this person's ability, experience, circumstances, timing, upbringing, contacts, and success? Not likely! Many motivational speeches are interesting and/or inspirational, but they won't change much in *your* life.

POLITICIANS

As we all know, politicians are everything to everyone, and they don't mind telling you anything you want to hear. They constantly contradict and correct (or clarify) themselves. Your best defense, since they will point the finger of blame at the drop of a hat, is a recorded statement brought up and played publicly at a later date (but be ready for the out of context defense). The more commitments you can get out of a politician, the more ammo you might have later.

Doctors

These folks have a distinct advantage over most of us who don't have medical training. The issues are pretty emotional and stakes are high when someone is talking about *your body*. An articulate physician with a good affect can convince almost anyone of their accuracy in diagnosis and proposed treatment. The only way to have total confidence in diagnoses and treatment options is to have another opinion; regardless of how much you like your doc. Consult a specialist at a teaching institution. Second opinions (vs. second-guessing) can be very enlightening, and at worst, reassuring.

Psychiatrists/Psychologists (also Counselors and Therapists)

The terminology emanating from these people will easily drive you to distraction. Their interactive style can be confusing, frustrating, irritating, and completely esoteric. That can leave you wondering how much of their elocution is founded in tangible facts, especially when they seem to grope for a diagnosis.

If you need the expensive attention these folks give you, then spend your money. If you have a chemical imbalance, then of course fix it. However, if you are faced with the classical terms "anger," "hostility," "cognitive dissonance," etc., get another opinion, apply a different theory to your troubles, take up a creative pursuit, or become a Buddhist. The biggest concern in psych areas is that many diagnostic, measurement, and assessment tools (like the ink-blot test) traditionally used in assessments are being invalidated as new studies are being conducted: illustrating the highly subjective, speculative, interpretive, and fragile nature of this field. Extreme cases are relatively easy, but for the bulk of people with often-temporary problems, diagnoses are far from being an exact science. And, you don't know if the practitioner is accurate or just "trying on" a theory and treatment to see if it works. Success rates in therapy are surprisingly low, so if treatments aren't working after a few sessions, try another theory and therapist. Don't be afraid to speak up and challenge a therapist if what they're saying doesn't make sense; remember who's paying for the "treatment."

ATTORNEYS

If you're working with an attorney, don't let them: stray from your agenda, let them persuade you that you're off base (unless you are), or talk you out of an aggressive stance (these folks will compromise/settle at the drop of a hat). Make them work for you, or get another attorney. After all, *you* are paying them: why make their life easier if you're right? Or worse yet, make sure you're not paying an inexperienced attorney to earn while they learn at your expense.

NEGOTIATORS

Good negotiators (of any type) rarely overarticulate if they are competent. If they are talking excessively, it's usually for a good reason. They tend to listen, patiently wait, internalize, process, assess, and then react without fanfare, glitz, or unnecessary moves. They always have options. However, if you run across one with loose lips, it is an advantage to you: definitely encourage him to keep right on yakking. He will give up useful information (implicitly or directly), as anyone would, if they're doing all the talking.

PUNDITS

When it comes to talking heads in other forums (TV, radio, panel discussions), the solution is relatively easy. Don't pay attention to them, their assertions are almost entirely opinion-based and slanted. Infomercials, even those featuring prominent, reputable personalities, usually lack substance. They only tout what the ultimate result will be through staged testimonials. The more you listen, the more you might get convinced that what they're saying has some merit. If that happens, it's probably because that's what you want to hear.

BANKERS

These people can make you feel violated by virtue of their severe risk-aversion, especially at a vulnerable time such as when you need to get a new mortgage or want to refinance anything. They seem to try and make you confirm your life history and reveal more about your personal life than you care to with their probing inquiries. Don't ever forget how much money they are going to make from you. If they need to collect certain documents, give them written permission, and let them do the work. Most important, don't be intimidated, and walk away to another lender if a banker is the least bit condescending. Let them know why you're walking away.

BROKERS

Investment brokers and analysts are usually parrots of a larger corporate agenda to bolster a given fund, stock, or industry on a given day. This is where you must do lots of research and your own financial analysis. You'll usually find out that the investment advisers don't know much more than you do, they're just more familiar with the language of their trade. Don't ever forget that brokers are commission-driven.

SALESPEOPLE

With salespeople, the important cues are: shallow interest in your personal life, excessive eye contact, interest in your hobbies, what cars you drive, where you live (real estate agents are most adept at this: as they gauge your net worth). Don't be fooled into thinking that sales-based relationships are real friendships: you've been profiled/categorized, and are being assessed as to how much they can get out of you and how quickly.

PROFS, RESEARCHERS, SCIENTISTS, ENGINEERS

Teachers and professors should be allowed to use the classroom to "soapbox" their beliefs only very sparingly. You're paying for an education, and not for an unsolicited opinion. Students are a captive audience struggling for a good grade, so it takes guts to stand up to someone who can make life tough for you. But someone needs to tell instructors to get on with the subject matter, preferably in front of the rest of the class (where someone else may jump in and help)!

The other technical types noted in this section can be pretty far out there for most of us to comprehend. A good reality check for these types is ask them to explain their rivals' theories or to ask them about solutions they have tried that haven't solved the problem (boldly declaring that it sounds like an execution problem). The result may be perplexity (for them), and perhaps a more balanced interchange if they begin to respect you following your bold assertion, challenge, or observation.

WRITERS, CRITICS, AND EDITORS

Clearly no love lost between these parties, but each is as opinionated as they come. And if they are articulate (which in these cases is not assured) they can be insufferable, since they tend to have many righteous opinions. After all, *they* have been *published*, have you? Try to confuse them with countervailing theories, or ask about their newest concept (that could fluster them, especially if they're not ready to reveal it). With editors or publishers, focusing on the success of their competitor(s) could effectively unnerve them, such as asking about the story or book that got away. Writers see critics and editors in terms of: "*Those who can, write! Those who can't, edit and criticize!*"

THE BOSS

If your boss is inclined to lecture, your tolerance will depend on how often it occurs, how much substance there is, and how much you like the job. If there is substance in the lecturing and it helps you learn, then listen. If the lectures keep you from doing your job, then let him know diplomatically (especially if it results in many extra hours for you to keep up with your work). If there is little substance, occurs infrequently, and you like the job, then don't worry about it, it's not much of a sacrifice.

CHARITIES

Charities such as those that aggressively purport to help foreign children, religious groups, environmental agencies, protect the family institutions, save the animals foundations, and similar special interest groups all need to be researched thoroughly. Think about how much money it takes to prepare an infomercial (much more than you think). The messages are eloquent, they address the compassionate, emotional, and vulnerable side of people, and they are intended to separate you from your money. The question is, how much goes toward doing "good" and how much to the commercial producers and promoters? Find out before you commit donations!

PREDICTORS

Prognosticators of all types (sportscasters, investment types, political pundits, pollsters, meteorologists, economists, volcanologists, etc.) are basically all astrologers in statistical and/or technically-correct disguise. If you buy into their assumptions, then you'll buy into their predictions. Unfortunately they are often wrong (with assumptions *and* predictions), and if you understand that, you will feel better. Second-guess these folks at every opportunity.

ROMANTIC EXCHANGES

Men don't need much in the way of talking: eye contact, a smile, and minimal indication of interest will get them involved (as women know, and use, quite well). Women, however, can easily buy into carefully presented flattery, and indulgence of their talking. In other words, women's frailty lies in hearing what they want to hear (especially if lonely), and smart men can play on this impressionability. But as we all know, it's tough to remain objective in this area, for men or women.

SHADY TYPES

Con artists, fast-talking crooks, and similar fraudulent types fall into the same group as astrologers, palm readers, and communicators with the dead (hopefully not you). Enough said.

IN SUMMARY

In today's day and age of often marginal ethics, it's up to you to sort out what's real, and what kind of impact a fast-talker's message will have on you. Protecting your interests is your job! Try to understand how someone's assertions and conclusions and recommendations will impact you: understand the situation, the nuances, and do your own research. With the World Wide Web, you have lots of resources at your disposal now. Above all, don't be inadvertently worked by that seemingly compassionate, articulate, passionate personality. Use your head, and be a little skeptical.

Occasionally you might find that articulate person you totally agree with and enjoy listening to. If you do, learn all you can and have fun.

19

Supervisor-Subordinate Relations

OF ALL THE seminars I have developed and presented, this one has been by far the most popular. Maybe it's because: you spend more of your conscious hours on the job than at home; your boss controls your career, livelihood, even your identity; and your boss creates much of the stress in your life. Since supervisors and subordinates each have their fair share of shortcomings, this relationship can range from mutually supportive to confrontational (sounds like marriage).

WHAT MAKES A GOOD SUPERVISOR?

In many respects, it's in the eye of the subordinate and what one wants from the work experience. There are some constants, however, and most people these days would say that desirable, effective traits of a good supervisor/manager include:

- Providing technical guidance
- Helping solve problems that are beyond the subordinate's grasp
- Providing the resources and/or training to work better
- Keeping priorities and deadlines clear and in correct order
- Keeping staff informed about the company or organization
- Correcting errors in a civilized manner
- Interceding in personality clashes
- Providing career guidance

- Giving credit when due
- Being firm, fair, and respectful
- Being enthusiastic about the work, making it invigorating and fun
- Demonstrating reasonableness and common sense
- Communicating intelligently, diplomatically, and completely
- Being a company advocate without going overboard about it, and understanding the intricacies of the business
- Being innovative and creative
- Challenging staff to be better, to make improvements, and expect quality results
- Being tough when needed and compassionate when it's called for
- Knowing each employee, what motivates them, and being genuinely interested in their careers
- Being a good reader, writer, proofreader, and editor
- Being technically up-to-date
- Being a good teacher, listener, and adviser
- Being ethical, honest, trustworthy, and demonstrating only the highest integrity

Wow, wouldn't that be nice. The reality is that very few supervisors have this (whole) profile. In fact, the preponderance of supervisors probably does not have a majority of these skills. Many supervisors simply aren't prepared (and/or "built") for their jobs, and some never will be. Supervisors have their own set of pressures and demands, and although *you* don't really care about that, the supervisor's pressures will impact you. The theoretical burden for good supervision must remain with the supervisor. In reality it's up to the subordinate to play a part in keeping the relationship constructive and in a sense managing the boss (up to and including firing the boss from *your* career, i.e., finding a different job if necessary).

WHAT MAKES A GOOD EMPLOYEE?

From the supervisor's perspective, there are a few very important traits any subordinate should ideally have. Of course, as reality would have it, these too are often in short supply:

- Loyalty: no "end runs" around the boss or discrediting to other staff
- Sticking with/meeting priorities and deadlines
- Technical knowledge, skills, and abilities (competence)
- Ability to read, write, and operate various computer programs
- Respect for the supervisor's leadership, knowledge, and experience
- Ability to suggest alternate solutions to problems
- Ability to be thorough, complete, and produce quality results
- Recognizing when a situation is developing into a problem (anticipating)
- Able to learn, grow, and not repeat mistakes
- Able and willing to communicate (good and bad stuff)
- Demonstrating a genuine interest in the job/career/organization
- Interested in taking on different tasks as needed
- Being motivated, assertive, and having a sense of urgency to correct problems
- Demonstrating honesty, high ethics, integrity, and trustworthiness (sound familiar?)

In other words, these are the characteristics valuable to the supervisor/organization. The person demonstrating a preponderance of these traits will likely be promoted, and will be protected (not laid off), if not coveted with extra raises. Now, if you cannot or do not want to meet the preponderance of this profile, you need to determine if you are in the right organization, job, or career.

"TAKING ON" THE SUPERVISOR

If you do not like your organization, supervisor, job, or career, you must still make every effort to meet the profile of a good subordinate. You are there, and at least for the moment it's all you have, so make the most of it. Exercise your options for improving your position as a separate project. This is no time/place to grovel in self-pity and wallow in "*they don't appreciate what I do*" attitudes. Take whatever supervisory wrongs you experience in stride and deal with them (if you're experiencing illegal discrimination, if you can prove it, and if you can't rectify it informally/internally, sue!).

Keep in mind that if you take on your boss, for whatever transgressions, you are not likely to get him fired. The tendency for supervisor's superiors is to believe them and give them the benefit of the doubt. It's easy for a supervisor to discredit you to other supervisors and management (where it really counts). The quickest way to be shunned by management is to be openly critical of (discrediting) your immediate superior. Most management levels support each other, and taking on your boss is like saying that *your boss's boss* screwed up by promoting him. It's best for you to *not go there*, the percentages are against you. You could be right, but *dead right* (as far as your career in that organization). The best course of action is to address issues with the supervisor directly, affirmatively, and diplomatically.

When it comes to formal grievances and lawsuits: unless there is a concerted action involving more than one employee, with clear patterns of behavior, and definitive unfair treatment, you'll have less than an even chance of winning (it all depends on your legal counsel's competence…no small consideration). It also depends on how badly you feel you've been wronged, how much real (incontrovertible) evidence you have, and how clean and credible *you* are.

ALWAYS KEEP IT A BUSINESS RELATIONSHIP

Remember that! Good supervisor-subordinate relationships sometimes have a tendency to cross the business line and continue developing by one party or the other, or both, into a personal friendship, or even an intimate relationship. If it's one-sided, harassment or uncomfortable come-ons can critically undermine the work environment. Even if it's a mutually wanted relationship, it will likely (sooner or later) become something you probably won't want to deal with.

The relationship must remain a business transaction. If/when performance and/or results slip, the tension, stress, solutions, and interactions become more difficult to deal with, and normal solutions are often overlooked or not even considered when a "friend" is involved. Both parties loose if/when that happens.

IT'S A DELICATE MATTER OF BALANCE

Since we've established that supervisors and subordinates both have their shortcomings, both sides must look upon each other in terms of *the preponderance* of attributes vs. deficiencies. If the preponderance of good stuff outweighs the bad, then it's much easier to overlook the bad; and the supervisor-subordinate relationship continues on a constructive path. If the converse is in evidence, with bad attributes on either side dominating, then a collision course is indicated—it's just a matter of time and what form it takes.

The interesting aspect here is that in many cases, it takes only one critical issue to disrupt the relationship for good. A subordinate who feels that the boss is continually taking credit for their work will immediately resent the supervisor, and even look for ways to make him look bad. A supervisor who feels the employee is critical of him to peers or even higher-level management will feel undermined, and will resent *that* behavior. Never mind that all other aspects of the work relationship may be good. These are examples, which if true, are difficult if not impossible to reconcile. Even increased communication may not fix the lost trust.

MORE TROUBLES WITH THE BOSS

Here are a few examples of what you as a subordinate may (negatively) think about your supervisor:

- Why should I work so hard just to make this idiot look good?
- I don't get paid enough to be unappreciated this much!

- How dare he correct and embarrass me in front of my coworkers!
- I have so many good ideas, be she won't give them the time of day!
- They (management) are just wrong in taking this approach!
- Why can't my boss just give me a raise, I work better than the others!
- My boss is burned out and she's a lousy role model, why is she here?
- Those were my ideas, and he took credit for them!

Remember, if on balance the pros outweigh the cons, learn to live with it; but don't let the boss get away without you being heard (tactfully, diplomatically, and behind closed doors). If you don't make even a humble attempt to express yourself, your wounds will become exaggerated, you'll lose your drive and won't be effective.

Besides not communicating effectively upward, another common mistake by staffers is to do *exactly* what the boss wants. If you have a better, more expedient solution, the deadline is looming, and you can produce as good if not better results, then by all means, go for it your way. The good boss will appreciate your efforts. If the result isn't that great, be ready to tap dance.

LOYALTY

Much has been said about loyalties having shifted from the organization (which seemed to nurture its staff for generations) to being loyal to your career and profession. This shift is largely attributable to corporations downsizing, reorganizing, and dumping excess staff to enhance earnings. There is nothing wrong with this shift in attitude (by either party: that's the way it works these days). It will actually help many people find the right organization and position for their abilities and interests (rather than falling into the make-work positions often created by companies that have too much money, or have exceeded their own sustainable growth: resulting in excess staff in either case).

Loyalty to your boss is important, because that person can help you develop your skills. Making your boss look good will probably create a reciprocal support (if he depends on you), and you'll probably learn something along the way. Also, don't bail out too quickly if you have a *tough* boss. These are the ones who you'll probably learn the most from, especially if they have a high energy level, know their stuff, have high expectations, and demand excellence. This is definitely the kind of person you want to be mentored by, and this type of boss is very hard to find.

COMMUNICATION IS THE KEY

Don't assume that your supervisor knows what you want out of your career, job, or work life. He can only guess at what motivates you. You need to express yourself. Forget the *"If he doesn't know, he doesn't care"* thinking, it doesn't work. Similarly, if you feel you've been wronged in some manner, you must talk it out. If you can't talk with that person, find someone in the organization that you can express yourself to, preferably informally.

MANAGING THE EMPLOYEES

The first thing you must ask yourself is whether you are really cut out for this responsibility. Forget that you may *want* to do this work, and that it gives you status and additional money. Many people are much better at being individual contributors who can function wonderfully at resolving complex technical issues rather than dealing with the intangible/conceptual/frustrating side of reconciling people issues and consistently demonstrating effective leadership.

One huge common misconception by supervisors is that they often believe they can truly motivate any one employee. You may be able to engage staff to complete specific programs or projects, but motivating any one is largely out of your hands and beyond your abilities. However, supervisors can *easily* and often inadvertently demotivate staff: losing their own credibility and staff support in a hurry. Demotivation results from not having very many supervisory attributes and/or being a jerk.

Let's assume you've done your job as a good leader and surrounded yourself with a capable, innovative, spunky, intelligent, action-oriented, outspoken staff. This is a very good situation to be in. However, that spunky staff will (without a doubt) occasionally put you to the test. When they do, remember, they are probably not doing it maliciously, and if they are, get rid of them. What if an employee presents you with an ultimatum, such as *"If I can't make as much money as Adam, I'll quit!"* or *"I've had it with my coworkers, it's either them or me!"* or *"If I can't be in charge of that project, I may as well go check out the competition!"*

The boss needs to be well grounded when faced with an ultimatum, especially if the staffer is a top performer. If it is from an otherwise good employee, and if they're right: admit it and accommodate them right away or with the next project (but let them know now). If the person is a poor or marginal performer, let them go (or better yet, accept their ranting as a resignation and set an example). In most instances, bosses can't let ultimatums rule the day or they'll lose control. It is sometimes important to remind staff that you have had more experience and there's a method to what may seem madness to the employee (assuming that is the case, and it often is). Anticipating and dealing judiciously/quickly/affirmatively with employee challenges is an important supervisory attribute.

The leader who habitually uses the *"It's my way or the highway"* line will quickly lose that smart, spunky staff (and deserves to).

THE MARGINAL EMPLOYEE

How does a good leader handle the marginal employee? The best solution is to not hire them to begin with: *don't ever forget that!* Assuming you've inherited a nest of hangers-on who have no interest in performing well, the best course of action is the same: get rid of them as fast as you can! Transfer, fire, reorganize, downsize, assess skill-mixes, expand jobs, redefine assignments, change workloads, but most of all: *immediately expect excellent performance and results from everyone!* Don't be shy about announcing your expectations, and reminding everyone daily if needed. Ultimately you will only be as good as your weakest link.

KNOW WHEN IT'S TIME TO GO

Similarly, if you're ambitious, don't waste too much time in an organization or in a job that isn't taking you somewhere (dead-end). If you're okay with a dead-end job and don't mind the work, that's not bad for people whose priorities aren't in the workplace.

The trick is to know when to leave. Two cases in point:

Early in my career, I was truly fast tracking it:

- *Promoted four times in three years,*
- *Received salary increases every six months,*
- *Was given responsible assignments at every opportunity,*
- *Worked six days a week, and did everything with a passion,*
- *Took on extracurricular activities to be more visible, and*
- *It worked! Until...*

I hit a ceiling, where more promotions weren't likely, because of the relatively young staff above me. I saw I would become unhappy soon with relatively slow growth. I looked for an opportunity elsewhere hoping to become a VP (at the brash age of twenty-six), found one, and my boss astutely announced: "If you're so stupid as to not take it, I can assure you I won't give you anymore raises or promotions!" He was actually being supportive and giving me good advice.

Later in my career, while in a key management position, reporting directly to an elected board of commissioners, I made many organizational improvements and changes (as I was contracted to do over a three-year period). In the process, since it was a consummate political organization (local government), I alienated a few career politicians and sensed that my impact/effectiveness was beginning to slip. When I resigned to move to my next career-enhancing position, one of the elected officials stated: *"The good ones always seem to know when it's time to go."*

In both of these situations, I was good for the organization and the organization was good for me...*for a while.* Knowing when to move on is a very important aspect of your personal and career development (for either managers or employees).

Message: *Power, control, and effectiveness are temporary attributes, especially if you intend to make significant changes and/or improvements in an organization.*

Second message: *It is very important to work at peak capacity at whatever you are doing and in whatever position you have been assigned. The employment relationship is a business arrangement: the employer has hired you to perform a service, and it is your responsibility to perform that service well! That's the tacit employment contract. If you don't like it, change something, but don't lower yourself to taking it out on your employer just because you don't like your current place in life.*

LEGAL ASPECTS OF THE EMPLOYMENT RELATIONSHIP

The following legal aspects are extremely critical in the employment situation and should be understood by anyone managing staff as well as by the staff members.

THE JOB AS A PROPERTY RIGHT

It must be understood and appreciated that jobs and careers have indeed become a *property right.* There's a good reason for this. Since the Industrial Revolution, most of us are no longer farmers and our work is our only means of sustenance. In the past, property rights protected farmers from losing their land, and therefore their ability to sustain their lives/families. Now those rights have shifted (correctly) to protecting the *job*. It's why noncompete agreements are hard to enforce, and why there are so many laws on the books protecting workers and their rights. All in all this is a good trend, and not as advanced as in many other industrialized countries. People management is not an area to be taken lightly, and those in the upper levels of any organization must actively monitor it. One of the reasons there are so many laws, adjudications, executive orders and regulatory agencies (local, state and federal) is because this area has historically been managed poorly. All of the laws/adjudications have created a healthy balance.

People-decisions within an organization are, in practical terms, the implementation and administration of a business contract. Like it or not, call it something else if you want, but that's what it is. If you begin thinking of staff relations in those terms, the correct balance begins to occur, it all begins to make more sense, and there is less manipulative thinking and behavior by both parties.

VICARIOUS LIABILITY: MANAGEMENT BEWARE

This is no longer a legal theory, but a mainstay strategy for employees to defend themselves and to turn the tables onto the supervisor and/or employer. When an employee is discovered doing something inappropriate, illegal, or has screwed up in any manner, the first order of business is for the employee to defend himself. Since supervisors and managers are not infallible (far from it), the employee's typical "defense" is to *shift the burden* for their poor behavior/performance onto the supervisor (or *company*). A typical defense looks like this:

- The employee admits to doing nothing wrong, and suggests they were assigned a job they weren't hired for.

- The employee may also argue they weren't trained for the assignment.

- The employee may contend that he was not informed of the expectations, company rules, and/or consequences of any failures.

- The employee may state that he had not been supervised, coached, helped, or given the needed tools or resources to perform the work as expected.

- The employee may assert that they were hired, then retained in, moved into, or promoted to a position they weren't capable or prepared for.

Once any (or all) of the foregoing assertions are made by the employee, the supervisor becomes obligated to at least explain (defend) himself and the actions taken. The question that often occurs to the supervisor is: "*Who is the guilty party, anyway?*" Even if the supervisor prevails, he will be gun-shy in future confrontations. Frequently the supervisor's enthusiasm for assertive action will be diminished. At best, the supervisor will be more restrained and cautious. At worst, the supervisor won't take any action that may even potentially reflect negatively on him (ironically creating problems for the supervisor and liabilities for the company through inaction).

Not knowing who may or may not be a problem on the job at any given time and who might turn the tables on you when an issue surfaces creates an environment that isn't particularly conducive to trust. As a confrontation approaches resolution, the truth becomes muddied and replaced with expedience, compromise, and a tendency to "*leave it behind and move on,*" and "*there are more important things to do.*" In spite of that tendency, the *empowered* supervisor will *not* let an employee who is not performing prevail, and will *not* be discouraged by threats and accusations (accepting them instead as a challenge).

Generally, unless wrongfully accused, good employees will accept responsibility for an improper action, not try to deviously shift the burden, and "vicarious liability" won't even cross their mind.

Note: See the chapters on "Integrity and Ethics" and "Trust" for more insights.

20

Negotiating

NEGOTIATOR CAN EASILY be a synonym for an *empowered* individual: cunning, patient, experienced, has a purpose, aware and alert, persistent, finds/seizes opportunities, always has options, moves only with reason, understands and notes patterns, understands the psychology involved, demands quid pro quos, takes risks, acts decisively, and goes for closure. Negotiating can be very confusing and difficult if your personality can't summon those traits when needed. However, if you are focused and feel you are exercising a reasonable amount of control during any negotiations, you will usually be more satisfied with the results.

WE'RE ALWAYS NEGOTIATING SOMETHING

Negotiating in the business environment is often made out to be a mystical process that is complicated and reserved only for those on the inside. These are the trusted ones who presumably have the ear of the board or CEO, the omnipotence of a prophet, the knowledge of a professor, the cunning of a fox, the survival instincts of a rat, and skills beyond those of mere mortals.

Subjects include: labor negotiations, consummating M&A and/or divestiture deals, completing international trade agreements, developing mutually beneficial terms for a joint venture, selling/leasing back property, getting the best price and terms from a supplier or service provider, establishing a competitive price for goods (domestically and internationally), negotiating settlements with regulatory agencies, obtaining the best terms for capitalizing/financing/refinancing, or simply coming to employment terms with a new key staff member. There are many more things that are negotiated, such as on the diplomatic front involving hostilities between nations, or when the risks are so high in hostage situations; but you get the idea, it can be a complex, overwhelming situation for the uninitiated or uninformed.

The concepts and principles of negotiating successfully on the personal front are really not much different: it's the subject matter and stakes that vary, with the biggest difference being *emotions,* which can confuse issues and make negotiations very difficult. Usually there are fewer intricacies/elements in personal matters, and the dollar levels are lower (although not in terms of proportionate impact on your personal net worth). Here we're talking about buying a house, negotiating the terms of a prenuptial/divorce, buying a car, checking out the best services (yard, pool, cleaning), remodeling, buying TVs and appliances, shopping for a vacation, buying a dog, finding the best cell phone terms, deciding how discretionary funds are used (with partner), or which movie you're going to see, or sorting out what you now want in a computer. When you back off and really look at it, you negotiate many more issues much more often than you think; and incomplete or one-sided results tend to carry frustration, stresses (and at worst, remorse or resentment). Successful, balanced negotiations can be satisfying and become the foundation for good future relationships.

Negotiating is really as simple as two (or more) parties starting from different perspectives, interests, and expectations, and eventually *converging* on terms acceptable to everyone. The parties usually compromise and understand the other's position a little better as the deal or understanding is consummated. If it's a conflict with stalemated positions, then mediators, fact-finders, and/or arbitrators may help clarify matters. Any way it occurs, careful timing and credible, continuing communication are the keys to resolving differences.

MIND-SET IS IMPORTANT

To be a successful negotiator, you must *not* make the discussions a personal matter, under *any* circumstances and at *any* time. Once it gets personal, emotions creep in and your objectivity slips away. If you can't be emotionally detached, then have an uninvolved individual guide you and do most of the interacting (definitely an attorney in legal matters).

In the business environment, you may be entertained extensively (especially in cross-cultural discussions). The usual intent is to develop more comfortable interactions (a relationship), to understand methods of operation, to get a feel for critical issues or financial parameters, and to perhaps distract you and/or use "time" against you. You must be very careful not to let friendly behavior soften you on the important issues. Setting ground rules for discussions (including use of time) before the parties meet is a good idea, especially in complex or international matters.

A common misconception is that if someone offers you a job, there is something personal about it. Get that out of your head! Being hired is as much a business transaction as anything else, and while you may *thank* someone for hiring you, they should also be thanking *you* for coming to work for them. Although it's hard not take business matters personally, it is an advantage to everyone in the long run.

In labor negotiations, when an impasse is approaching, the union side is usually adept at trying to unsettle management negotiator(s) by bringing style differences into play, trying to make matters "personal." The strategy is to try and make the negotiator mad and unsettled or flustered. If you get mad, you'll be on the defensive, vulnerable, and distracted. Don't go there, take tactics (even epithets) in stride, and keep hammering away at the issues.

On the home front, even your own real estate agent may try and sway to into making an offer that will be easy to sell. The most common tactic is to not so subtly suggest that there may be another offer pending on the house today, and your kids would just die if they couldn't live in that neighborhood. Make sure your agent has presented you with more than one acceptable home to choose from!

Message: *The successful negotiating mind-set means: take nothing personally, don't be distracted, and don't be pressured. The good negotiator can intuitively sense a problem even if it can't be readily identified: if it doesn't "feel" right, step back and slow down.*

BE VERY CAREFUL HOW YOU DISCLOSE INFORMATION IN SERIOUS DISPUTES

In an adversarial situation such as a lawsuit, administrative law hearing, regulatory agency deliberation, labor impasse, divorce (or any time a third party, like an impartial mediator, is involved), the amount, kind, sequence, and timing of information disclosure is a critical strategic matter.

The accuser *(plaintiff)* is often all too eager to put the whole problem (arguments, issues, motivations, etc.) on the table. The accuser wants justice *now,* aggressively attacking the problem and the perpetrator, perhaps intending to unsettle the party who has purportedly done something wrong. The accuser tries to carry the banner of fairness, law, and good faith (securing the ethical/moral high ground as much as possible). Unfortunately the accuser usually has the burden of proof, and must conclusively show that the accused (the *defendant*) is guilty of something beyond a reasonable doubt.

Tactics become especially important, and regulatory agencies (IRS, customs, EPA, prosecutors, EEOC, labor boards, etc.) are often quite good at *bluffing.* They'll overstate their case against you, and then use time as a weapon: *"Here's the deal, but you must decide now, or we'll go for more in court!"* or *"Agree to this extension, or it goes right to the Justice Department!"* Or, an ostensible settlement may be deferred to a higher level for finalization (once you've shown what you're willing to pay), and another negotiator takes another bite out of your pocketbook.

Regulatory agencies have lots of resources, they've had lots of practice, and they don't necessarily have to negotiate in good faith *(Note: Someday the Supreme Court will put an abrupt stop to misleading tactics, and there have been a few hints to that end already).* These are prime examples of where you should not allow yourself to be bullied: think in an *empowered* manner and be as (or more) aggressive as they are *(unless, of course, you've really messed up: in which case you should cut a deal as quickly as you can and put the issue behind you).*

Showing all of your cards (facts, arguments, and settlement goals) too quickly may have a result opposite from what you may expect. Instead of overwhelming the *defendant,* it may allow the defendant to pick and choose what wants to respond to, giving a distinct advantage *to* the defendant. The typical result is that the accuser's points and arguments (factual and meritorious as they may be) can be assessed and selectively picked off one by one. Important items (for the accuser) can be labeled as insignificant; and minor, more vulnerable points can be blown out of proportion, made fun of, and discredited. Another typical ploy is to introduce devious or misguided intent by the accuser into the defense, suggesting the accuser is greedy, seeks vengeance, wants to eliminate the competition, or has some other less-than-honorable personal agenda (all to detract from the facts of the case and suggest unethical, ugly intentions/motives): and it can play well to a jury.

LETS PUT THE PAST BEHIND US

The *defendant* will take the seemingly salutary and conciliatory position that groveling in the past is unhealthy and impedes resolution of the issues. The argument takes the form of *"Let's not dwell on the past, and move forward."* The defendant may bring up this angle early and often, and usually to the disadvantage of an overaggressive accuser (especially if they have indeed wronged the accuser).

This presents an appealing point of view to any unemotional third party such as a mediator, judge, or jury who is interested in getting the matter overwith. No third party wants to listen to (or has much patience for) a *"he-said, she-said"* name-calling case. The premise by any outside party, before any case is heard, is usually that *virtue is not reposited in either camp.* This is exactly how and why no-fault, community property laws have become so prevalent in car accident and divorce cases: too much noise, fog, and clutter to efficiently sort it all out.

JUST THE FACTS, PLEASE

The *defendant* is always well served to sit back and receive information, providing little or nothing in return, and responding selectively. The *plaintiff* on the other hand must either bluff and/or show restraint: bringing out evidence in a sequence that gradually builds a compelling logical case and a factual representation of the issues. The *plaintiff must at all costs* resist diatribes, outbursts, accusations, name-calling, ascribing intent, or labeling behavior (very difficult to avoid in an emotionally charged issue). To do so usually results in meaningless exchanges and a burdensome obligation to repeatedly clarify what you mean (detracting from your arguments and your intent to presumably be made whole).

In a business negotiation (mergers, acquisitions, pricing, etc.), full disclosure is expected and a thorough due diligence will usually bring out the issues anyway. Timing is not as critical of an issue. To not be open and conversant only creates suspicions, distrust, and begs for a fraud accusation if one party or the other feels they've been taken advantage of (often well after the deal is done).

SHIFTING THE BURDEN

This is where the rubber meets the road. If you feel the pressure to have to do something significant without feeling there will be a quid pro quo or some reciprocal movement from the other party, and if your move doesn't close the deal, you're probably at a disadvantage and may very well lose, or be compelled to concede or at least significantly compromise your point.

A shift in the burden can happen several ways. Someone may simply run out of sensible arguments, and it becomes obvious it's time to drop it. If a demand is a small one, giving it up may be a good tactic: inherently shifting the burden back, and waiting for the other party to move (or give up) something in return. If your point has stalemated, and you believe it is a righteous one, putting it aside, but only for a while, is often a good move. If you can create even the illusion of being quite capable of walking away from the deal, you shift the burden and pressure. Sometimes theatrics can be effective, but be very careful about bluffing because it can easily backfire.

There is an old adage that says *"The first one to put a viable number on the table loses."* In other words, don't offer too much too soon, you may be overburdening yourself. In addition, you must try and determine, or at least have a feel for, the other party's pain level and threshold. This is where careful listening and probing is necessary.

When *time* is used as a pressure tactic, it's good to let issues sit (even forcing delays) until there is some time pressure on *all* parties. Then bundle up all of the issues (which tends to defuse the remaining demands), and settle/compromise at the eleventh hour.

BEING INTENTIONALLY VAGUE

Vagueness often *seems* to be a failing in labor negotiations and in many business deals. However, *vagueness* may facilitate reaching an agreement when it would not otherwise occur. If *principles* are important, politically dual-purpose (even duplicitous) language that allows both sides to claim they won may not be that bad. Unfortunately, it may create conflicts later, as a result of applying those divergent *principles* (interpretations inconsistent with what the other party expected). Negotiators usually know what's up, however, and reaching an agreement usually outweighs the risk of relatively minor litigation and/or ADR (alternate dispute resolution) at a later time. That's where independent third parties such as mediators and arbitrators have a useful role. On balance, although awkward, vagueness may be the only viable way to go.

THE STRENGTH OF OPTIONS

Having *options* is probably a negotiator's single most useful weapon (other than reasonableness, flexibility, and intelligence). You may have a specific goal in mind in one aspect of a negotiation, but that goal may be acceptable to you in a multitude of variations (shapes, sizes, definitions, configurations). A capable negotiator will have *many* possible *options*. If the first proposal doesn't work, the good negotiator will try another angle (*option*), and as many more as needed. Persistence is the operational term here!

The best way to remain objective is to have more than one option, and the party with whom you're negotiating needs to know that (although not in detail). If the other party knows you can walk away from the deal (and they don't want you to do that), you have a clear and distinct advantage. You can dig your heels in on matters important to you with much more confidence. It's of course much better and more persuasive if you *really do* have another viable option. This is true in *anything*: buying a house or car, consummating a merger, discussing a prenuptial, completing an acquisition, you name it.

Negotiations become a little more delicate, however, when you're dealing with a party with whom you must continue a relationship (important supplier, customer, labor union, spouse, governmental agency, etc.). In these cases you simply don't want to threaten the other party. Finding a reasonable compromise is usually the best strategy, unless the other party takes an outrageous stance. It may take or warrant a cooling off period at times, but find that common ground, or bring in a third party (when it makes sense) to help you get there.

CREDIBILITY

Credibility is the most critical personal component in any negotiation and there are many aspects to it:

- Your word is *everything!* You must keep your promises and commitments regardless of how small, and you must follow through on time and as promised, In other words, you must deliver! The slightest break in this trust is extremely difficult to recover from. Sometimes this is the most difficult part of administering an agreement, if only because it's often the case that *"you can trust the other side to deliver, more than you can trust your own."*

- You must be perceived as having the authority/power to make decisions and commitments. If you have a superior, make absolutely sure that she commits not to preempt your efforts behind the scenes by communicating with the other party.

- You must be true to your personal style of delivery. Don't change your personality in a negotiating forum, because it will only come off as contrived. Style is not that important, provided you remain upbeat, logical, factual; and most importantly persistent, tactful and diplomatic.

- You must give deference to the other side's interests and give them due respect. This is especially important in cross-cultural discussions. If you don't, you'll offend them, and things will be much more difficult if not impossible. Listening *and* understanding are vital attributes.

- You must be infinitely prepared with facts, logic, consistency, and accuracy. If you choose to shade the truth or bluff, don't get caught—it's offensive and it will damage your ability to persuade and gain any confidence (it's best to not even consider this type of manipulation).

- You must be able to compromise. But you must not capitulate too early either: timing is important, and you must not be worked by artificial deadlines, it will show a major vulnerability.

The absence of any of the foregoing personal characteristics doesn't bode well for a successful career in negotiating. If any aspect is missing, you can expect to be ignored (with an end run to your superior, or governing board) and indulged while the deal is being cut elsewhere.

BE THE WRITER

Once the conceptual deal is done, try to be the party actually writing or at least controlling preparation of the written language. Nuances in language often clarify processes or help define situations, and those types of details can prove to be useful at a later date, especially if favorable to you: provided you don't try to sneak in something significant that you couldn't attain in discussions (if you do that, you've trashed your credibility).

HELPFUL THOUGHTS

- A good negotiator will occasionally be faced with having to stick his neck out and make a commitment he may not be authorized to make. Usually this will take place toward the end of a negotiation when a few "tidy up" issues can come up quickly (and it can work both ways). As long as there is a quid pro quo, the "sell" to governing management will be easier. All good negotiators will experience this situation: they'll usually take a risk to close a deal, they'll feel the pressure, and usually the matter will work out well.

- Never lose your temper, regardless of how much pressure you feel. Take a break, have a caucus, lighten up, but don't get trapped into an emotional outburst, even if you are being attacked personally.

- Don't compromise your principles if you don't have to, but realize that a pristine and idyllic righteousness doesn't work either.

Protect your (or your client's) interests, but not to a fault.

- Be sure to ask for whatever you need. Don't be shy on this front. If you don't ask, you definitely won't get it.

- Some things are simply not negotiable. That should be made clear up front, and stuck with throughout the discussions. But also remember that there usually are no "absolutes."

Note: Kids seem to make perfect little negotiators. They are persistent and purposeful (although maybe not logical), they make you feel guilt (shifting the burden), they are emotional (making you emotional, too), and they insist on an answer NOW! They seem to win often, too. But, of course, you forgive them for their tactics, and their credibility seems to remain consistent (whatever it is).

SECTION 3

PERSONAL REALITIES

21

Un-Stressing Your Life

Message: *Some nervousness and/or pressure prior to a presentation, meeting, competition, or any activity can be a stimulant for excellent performance. However, if you are stressed you are unlikely to perform well at anything you try. You won't think clearly, you'll be consciously or subliminally preoccupied, and results will be less than optimal. That's all the reason you need to take any action possible to reduce and eliminate the problem(s) and minimize the stress. Potential stress is all around, so if you want to function well, you must learn to deal with it!*

STRESS IS A CONSTANT

THERE'S AN OLD adage that states: "*It's the bullet you don't see that gets you.*" If you don't see a problem developing, haven't prepared for doing something about it, or simply "*can't deal with it,*" you may get emotionally hammered.

Many stresses are unexpected, such as: the loss of a relative, friend, or loved one; illness with you or family; a home burning down; being victimized; witnessing a crime or a severe accident; arguing with your boss; or it could be the loss of a pet. It may be a continuing problem, such as: living in a crime-infested area; bankruptcy; having to leave your hometown to accept a new job (uprooting the kids from school and your family from the community); a difficult divorce; or discovering your child is taking drugs. It may be not having enough time or money to go to school and improve yourself, or it could be as severe as not having enough food for your family. The list can go on and on. It's not easy dealing with even one of these problems, for even the toughest personalities, and many people experience multiple stressors simultaneously.

Daily stressors are all around us and they are unavoidable: the unexpected traffic jam, a stranger flipping you off or yelling at you, investment losses, unruly kids, an overwhelming number of things to do, and many variations of social/interpersonal struggles. Then there is the personality side: fears, guilt, feelings of inadequacy, failures, insecurities, making a mistake or committing a crime and fearing discovery: it happens to all ages and sexes. Some fear and insecurity is probably good for us, but too much isn't. For some people even a little stress creates significant and undesirable psychophysical reactions.

Then there are the symptoms: sleep loss, bad attitude, feeling unmotivated, weight loss or gain, illness, increased blood pressure, lethargy/withdrawal, feelings of failure and helplessness (often creating self-fulfilling prophesies), and depression. Unfortunately, stress causes all too many individuals to overmedicate: legally or illegally, creating other issues and unhealthy dependencies.

Of course each problem has its own solution and each individual has a particular way of dealing with matters. Luckily, most problems are temporary (at least that's the attitude that one should have), so the sooner and more affirmatively you deal with the source of the difficulty, the sooner you'll reduce your stress and resume functioning at a more productive level.

WHO/WHAT CREATES STRESS AT WORK?

For some people, just to get up in the morning and drive to work is a stressing experience. If you don't like your job, you certainly have a problem. Heavy stressors include: getting a poor evaluation, getting disciplined, getting demoted, and/or losing your job and then dealing with the adjustments associated with that (no money coming in but the bills are, finding a new job, or having to sell the house and relocate).

Typical job stressors include: tough (or crummy) bosses, errors, poor performance, lost sales or accounts, short deadlines for critical projects (or missing the deadline and messing up the project), not having the resources or information to complete a project well, poor staff relations or inadequate communications between bosses or coworkers, and there are *many* others. Some very serious stressors could result from trauma (such as paramedics working at a multiple fatality scene, an act of terrorism, an injury, police or firefighters at a call where a colleague is killed, and so forth) and may require professional debriefing.

Since bosses usually discover problems and do something, they tend to get the blame for creating stress (when in fact they are reacting to a problem). No one in an organization is immune from stress: there are plenty of problems to deal with on all fronts. If it isn't machinery breaking down, it's an unhappy client or customer. If it isn't enough sales, it's your banker capping your line of credit, or your supplier missing a delivery date and shutting down operations. Or it might be an electrical outage (or lightning strike) blitzing your operating systems and creating lots of anxiety.

Interestingly, it's the top brass in an organization who tend to have less stress than anyone else. They seem to love generating and passing stress out with their orders, directives, expectations, and deadlines. They also have the most security if they lose their jobs (golden parachutes). Don't believe for a moment that stresses get more pronounced as one rises in the organization. Stresses will be different for managers, but only greater if they aren't good at what they do.

Nothing in the work-world can be more stressful than the single mom in a low paid, time-consuming job, not having the time or money to break out of her situation (perhaps having to work more than one job, living in crowded and/or unsafe conditions, barely making ends meet, and unable to pay enough attention to her kids).

FAMILY FOUNDATION

In seriously tough times the fabric of a family gets tested. These are the times that demand a strong focal point, someone who the rest of the family unit has *confidence* in and can feel has the matter *under control* (or is at least in process of helping *stabilize* the problem). This is the time someone needs to be: *strong;* have the stability and presence of a *"godfather";* the *leader,* generating action and inspiring confidence; providing *wisdom* and *compassion.* That someone could be you, someone else, or several people. Often the patriarch or matriarch of an extended family is a good choice. In really serious times, rally the full strength of the family (perhaps close friends, but family is best).

PERSONAL RESPONSIBILITY

With issues that are stressing, but which don't necessarily require an extended family commitment, the matter will rest squarely on your shoulders. All of us deal with lots of mini-stressors, that most people can joke about later: loss of a girl/boyfriend, poor grades, tough teachers, messing up that critical test or report, not having enough time, too much to learn, not having the money to buy something you want or need, being unprepared for an athletic competition, not being able to live up to a commitment, getting caught in a lie, kids acting unruly, and so on.

In the aggregate, how you deal with this stuff shapes and defines your character and you as a person. Learning to cope with and handle everyday stresses will undoubtedly help prepare you for the major stresses you will likely encounter sometime in your life.

DEALING WITH STRESS

Some people can handle stress as a natural extension of their personality, and many have found that even one simple activity eliminates any and all stress from their lives: like going fishing, taking a walk, talking to a friend, or just sitting in a church. Others must learn how to destress as a conscious activity, and often they must force themselves to unwind.

Stressed or not, before you *do* anything, get your health under control: see a physician, and if indicated, a therapist (psychiatrist, psychologist, counselor, clergy). Make sure any/all physical symptoms are addressed! Without your health, you'll only get more stressed and feel worse. Get a checkup, and be honest with the Doc, even if you don't have significant symptoms. If you're depressed, get treated! Don't rely on alcohol, self-medication, or illegal drugs: they can easily take you where you don't want to be. If needed and within reason, lose weight, change your diet, and exercise (sound familiar?). Be extra careful on the exercise, and follow your doctor's advice, because it could kill you as quickly as it could help you.

Here is a partial list of possibilities. If you're already good at dealing with problems, these ideas may increase your repertoire. If you're lousy at destressing or "debriefing," try anything and/or everything on this list until you find what works for you. The operational keys here are: take control of yourself; think in an assertive, *empowered* manner; and believe you can take care of *any* problem facing you! The trick is to affirmatively manage the situation, and do something about it! Once you take some action, your attitude and emotions will stabilize and things will begin falling into place. *Note: Sometimes surprisingly little, seemingly insignificant actions can have a profound impact on making you feel better; you just need to keep searching until you find what works for you.*

- Use Kaizen concepts, and take unnecessary clutter out of your life: organize everything, and keep important things where they are easily found;

- Distract yourself by doing something atypical: a skydiving or hang gliding lesson, drive a dune buggy, go sailing, go hunting (with camera or binoculars only, of course), have someone take you rock-climbing...

- Window shop for something *big* like a house or car (be sure you can afford it before you commit to anything or you'll end up with more stress);

- Contemplate: look at Indian ruins and their etchings, watch fish, watch a storm, sit by a river and feel the energy, sit on a mountaintop and enjoy being there, watch animals in a zoo, go to a museum or an art show;

- Reassess your circle of friends, make sure they aren't part of the problem, and if they are, begin associating with people who can help inspire and support you;

- Seriously consider emphasizing your spiritual side: religion, yoga, martial arts, tai chi, biofeedback, etc.

- Spend more time with your kids: playing, teaching, just having fun;

- Build something with your own hands: a birdhouse, a toolshed, remodel your house, repaint a room or two;

- Turn your creative side loose: sculpt, paint, write (a poem, a story, an article, a book), take photographs, memorize great writings, play a musical instrument;

- Get a dog and take the time and effort to train it;
- Take a trip, change your venue and perspective (but don't run away);
- Study something you've been interested in but never got around to: astronomy, philosophy, Shakespeare; or just read a book (especially good if you don't generally read); attend a concert or cultural event;
- Change your job, company, department, assignment: especially if you don't like what you're doing or if it's a bad fit for your personality;
- Resurrect old friendships from the past. Look up old classmates you were once close to (the process of finding them can be challenging and rewarding);
- Interview your parents on video: this will be invaluable when they pass on. Ask them about their past, growing up, how they came up with a name for you, how they met, all that little but important stuff;
- Donate time to your favorite charity or cause;
- Take up a competitive sport (or any sport);
- If in an unhealthy relationship, change who you're with, but be careful not to inadvertently jump into a *different* stressful relationship!
- Try out for a play, sing to yourself in the car;
- Music may be good, but it may also bring you down further; be careful what you choose to listen to!
- Hit a punching bag, or do any other activity that gives overt, physical release (as long as it isn't against a *person or pet*);
- Attitudewise, allow for a little reflection and even reverie, but don't stay there: convert your anger, fear, frustration, hurt, and/or disappointment into attitudes and *actions* that move you forward quickly;
- If you're concerned with your sexuality or impact, do a makeover (men *or* women);

- If you've been doing things for others, and your needs have been somehow forgotten, become just a little more selfish and expect reciprocity/balance from others;
- If you've been betrayed by a loved one, take action: make yourself feel as though you can control at least a little of the situation (being careful not to be irrational or overreactive);
- Whatever you try, do it with enthusiasm! Also look for possibilities under "*In The Zone.*"

Your self-image and self-esteem are most important in dealing with any stress. Confidence in yourself is critical. No defeatism is allowed, no "pity-parties," no selfbelittling or denigrating, and it's okay to brag a little.

HOW TO LOOK AT FAILURE

Failure is a state of mind (it's just a label and an opinion), unless you let it get you down, get preoccupied with it, get locked into inaction, and get stressed by it. When any of those conditions exist, "failure" *is* a problem. If you look at failure as one option that didn't quite resolve a dilemma, as a minor setback on the way to a solution, and you have other options ready to try, then a failed approach is a learning experience. Just make sure you learn from it.

GRIEF

Handling grief is a particularly individual, personal matter. Most of the clichés don't seem to help much, although people seem to want to use and repeat them: *forgive and forget, it's time to move on, the healing process must begin, you can't dwell in the past, trust in God, etc.* When you're grieving, those phrases can all seem trite, banal, patronizing, and hardly helpful; but that's about all that well-intended people can really say. You'll be as emotional and "down" as your personality allows, and there's really nothing wrong with feeling sad, lonely, angry, and even hateful. Start doing things that keep you distracted, that improve your situation, and the grief will dissipate in due time. Seek medical intervention if it really gets you down.

22

Protecting Your Assets

WHEN FACED WITH a threat to your assets, your *empowered* instincts *must* be in top form, or you're likely to be victimized.

A SAD BUT TRUE STORY

The son of a close relative learned a skilled trade in the military. He worked for a defense contractor after leaving the service, but was laid off and called back several times within a few years. During the off time he started using and selling drugs.

Following a layoff, his father (with substantial but not extravagant assets), who didn't know about the drug activity, set the son up with an apartment, new truck, and money to get restarted. The son found a lower paying but good job in the electronics industry, and everything seemed on track until the son showed up at his father's house (when the father wasn't home) with an extortion-minded drug dealer, demanding thousands of dollars from his stepmother or someone would be harmed. The son purportedly owed the drug dealer money. The dealer was diverted to the father's place of work, where an ugly face-off occurred. The dealer drove off in the son's truck, and the son ran off.

The dealer visited the house again at night, with an entourage, and several veiled threats, including one directed against a one-year-old in the family. The dealer was again diverted to the father's place of work. The indirect but clearly understood threats later became an important point. The dealer knew just how much to say, because neither the police nor the prosecutors (local or state) would take any action since there was technically no law broken (never mind the clear implications of physical harm, the intimidation, the demand for money, and the fear and emotional damage

GALLEY PROOFS © PARAGON HOUSE

inflicted). The authorities would not even release the drug dealer's name so a civil suit could be filed.

Moreover, when the dealer appeared at the place of work, the police had been alerted but failed to respond because they were consumed with paper-work. A private investigator discovered the dealer was driving a stolen car at the time.

The result: The son disappeared, not to be heard from again; the dealer got away without any cash; and the family relocated a to a secured/gated community, using a corporate identity to keep from being traced. A guard was hired to watch the house until they moved.

DON'T COUNT ON THE AUTHORITIES

Message: *Don't count on the police or prosecutors to help unless you are severely victimized, and perhaps not even then. Assuming the authorities were interested in your case, their success at finding a perpetrator and successfully prosecuting him (contingent on any number of legal technicalities) would be dubious at best.*

The reality in the case study on the previous page is that if a criminal or civil action were filed against the drug dealer, it would have probably resulted in a drive-by shooting (to at least intimidate the plaintiffs). If the father had physically hurt the dealer (something that could have easily happened), *he* would likely have been prosecuted. The dealer received more protection than the victim(s). It's incredible, it's intolerable, it's unfair, and it's true. More on this in the *Epilogue*.

While this seems like an unusual example (which it isn't), it illustrates that protecting one's assets is more than just a matter of money. Yet another acquaintance experienced fundamentally the same extortion/victimization process. In his case, he mortgaged his house, paid the extortionist(s), abandoned his house, moved far away, and filed for bankruptcy. His family was together at last contact, but he was heavily in debt. An important awareness to have is that extortion and even kidnapping appear to be on the increase, and taking precautions commensurate within your comfort level is advised.

Security options (some of these actions may seem a bit extreme, but only until you are victimized): *Note: this list is by no means all-inclusive, but intended to help you start thinking and considering reasonable precautions.*

- Install a high-end, monitored home security system, and use it (this is not really optional if you have any assets at all);
- Be sure your kids are escorted to and from school and at playgrounds (also not optional);
- Make sure your cars have alarms and even tracking systems;
- Learn self-defense techniques;
- Learn evasive driving and emergency driving methods;
- If your car breaks down, and especially if you're a woman, call for help and wait;
- Consider learning to use various defensive weapons (within your ability and comfort range…but first consider the kids), including securing a CCW (carry concealed weapons) permit;
- Live in the safest community you can afford;
- Deal aggressively with any hint of drug use by your children; better yet, preempt it with good training at a very early age (they *will* be exposed to drugs);
- Don't even think about experimenting with drugs yourself, it's pretty stupid any way you look at it!
- Consider filing every conceivable civil lawsuit (in addition to following through with criminal charges) against anyone who would threaten you, your assets, or your family. Find the right attorney, change your residence at least temporarily, and hire a bodyguard if needed.
- Consider an armored car or SUV if you have considerable assets;
- Also at higher asset levels, use a driver who can double as a bodyguard;
- Visit Mexico/South America carefully. If you drive, buy local insurance; don't give much lead notice if you travel on business; and always have a trustworthy, knowledgeable, language-capable, local escort.

- There is something to be said about being a little understated when out and about: cars, jewelry, etc.

PERSONAL LIABILITY

Here are four true incidents that may give you reason to pause:

CASE #1:

A CEO of a prominent medical center lived in the middle of an apple orchard. He was a member of the clergy and well respected in the community. One day he was visited by a good friend and family, which included a preteen boy who loved to climb trees. The boy fell out of a tree and injured himself, resulting in temporary paralysis. The "friend" filed a million-dollar civil liability suit against the minister, assuming there was plenty of insurance and/or assets to take care of the recovering child. The lawsuit was settled for an undisclosed amount. You can guess what happened to trust and the friendship. The minister retired and became more reclusive.

CASE #2:

A young boy wanted to drive his minimotorcycle in the cul-de-sac. Little boys like to show off, so he told an older neighbor he was about to ride the cycle. The little boy's mother indicated he might want to share and let the older boy drive it, too. The boy's father intervened in front of the older boy's mother, suggesting there may be too much risk and liability. The older boy's mother understood, and graciously stated: "Don't even offer, I understand perfectly." No one was offended and a risky situation was averted. In this case, the older boy was a bit "adventuresome," could easily have driven too fast, possibly losing control and hurting himself.

CASE #3

A couple is playing with their miniature poodle at a school playground. The dog is running free, and there's no one else around. Another couple walks onto the playground with their toddler. The poodle decides to play with the baby, and in its excitement nips the baby, breaking its skin. The baby is scared, screaming, and the parents assume their protective mode. The couple with the dog is culpable, and the couple with the baby totally controls the situation. Their options include: impound the dog, test for rabies, sue for assault, file criminal charges for not controlling the dog, file civil charges for emotional distress, demand payment for emergency room costs (and maybe for counseling); and if they have an attorney (who has a feel for your net worth), your personal liability insurance may be tested. In this instance the couple consoled the child, gave the dog-couple a dirty look, and both couples left a little distressed: extremely fortunate for the dog owners!

CASE #4

At a three-way intersection (also a three-way stop), a woman is making a legal and proper left-hand turn. Another woman coming from the opposite direction fails to stop and plows into the car. No one seems to be hurt, however, the one who failed to stop immediately holds her neck and tries to find every reason why she was not at fault. Luckily for the first woman, two witnesses come forward and describe the incident to the police, who issue a citation to the second woman. Were it not for the willing witnesses, it appears clear that fault could have been difficult to establish, with the second woman looking for ways to confuse the facts and avert responsibility. If she were successful, the first woman and her insurance company would probably have been looking at shared medical and damage payments, and who knows what other allegations may have come forth.

MORE POSSIBILITIES

What does one have to do, isolate oneself from the rest of the world?

If you are wealthy, someone will want to "share" your wealth with you, and not just burglars. Insurance fraud and theft are much more common that people realize, and if you have assets, consider yourself a target. Other typical examples:

- A setup accident where a pedestrian fakes being clipped by your car as you accelerate from a stop sign or stoplight;
- A twisted ankle as someone walks down the steps from your home;

- A fall on the sidewalk in front of your house just after you've shoveled the snow and chipped most of the ice away;

- A credit card left in a drawer, seldom used, slipped away by a housekeeper; or a book of checks left out by accident, with a check at the back missing;

- A small team of roofers works on your home while you are away. Since you negotiated a lower price than they wanted, someone evens the deal when a high-end bicycle disappears from the backyard.

Message: *Get it into your head that these instances (or variations thereof) will happen to you if you are perceived as having assets, it's just a matter of when you are targeted. Having a sufficient level of insurance is important; and having an alert, empowered mind-set that you will prosecute transgressors and be aggressive in proactively protecting your assets is just as important.*

FINANCIAL ASSETS

The investment industry is theoretically set up to help people increase their wealth. That is a very compelling and seductive concept, and the industry has many kinds of products you can buy to help the industry increase *its* wealth with much more certainty. *Buy* is the important operating term, because when you become involved with any financial investment, that investment has many ways to keep tapping into your earnings, *whether it grows or not*. Besides the up-front commission or sales fee (which can easily eat up the first year's earnings), consider the ongoing administration costs for the investment itself; the ongoing administration costs for the agent or institution who sold it to you, the transaction fees when you liquidate, the change fees if you make any modifications, taxable transactions and distributions (mutual funds) and back-end loads or penalties if the investment isn't retained (in full or part) for a certain period of time.

All of these (and often other costs) dilute the thrilling, *pre-fees* growth and return that is always touted in the marketing pitches and materials. This is why all investment advisers tell you to consider investing as a long-term strategy. In the long-run, as growth *has* occurred, the adviser's fees and the institutional charges become buried, muted, seemingly insignificant or transparent, and the investor may not be sophisticated enough to know or care.

There is also good reason to be careful about self-directed investments with IRAs and 401Ks (where returns are notoriously lower than if the company invested for you, as in a pension plan). Uninformed or impressionable investors can easily make "knee-jerk" investment changes at inappropriate times and be persuaded to change investment strategies, the changes all costing money in some way. Don't allow yourself to be worked by less-than-ethical financial advisers (remember, they always get their transaction fees).

People *sometimes* start realizing just how much they can lose when the markets take a dump. Administrative costs can be even more apparent after you decide to retire, and wish to protect your assets *more* than you want to risk increasing them. Computer models for maintaining and efficiently working down your wealth/assets vary widely and are extremely sensitive to (and dependent on) tenuous assumptions: all projecting/prognosticating how the economy (and which markets) will perform in the future. Programmed projections or models may not have any relevance to you if you're looking at twenty-five years of retirement. Retirement models become useless and require *adjusting* as soon as frequently *uneven* markets decide to adjust themselves (usually downward). Recovering from projected earning losses in down cycles is very difficult, usually takes years, and you may be back to work before you know it.

KNOW AND UNDERSTAND THIS!

Protecting yourself from financial invaders can be more difficult than it seems, because you want to trust them. Just remember, *all of them are in sales,* and they usually don't have viable insights that you can get yourself from reading reputable journals. Brokerage sales staff often receive marching orders based on which markets, industries, products, stocks, or funds need to be supported or promoted, usually for institutional profitability; and sales staff are evaluated on whether or not they have sold enough to justify their value to their employing institution. Brokers' lives are not dedicated to making you wealthy, although they would certainly have you believe that.

A few good points to consider:

- If you aren't a truly well read, up-to-date, informed investor, stay very conservative, you'll fare much better that way.

- Never wing it when it comes to listening to pitches on great deals, special IPOs and other "terrific" investments. You'll run out of good money *well* before you run out of all those purportedly good investments.

- Trusts of various kinds can be exceptionally useful, but see a reputable, financially astute tax/trust attorney, *not* an investment adviser, for this information.

- Tax planning is important, as well as which investments you convert and when as you dip into your retirement funds. Use a big-five accounting firm for up-to-date guidance.

- Try and live a notch or two below your means. Use some of the concepts you've learned from good, basic management and cut out extraneous expenses. Usually there's lots of nickel and dime stuff you've just assumed is *necessary* (when it really isn't), and it can add up.

- If you are very wealthy, consider incorporation on several fronts in several ways, even internationally, depending on where you have financial interests and where you want to hold citizenship. If married, consider splitting assets legally (without divorcing). These actions may help protect at least some of your assets in case of damaging legal determinations against you, your spouse, or your offspring (during the years when you're responsible for their actions).

- As investments appreciate, consider converting them to real, tangible assets to help ensure *realization* of the growth (vs. paper increases), and then rebuy the same (or other) investment at a lower cost, living on the appreciation (spread). That way you can protect the basis and capitalize on the upside. Watch the taxes (capital gains vs. ordinary income), and any/all transaction costs.

- If you decide to invest in an unusual project of any type, get good legal advice and do plenty of research on all involved parties.

- Be exceptionally cautious about *tax loophole* sales pitches: IRS rules can change, and there are usually inordinately high fees associated with these kinds of products.

- Do lots and lots of reading and get a feel for traditional markets as well as individual companies if you decide to day-trade or make investment decisions. Know much more than you think you need to before you do anything! *Important: first get rid of most or all of your debt!*

BE ALERT TO BECOMING A VICTIM

Here are a few additional examples of situations in which people can be victimized and lose some of their assets:

- The more pious someone is, the more it seems those individuals contribute time and money to charitable organizations. The more they contribute, the more they are asked to contribute, being made to feel guilty if they don't. There is plenty of room for becoming a victim, especially older individuals, so investigate every organization before you contribute anything.

- If you are a recent widow, widower, or divorcee with money, be very careful who seeks you out and comes on to you. Gold diggers can be caring, attentive, and sympathetic until they have access to your money.

- A poorly constructed and/or executed prenuptial can pose problems. In one case, a woman in a "community property" state alleged she signed a prenuptial agreement under duress (claiming she was taking medications and didn't have a complete understanding of the terms). She tried to nullify the prenuptial after a legal separation, and just before the man became wealthy from the sale of his company. He (sort of) prevailed.

- A postnuptial agreement in a community property state can pose problems as well, when one party or the other makes the argument that one can't contract away one's constitutional or legislated rights: as additional assets are obtained in subsequent years. Use experienced legal advice in this area.

- Remodeling and construction companies are notorious for conning people, especially elderly homeowners.
- Be sure to always take along a good negotiator when buying a vehicle. Buy a dinner for the negotiator, who might save you thousands of dollars.

TAKING PERSONAL RISKS

Here are a few areas where you really don't want to take any risks, threaten your assets, and tempt fate (so to speak):

- Keeping your word: commitments, promises, obligations of any type; and maintaining your honesty, integrity and ethics;
- Your family relationships: marriage, kids, extended kin: most are worth preserving in spite of petty squabbles and differences;
- Protecting and preserving your personal assets and family security (as discussed earlier);
- Addressing health and stress matters aggressively;
- Raising your children in the best way you possibly can;
- Continually improving yourself and/or your career;
- Doing whatever you can to live a (generally) happy and fulfilling life.

You can probably add many more items to this list, but you get the general idea. Risks that are common, and which should be handled judiciously include:

- Playing the investment markets (funds, stocks, futures, annuities, etc.) and fundamentally with your future;
- Decisions to change jobs, and especially occupations;
- Participating in risky sports and activities that will likely result in injuries;
- Extreme specialization in your job and/or career;
- Deciding to go into business for yourself and assuming the financial risks (be sure you're cut out for it);
- Not using safety precautions in day-to-day activities: seat belts,

speeding, driving under the influence of something, using ladders carelessly, using power or hand tools incorrectly, sloppy kitchen activities, etc.

- Taking any "professional" advice on face value (lawyers, accountants, trainers, politicians, medical practitioners, etc.)...

Message: *Always second-guess the cost/benefit of taking any risk; and don't foolishly risk your well-being for any temporary rush, for time-saving shortcuts, or because you're too lazy to pay attention to what's important.*

A SIMPLE CONCLUSION

In protecting your valuable assets (family, investments, yourself, property, future, etc.), don't make too many compromises unless you're willing to potentially pay the price for not being alert, not being a little skeptical, not being fully informed, or for being just plain careless.

The military actually has a pretty good philosophy in this area, with its *defensive weapons* (seemingly an oxymoron). This may be a political way of describing a retaliatory device, but the concept is fundamentally valid. Often, the best defense is a very affirmative offense. It's like a small kid standing up to a bully: if someone knows you won't be an easy target, they'll think twice about pushing you around or wasting their time on you.

23

Hosts and Houseguests: Rules of Engagement

THE PURPOSE OF this chapter is to illustrate how an *empowered* approach can help you address and manage a sensitive aspect of your personal life. The following rules apply to any situation or event: holidays, vacations, weddings, funerals, anniversaries, concerts, ball games, etc. and they pertain to your home, your cabin, trailer, motor home, boat or any other personal space. Entertaining houseguests can be very stressful and taxing on the household, especially if space is at a premium. This is one area where preplanning, and then following the plan, helps increase the odds of having a pleasant experience.

There are a few good, well-mannered guests out there; but it appears that most need instructions. For those needing a crash course in courtesy, this is it! Good houseguests seem to have an instinct for being polite, for not disrupting the household, sensing when their presence may be creating discomfort, and knowing how to make it fun.

Indulgent guests who expect you to give them your undivided attention and to fully entertain them have few reservations about turning themselves loose on you and your household. After all, they're out to have fun on their time off, but they're using your time, too. Don't burden yourself with what you'll soon see is at least partly *the guest's* responsibility.

These rules are a reasonable set of expectations; but if you want and choose to be totally accommodating regardless of cost and impact, that's up to you. And sometimes you may want to do just that, perhaps for relatives, very special friends, or for business entertaining (judiciously, of course).

RULES OF ENGAGEMENT:

INVITATIONS AND SCHEDULES

HOST: If a potential guest invites himself to stay at your home, *do not commit* until after you've considered your own schedules and activities.

A self-invitee is like a telephone solicitor; there is no logical or moral reason to categorically accept someone else's inclination to jump into your private space. Also, if there is any stress currently between any family members, houseguests can make matters worse.

GUEST: Don't ever be so presumptuous as to invite yourself into someone else's home! If they want you there, they'll offer.

LENGTH OF AN IN-HOME VISIT

HOST: No one should be allowed to interrupt your life any more than you want them to. Whether or not you choose to use up your vacation time is a serious consideration. Keep in mind that if you are working, there will be no unwind-time when you get home, only more expectations. If you have a busy stretch at work, or a hard day or two, the added burden of guest(s) in your home can be very taxing, especially if you take it out on your spouse. The *maximum* tolerance time is usually four days (preferably less).

GUEST: Your host decides this one, not you!

THE HOUSEHOLD ROUTINE

HOST: Don't feel compelled to change your routine: work, school, children's activities, meals, church, etc. You certainly can change your normal routine if you want to, but the more you do so, the more disruption you'll create. The more you're stressed, the less comfortable everyone becomes, and little things can become big irritants. *Do not* stuff visitors into occupied bedrooms. *Do not* dislodge kids from their rooms (or yourself). If you have a spare room, that's where the guest goes. If not, the visitor sleeps on the couch, assuming you would want him there; otherwise, they're in the nearest motel! Remember that high-density breeds tension in a hurry. There's a good reason people build guest houses: even the slightest distance and separation helps immeasurably.

GUEST: If you notice that people are physically moving around the house to accommodate you, get to the nearest motel: you don't belong there! If you can't afford it, then you can't afford to be a guest.

ITINERARY, SCHEDULE, AND PLAN

HOST: Ideally, make a daily plan and schedule of events/trips for the duration of the visit. Allow some flexibility, but not much. Things can get sloppy pretty fast if you get too relaxed. One of the more frustrating experiences is to have guests who demand attention, are indecisive, are getting listless and bored, and no one knows what to do with them. Better yet, prepare a plan, send it to the guest(s) ahead of time, and agree on the details.

GUEST: Stick to the plan and stay organized. If you want to free-wheel it, then don't bother staying at someone's house and don't involve others in your impulsive or indecisive whimsies.

TOUR-GUIDING

HOST: This one's up to you. If you enjoy it, have at it. Remember that you may need to take time off to do so. Don't make your kids feel like they are being preempted with your attention to the guests and *their* kids. Remember that children are particularly sensitive to changes, about who gets how much attention, and moreover, who may be messing with their stuff! Spouses pay attention: don't burden your spouse with entertaining *your* guest(s), unless you've broached the matter ahead of time (it could be more sensitive than you think).

GUEST: It's the host's decision, not yours. Don't pressure the host to drive you here, there, and everywhere. You should have your own transportation anyway. For long trips (over one hour of driving one way), you're on your own! If the host drives you somewhere and especially on a longer trip: pay for the gas, pay for any meals, pay for fees to parks/events, and do your share of the driving! Remember that you're getting a private guide. How much would that cost if it weren't for your host?

CHILDREN AND BABIES

HOST: Don't underestimate this issue! If kids aren't getting along (and this can be in any number of ways), be ready to move the guests to a motel. If even one child is having trouble adjusting to visitors, make the move! Also, you have a household to maintain, plus worrying about what to feed the guests, don't even think about being a day care service. Their kids are *their* responsibility. Consider the impact on you if you have a baby keeping you awake: especially if you have an important meeting the next day.

GUEST: Don't ask your hosts to babysit! And if they offer, don't accept! You do not dump the kid(s) and take off cavorting while you leave your hosts holding a bag of dirty diapers plus attending to all of their other responsibilities. Don't expect to have dinner waiting for you when you show up later in the evening. If you have a baby, make sure you bring a portable crib; and make sure all of the baby stuff doesn't monopolize the kitchen. Take care of the diapers yourself, and don't make a mess when you wash the baby. If the kids are older, control them, because they are not at home. If your kids crayon the wall, don't just clean it up, it will look worse. Find a painter, make the appointment, and pay for the time and paint, even if the host says, "It's okay."

ANIMALS

HOST: This is your house, your pets are your family members, and you don't have to make any accommodation for your critters. But moreover, bringing other animals into the house or onto your turf (literally) can pose difficult problems, not the least of which can be allergies. Often pets do not get along (sometimes to the point of an unanticipated trip to the vet.). Even if they do get along, dogs like to stake out their territory (inside and out). The rule is: houseguests do not bring pets!

GUEST: Don't ask if you can bring a pet along, because you can't. Leave it at home and make arrangements to have someone look after it. If you know that your host has a cat, and you are allergic to cats, don't stay there! If you go anyway, don't complain!

BATHROOM/LAUNDRY USE

HOST: Tell the houseguest(s) which bath is for their use, and no exceptions! This is *really* personal space, so protect it. Think of your frustration: going into a bathroom and smelling unfamiliar cologne, seeing toiletries all jumbled up, unfamiliar hair here and there, towels rolled up and tossed in a corner, sticky stuff spilled on counters, medicine chests open...get the picture? The same applies to dirty laundry, wherever it happens to pile up.

GUEST: Make sure you bring your own toiletries. Be extremely meticulous and clean. Don't leave a dirty commode. Ask when your hosts need to take showers so you don't use up the hot water (guests seem to love to do this). You don't need to take several showers a day or use a new towel every time you wash your hands. DO NOT walk around the house wearing only a towel or underwear, or less. Wash your own dirty clothes separately from your host's clothes, and do it when it doesn't inconvenience them. Confine yourself to your assigned washroom.

THE KITCHEN

HOST: This is clearly another sacred area. Set strict ground rules and control movement in and around this space. Show guests where the cold cuts and bread are located, but if you turn them loose on much else, your blood pressure will double up in a hurry. Also, it's too dangerous for kids to be rummaging in the kitchen. Remember, nothing returns to its proper place if strangers have access.

GUEST: Stay clear except to help clean up. And clean up you will! If the host has made a nice dinner, YOU pick up and clean the dishes, pots, pans, glasses, and silverware. And you do so even if the host insists you don't need to help, no exceptions and no excuses! Also, YOU clean up after your kid's spills and messes.

CONVERSATION AND GRACIOUS OFFERINGS

HOST: Here is where things can get a little tricky. A gracious host will often make nice offerings about doing things, entertainment options, going somewhere, etc. A not-so-gracious guest may accept the offering and assume since it was your idea, you'll pay for it. Often this stems from the host appearing to be better off than the guest, and the guest not even considering contributing. If conversations probe your net worth, redirect the conversation: it's none of their business. Also be careful about offering future visits in your home: the lousy houseguest will accept, remember, and return.

GUEST: You DO NOT accept offerings that may occur in the course of a casual conversation, such as "maybe we can…sometime" or "it would be nice to go to…" and so forth. If a chat evolves into an action plan, you pay your fair share of the cost, and preferably the cost of your host! Also, it is your responsibility to be interested in your host. If most of the conversations revolve around you and your interests, it comes off poorly: basically self-indulging, boring, and even rude. DO NOT drop comments about how well off the host might be or ask about your host's investments: just don't do it!

DINNERS, FOOD, AND DRINKS

HOST: Making dinners, going out, or ordering carryout is your choice, based on your preferences. Don't feel pressured beyond your comfort zone. Having the guest(s) eat with the rest of the family, consuming your normal foods is just fine. Allowing guests access to drinks, snacks, and/or sandwiches is fine. You do not have to go out of your way to buy or prepare special diets or foods: that crosses the reasonableness line. The same with alcoholic beverages: purchasing what you normally consume and a little more is okay. Special whiskeys, wines, and beers can be overly and unnecessarily pricey and there is no reason to go that far.

GUEST: No free ride here. Take your host and the host's family out to dinner (don't just offer: find the restaurant they like, make the reservations, drive them, and pay the bill). And, on another night, cater in some really good food, and YOU pay. If you like certain alcoholic beverages, bring your own. Find out what your host likes, and secure a bunch of that as well! Don't offer to do it, JUST DO IT! And, bring some fresh flowers while you're at it! DO NOT offer your host money for food as you are leaving: (it's tacky), you know they won't take it, so don't bother. Do not expect to be served or waited on: help set the table and pick up your plate afterwards (remember, do the dishes too).

PERSONAL HABITS AND RULES

HOST: Always remember, you are in your space, and you have control over it. It is your home, and you make the rules. It doesn't hurt to have a list of rules posted on the refrigerator. If there is no swearing, if there are no long-distance calls allowed by teenagers, if you can't wear shoes in parts of the house, if you are expected to clean up after yourself, if everyone goes to bed at a certain time, if the TV can only be so loud and the kids can watch only certain shows, if you can't walk through the house after being in the pool, if you sit in a particular chair to watch TV, ...*then that's the way it stays!* Remember, the guests are not at home, YOU are, and they must respect that fact! You do not have to change your lifestyle even temporarily.

GUEST: You are not at home so don't act like it! No underwear strewn around the house! No socks left in the car! No grossness or stinky feet on the coffee table. No off-color jokes, pictures, or videos. Your kids can't be turned loose or be overly noisy. You can't get drunk or bring drugs into their home.

BROKEN ITEMS

HOST: Having someone in your house is the same as if a neighbor borrowed something from you. If they break or lose it, they make you whole: that is proper, correct, and courteous. Guests are responsible for any damage, so don't be too quick to say *"that's OK, don't worry about it."* It's *not OK*, and you will be angry about it.

GUEST: Not only do you pay for any damaged item(s), you arrange for their repair (find the repair shop, take it there, pay for it, and bring it back). If an item is lost, go to the store and find it (or better yet an upgraded replacement) and present it to the host. This means anything the kids might break or you, accidentally or otherwise, regardless of the value. Just paying for it isn't enough, much of the aggravation is in the replacement process (the trips, locating or ordering items, etc.).

LET'S SUM IT ALL UP

If the purpose of an in-home visit by a friend or family member is to spend quality time and nurture the relationship, then the guest *must* be as (or more) gracious and polite as the host. If you as a guest can't afford to make it a mutually positive experience, then don't make the mistake of ruining the relationship by visiting and making a mess of it: spend time on the phone, use the Internet, and exchange photos or camcorder videos instead.

Your host isn't running a resort just for you: it's their home; and your host isn't there to serve you. Mutual understanding, respect, and reciprocity are the names of the game. It makes absolutely no difference if the host is of means and can afford to keep you. If the experience is one-sided, a comfortable continuing relationship may be doomed.

When it comes to reciprocity (balancing the activities, interests, costs, conversations, etc.), no one keeps precise score, but it's intuitive, it's real, it's important, and it's expected. The consistent factor seems to be that crummy guests tend to be equally crummy hosts. So don't think that events will balance out if/when you visit them, because they won't. Crummy guests just don't seem to have a clue, and they don't want to put out the effort to learn or to be accommodating (although they expect it from others). My personal experience (several times over, but I think I've learned now) is that the crummy guest will make you feel violated fairly quickly. They'll get into things like a two year old, sometimes snooping, while leaving a trail of expenses, servitude, litter, dirt, and disorganization for you.

The burden of making a visit successful is always on the guest! The guest is the alien in the household and must offset and compensate for that fact. The guest creates the aura of comfort or disgust, fun or one-sided obligation. The guest must make the host feel like the *host* is the guest. The good host will always say, "*You shouldn't have*" to your swarm of niceties, but the reality is *you must* do lots of nice things for the hosts and their kids. With that mind-set, you start developing balance, mutual respect, and courtesy.

A GOOD SCENARIO OR TWO

One houseguest or a couple occupying an available room with a bath can be pretty nice, provided, of course the guests are cordial, courteous, tuned-in, polite, and capable of taking care of themselves. If they have all or most of those characteristics, they are probably pretty interesting people to be with as well.

More guests (than a couple) at one time (such as those with kids) should stay at a resort or motel and invite the hosts to off-site activities. The host could certainly invite the guest(s) to their home, briefly (two to four hours), for certain activities, and then have the guests go back to their own space. This is as if the guests were living in the same city and visiting briefly before returning home: *very* nice alternative. Everyone keeps their personal space, and everyone is likely to enjoy the encounters. This option creates a sense of order to the visit.

If you don't know the guests very well, or if it has been a long time since you have seen one another, the hotel/off-site route is the only alternative, at least for the first visit. A good guest wouldn't even consider staying with a host under these circumstances.

Regardless of my cautions and suggestions, hundreds of thousands of gracious hosts will encounter and be savaged by ungracious house guests. But the sooner we operationalize these "Rules of Engagement," the sooner we can improve these encounters and begin to make these experiences a little more civilized.

24

Let's Talk about Religion

THE INTENT OF this discussion is to offer a few observations, provide relatively neutral/objective thoughts, and explore the notion that while religion can indeed be very good for people, even helping them vicariously experience *the Zone*, organized religion can also foster unproductive guilt, mediocrity, and serious conflicts.

If you find the discussion in this chapter offensive, stop reading, and go to a different one. Be absolutely assured, however, that no attempt is being made to convert anyone to or from anything. Whatever religious/spiritual theory you embrace and have faith in is totally your choice. If it helps you and doesn't hurt others, excellent!

FATE VS. FREE WILL

Mainstream religions, in their many forms are not particularly tolerant of independent thinking (exercising free will), and only their anointed clergy are authorized to and capable of understanding and interpreting supreme will. Most of us attribute actions that are out of our control or understanding to fate, the will of a supreme "loving" being; but at the same time no one can logically or adequately explain why God would allow so much pain, evil, and hate to exist in so many parts of the "civilized" world.

Comments made throughout this book that encourage exercising free will and independent judgment under the rubrics of ethics and integrity are totally congruent with the ultimate philosopical goal of most religious teachings. If religion helps you organize your life and be a good, ethical, and tolerant person, then it works for you.

The suggestion in this discussion is to consider not letting fate and unquestioning submissiveness/obedience to any single belief system become your only way of thinking. If that happens, individual responsibility is delegated, you lose control over your reasoning, you become blindly compliant and unquestioning; and you outrightly dismiss other potentially viable possibilities.

Message: *When thinking is controlled as effectively as it is through programmed beliefs (organized, mainstream religion), individuals don't necessarily feel they have control (free will) over their status, their needs, and what is best for them, instead accepting their situation (be it good or bad) as their predestined fate. That is the power, and the shortcoming, of unquestioning, submissive, obedient faith.*

RELIGION AND THE ZONE

Recently, scientists isolated the portion of the human brain that accommodates religion, faith, superstition, and similar matters. They found that some people have a physically larger receptor and corresponding need in this area than others.

The evolutionary theory is that this receptor was associated with humans clustering for protection, from hostile entities (probably mainly from other humans). Accordingly, social systems developed, and if you wanted to be part of the group and be protected, you needed to believe in what everyone else believed (i.e., what you were told by the prevailing leadership). Being compliant in religious circles, or in any social order for that matter, provides comfort, direction, reinforcement, security, and strength in feeling a part of something that's important and "big."

Researchers have also found that individuals experienced in various forms of meditation and/or deep concentration (including intense praying, yoga, biofeedback, revivals, etc.) are capable of turning off or blocking portions of their brain so that perceptions of time, space, and self are put aside or on hold. This creates a sense of euphoria: a perceived freedom from social and physical (worldly) constraints, a sense of floating, oneness with everything, and a feeling of being omnipotent and serene. It makes you wonder if this is the same peacefulness experienced as people pass on.

Those who can attain this detached state of mind are unquestionably in a different perceptive zone. They sense they can sort out the fog of extraneous confusion and find truth, significance, and insights to perplexing problems. If they believe their "energy" can somehow enable miracles or other constructive events, then encouraging praying or meditating can only be a good thing. If they can harness useful insights while in this *Zone*, be it a dream state or not, and regardless of how their enlightenment occurs (drifting through time and space, levitating, controlling involuntary physical functions, or just cruising peacefully in their own reality), it is a state of mind worth pursuing and attaining. It's probably quite an adventure.

For those who aren't inclined to accept organized religion and its lack of logic as their philosophy, using a more neutral approach may be something to consider. If you're interested enough you'll eventually find the vehicle that will get you there: rituals, mantras, repetitive/ hypnotic chants, self-hypnosis, inspiring group singing or dancing, holding a mojo, praying, communing with nature, gazing at stars or other natural objects, focusing on a crystal, fasting, and/or martial arts. All have a few things in common: discipline, concentration, active participation, dedication, and commitment (including the *belief* that some level of truth and direction will be realized). Getting "caught up in the moment" of any of these events can be a very inspiring experience.

DEVELOPMENT OF "ORGANIZED" RELIGION

So here we have the classical human paradox: the highest level of intelligence coupled with fear and insecurity and the need to have a paternal "being" for protection. With intelligence came imagination, and lots of it. Any natural phenomenon that was not readily understood was given creative significance by the elders, who were probably the most intelligent members of the tribe. Rituals and customs gradually evolved, creating the protective, reassuring, cohesive framework and philosophy everyone needed. Religion filled in the missing element: an intense belief system that could focus the group, give its members confidence, and give the pack an identity. In other words, pretty powerful stuff; and that *really* distinguished humans from other critters.

SIMILAR THEMES THROUGHOUT TIME

If one were to objectively examine the themes that humans found compelling through the ages, you would find that things haven't changed much. Examining the evolution of mainstream cultures and religion from a comparative perspective (Sumerians to the Egyptians to the Romans and Jews, to Mohammedans and to Christians, for example), it becomes unquestionable that each borrowed from the others and adapted the faiths to the prevailing social conditions and needs.

The principles and behaviors expected of people in any organized religious or philosophical order are not that different from one to another. From followers of Confucius to Hindus, Taoists to Romans, Greeks to Nordic gods, Christians to Islam, worshiping nature to worshiping idols: there are more commonalities than differences. The differences are greater in the *forms* gods take and in the rituals, and less in their fundamental message or purpose (to make socially compliant citizens).

Common reoccurring and compelling themes have included immaculate conceptions, exaltations/resurrections (mummies), miracles, being granted godlike or sainted status, and some form of damnation or shunning for those without belief in the "only true faith." Most Christian scholars, when asked, will admit that the Bible was written as a series of metaphors, not to be taken literally. But yet in practice, interpretations, rituals and customs all suggest that its words should be accepted literally. This is in part how organized religions keep their following compliant (ingrained ritual and literal acceptance which quickly becomes a habit, and eventually a need).

WHAT MAKES A GOOD PERSON?

If you are totally into the dominant religious scene around you, then to you a good person is one who conforms to the beliefs/rules you subscribe to, and "unbelievers" are shunned, cast out, avoided, and perhaps even killed. If they survive, they'll be leading a lonely life...unless they find an alternate societal group that will accept them, and these days there is usually one for everyone.

Religions would have you believe that you are fundamentally/

inherently bad (especially Christians), that you must redeem yourself, and that without salvation you're doomed in the hereafter. In addition, apparently no matter what you've done and how heinous your actions, your misbehavior can be forgiven and you can be back on track for heaven by restating your commitment, doing good deeds, and giving money. It just seems there's something very contradictory, self-serving, and incomplete in this concept.

Case in point: *There is an old popular Russian folk song entitled "Twelve Robbers." It has a beautiful melody, and borrows phrases from liturgies. In the song, a band of robbers kills many god-fearing citizens. The leader steals a maiden and, while devastating her, receives a holy enlightenment. He is transformed, becomes a believer, and goes to the monastery to serve people and God.*

If the story means he was effectively jailed and made to do good things, then perhaps justice was partially served; but the compelling interpretation is that God changed and saved a dastardly soul. But what about all the victims? The element of justice is clearly missing.

Religions would have us believe that without religions, there would be moral anarchy; and to some extent they are probably right. If you allow humans to carry on without social expectations and discipline (i.e., law), then many would be vile, obnoxious, self-indulgent scourges. But in today's world most civilizations have laws (which evolved from religions) to control outrageous behavior. In the school and work environments we also have sets of principles and behavioral expectations. We seem inundated with rules, regulations, policies, procedures, philosophies, and controls. If we all subscribed to and followed all the social orders around us, perhaps (together with integrity and ethics) we could create a lovely world.

If subscribing to a religious philosophy, organized following (mainstream or not), or even cult provides you with integrity, ethics, principles, values, practices, and/or habits that make you a good person *and no one is harmed in any way as a result of your faith and convictions,* and as long as it isn't inadvertently restricting you from making the most of yourself (continuously improving), then by all means follow those teachings. Do so as long as you aren't being taken advantage of and as long as you respect others and their beliefs without prejudice.

Unfortunately, there are many ostensibly religious people without scruples. There are also many people without formal religious attachments who are infinitely humane and fundamentally *good*. If history has any accuracy, then religions, largely synonymous with "government," have been responsible for countless atrocities, bigotry, ethnocentrism, nationalism, hatred, and all that is bad about mankind. Any way you look at it, the power of religion is very impressive.

INTOLERANCE: THE DOWNSIDE OF RELIGION

True religious believers tend to have little tolerance for those outside their system of beliefs and circle of followers. Extreme *belief* can (and does) become disdain, bigotry, controlled thinking (even brainwashing), discrimination, and a foundation for hate. Most religious teachings are not inherently "bad," but convolutions of those teachings and what some people do in the name of their faith has been demonstrated many times over as *inhuman*. It's amazing how, historically, the most pious (and incidentally the most educated) have also been the most intolerant and cruel.

It is very difficult for people to distinguish religious teachings from political ideologies and ethnocentrism. As a result of religion being totally entwined with governance, some of the world's worst atrocities have been committed in the name of one God vs. another or one belief system vs. another. Often the precipitating event is economic hardship, such as starvation, and the need to take over someone else's food suuply.

Causes of any kind will coalesce people easily, and the cause will thrive when there is a perceived, fabricated, or real enemy, persecutor, or adversary embodying the devil, some form of evil, or some kind of threat. U.S. patriotism reached a new high after the World Trade Center (and related) disasters, literally unifying the country overnight. For Americans that was a good thing.

Other less admirable examples, to name a few, include: the Inquisitions, Crusades, Soviet/Communist atheism, Nazi annihilations, Balkan ethnic cleansings, Islam/Judaism strife, Hutu–Tutsi warfare, right-to-life bombings, jihads, the IRA, witch-hunts, and other religious-based persecutions. In other words, when religion controls or has some significant influence on politics, government, terrorists, soldiers, or armies (real, tangible power), things get ugly. That's one reason why the founders of the U.S. made it a point to try and separate church and state.

There is always a cause to pursue, a devil to purge, and someone to hate. People have always found those concepts irresistible (allowing a vent for their frustrations, aggressions and perhaps relieving their boredom by conquering and plundering, or at least trying to). And, of course, if you die while pursuing a holy, righteous cause, you are assured immediate access to Valhalla, heaven, or somewhere similarly nice.

DECISIONS, DECISIONS

Here are a few logical points to consider about religious faith *(You'll have to decide what piques your curiosity. If you can accept that there is no right or wrong in the following ideas, that's a good thing. If you can't accept that notion, believe whatever you wish, but be a tolerant individual.)*:

- Being a moral person and being a member of an organized religion are not necessarily dependent on one another; being at peace does not necessarily require adherence to mainstream belief systems; objectively, it's conceptually difficult to put total faith in any god that threatens you into obedience (why does a god need to be worshiped anyway?); and it isn't likely that all those people who don't share your faith will end up in hell;

- A good argument can be made that faith in an organized religion is much less important (as far as your impact on others) than spirituality (morals, ethics, values, open mind,etc.).

- It's much more convenient to be told what to believe than to figure it out for yourself;

- It's harder to take personal responsibility for the sum total of your actions and make those you've injured whole, than to conveniently be allowed absolution/redemption for your sins by theological decree;

- It's harder to exercise your free will, and take control of your life, than to declare that "fate" is somehow responsible for your shortcomings and/or inactions. Eric Hoffer stated it very succinctly fifty years ago in his book *The True Believer: "Faith in a holy cause is to a considerable extent a substitute for the lost faith in ourselves."* Being totally submissive, obedient, and compliant can perhaps help you feel satisfied and comfortable, but it also has a very averaging (noncreative, nonquestioning, bureaucratic) effect;

- The power of religion and the righteousness it brings out in people to act in concert, seemingly unselfishly, right or wrong for a noble cause, and to *move* people into action (including war) is nothing short of incredible. Similarly, the strength *extreme faith* has to at least facilitate the healing of emotional and sometimes physical problems is awesome.

- No single organized religion can possibly embody all of the truth, virtue, and answers for all mankind; "God" can, and does, take many forms as demonstrated through so many different faiths; not any one "God" that we can comprehend is probably complete or right; and having respect for the good attributes of all gods and religions seems more of what any god would want (otherwise we wouldn't be giving "God" enough credit);

- Religious intolerance is a very bad thing. If bigotry and ethnocentrism are by-products of any religious order, then it is not a good religion to be a part of (in our global world, religiously based cultural clashes are out of date and totally unnecessary);

- Organized religion has little value in our workplaces (speaking of the U.S.); however, the principles and values often gained and practiced as a result of being a part of a religion, are invaluable anywhere (but only if exercised in a nonprejudicial manner);

- There is much that we (and religions) just don't know: historical accuracy and facts are always in question; quantum physics theories suggest other worlds, dimensions, and/or universes that we can't begin to comprehend; no one really understands what "time" is. If there is a heaven and/or hell, how do we know we're not in one right now? Can praying and/or someone's aura create a transferable energy field enabling healing? Why doesn't God elect to "reside" here on earth, instead of remaining an abstraction and a concept?

- Religious and spiritual people have the ability, perhaps even more so than noncommitted ones, to occasionally experience *the Zone* in a very personal, intense, and fulfilling way.

Message: *Believe in whatever helps you with living in a complete, wholesome and fulfilling way. But concurrently, be tolerant of others, assume full responsibility for your actions, and maintain an open, reasoned perspective on everything around you...never stop exploring ideas, concepts, and philosophies. Developing and nurturing faith in one's self is as (or more) empowering than anything else.*

25

Sexuality and Managing Relationships

I WILL ALWAYS wonder how often this chapter will be the first one read out of all the possibilities in this book. This is truly compelling subject matter, and one of the strongest and most driving behavioral motivators. Many of the principles described in this chapter apply to other situations; but this area is the most intense, has the most components, and provides a good example of how an *empowered* mindset can help by assertively resolving conflicts and actively managing personal relationships.

More can be found on love, sex, and relationships in the chapter on *Happiness*.

IT ALL BEGINS WITH PRESENCE

The previously discussed concept of presence is totally related to a person's sexuality. *Webster's Collegiate* defines sexuality as *"expression of sexual receptivity or interest."* For the purpose of our discussion, the term *sex appeal* could be synonymous with *sexuality*.

Everyone wants to be noticed positively for their sexuality, it is unquestionably in the natural order of things. People go to great lengths to look desirable, appealing, attractive, alluring, fit, and sensuous. People also act to emphasize (or deemphasize) their sexual receptivity: clothes, discourse, body language, dancing, flirting, language, eye contact, and any number of gestures.

A person's *presence*, and especially how that presence enhances (or suppresses) their *sexuality*, often determines how the person sees (and defines) him or herself. A person comfortable with their sexuality is probably having their needs met, they are in their comfort *zone*, and there is reciprocity in their relationship (not a small achievement in this hypersensitive area). A person who is comfortable with their *sexuality/presence*, will also have a sense of confidence that helps them fare well in that (and many other) arenas. If they don't have a reasonable level of comfort, insecurities and/or maladjustments can develop into serious problems. Developing a presence is discussed in detail in *"How Do You Define Yourself?"* In this chapter we'll focus on the importance of understanding and managing an intimate, personal relationship.

At any age, it seems, a person's needs vis-à-vis their sexuality are also their vulnerable area. The drive is so strong, people will go to great lengths to find what's missing in a relationship, often taking risks and/or breaking rules. Problems arise when people can't control excessive, unfounded, unreasonable urges or if they don't try (make the effort) to strengthen their current relationship. If you think you're in a bad relationship, make sure you're not the problem, or you may repeat bad relationships. If the relationship is truly detrimental, and there's no reason to salvage it, know when it's time to go and move on.

Speaking of age, your sexuality shouldn't change much during your life span (although illness can set you back). If it is changing negatively or going flat, fix it! At the same time, don't expect to attract 20-some-things when you're 60-something (unless you're rich, famous, and at least somewhat attractive). Even if you do, don't expect it to last.

THERE'S NO AVOIDING THE TOPIC: IT'S EVERYWHERE!

There are endless jokes, films, stories, novels, and commercials/ advertisements dealing with every conceivable aspect of this topic. There are many observations about the mechanics of sex and/or love, difficulties males and females have in understanding one another, and difficulties men and women have in adequately satisfying each other's needs. The disparate needs are at least generally known to most people, but worth a quick review: because even though men and women think they understand each other's needs, they sure seem to have trouble figuring out what to actually do.

The following two "needs" sections are clearly abbreviations, and should by no means be considered complete, but they'll serve as a reminder of what you've heard and read before, and you can fill in the gaps.

MEN'S NEEDS AND MOTIVATIONS

Men are visual, mechanical, and they want to touch everything. They are constantly searching for/pursuing/chasing a sexual partner, and their testosterone causes a physical need to periodically relieve "pressure." When that doesn't happen, they can become moody or aggressive. They tend to want to protect their partner from any other interested males, making them a little more possessive if only because it's tougher for them to find a receptive partner. Men try to emphasize their musculature (sometimes coming off as bizarre), they compete in speed/strength-testing sports, and their toys focus on "power" (cars, noisy motorcycles, guns, etc.): all to get attention. The smart ones write poetry for women. They want women to admire and respect them, and they tend to prefer affectionate women who also like to touch and maintain physical contact. Relationships are important, but communication (especially conversation) is more difficult than for women. Men tend to be flattered by the attention of any attractive woman, often misunderstanding their friendliness and/or intent. They struggle with conceptualizing, fully understanding, appreciating and then managing women's drives. Men tend to be impatient, and they like to take charge of the relationship.

WOMEN'S NEEDS AND MOTIVATIONS

Appearance-wise, women are much better equipped to get attention than men, and they are excellent at emphasizing their strongest physical attributes (compensating with the correct clothing as needed). Women can (and know how to be) much more physically attractive than men. Women are security-driven, and they do the choosing. Security means many things: physically appealing but not "pumped," not overbearing or abusive, polite and courteous, affable, of-means, stable, faithful, interested in/attentive to them, willing to protect them and any offspring, compatibility (social, racial, religious, ethnic) and they expect men to be not so reckless or independent they won't settle down (even though they may be initially attracted to the wild side). Accordingly, it takes women longer to figure out if they want to be with any one male. To be sure they aren't being tricked, they take their time; and they tend to be choosy, and play the field (investigating as many "acceptable" candidates as they can attract) until they *are* sure. Women can also manage men's relatively shallow physical and emotional drives very effectively (men *try* to fight it). Women have a need to be wanted (not left alone or abandoned) and fear being rejected. They love to be collaborative. Many women feel *they* must have full control over the relationship to be secure. Women tend to look long-term, in contrast with men's often short-term interests.

YOU'D THINK IT SHOULD BE EASY

You would think that once you've read these and similar comments (and everyone has over and over), that appropriate actions would be easy to figure out: addressing and satisfying the other party's needs, compromising, and thereby improving the chances of having your own needs met. You would also think that a little insecurity (both ways) might prompt each to try a little harder. *Now, that's optimistic thinking!* The other aspect we haven't mentioned, confusing matters immensely, is when either (or both) is in *love:* thinking becomes anything *but* rational.

The man-woman relationship has more intricacies than managing a complex organization. The same kinds of issues you face at work, you face in the relationship, but amplified with intense emotions. It requires very skillful negotiating and diplomacy to navigate through relationship issues smoothly. There are lots of challenges, conflicts and unexpected reactions and problems to resolve. It takes lots of thinking, planning, anticipating, understanding, and prudent acting to keep things from getting confrontational, or simply boring. Self-fulfilling prophesies really work here: think/act positively and it happens, think negatively and it *definitely* comes to pass. The relationship and those in it are constantly changing; and you must understand that shifts in interests and priorities will occur, so complacent thinking will result in staleness. Remain continuously alert to changes and make sure, as much as you can, that changes are often improvements.

CONTINUING MANAGEMENT IS ESSENTIAL

The interesting thing is that any and/or all of the parties' needs don't stop and all needs aren't necessarily met once a man and woman get together. Often, one or the other (or both) forgets to continue trying to fully discover and understand their partner: taking the other for granted, and/or letting less than desirable behaviors creep in. That scenario and many like it can begin to erode the relationship's "sweet spot." When the needs of either party aren't met, those needs become a big deal, manifesting themselves in emotional (if not desperate) ways. And then, if communication slows down or stops, the relationship will undoubtedly deteriorate. This is where an *empowered* mind-set can help.

Message: *Good indicators of when it's time to step up attention to the relationship is when practicality (day-to-day obligations) override and disallow spontaneity, fun, and random playful acts and/or when casual conversation and touching are missing.*

WHAT TO DO, AT LEAST CONCEPTUALLY

Once again, you may have heard or read these before, but they're definitely worth repeating; but moreover, certainly worth practicing and trying (feel free to add to this list) *Note: be careful not to overwhelm the other person to the point they "can't breathe" or they "need space;" some restraint is good*:

- Continue to do the appealing things that got you into the relationship you wanted. It took a lot of effort, you were focused, attentive, and probably acting with lots of passion (perhaps even irrationally);
- Try new variations of those appealing actions: the secret is to not get mired in the same, repetitive activities (they'll eventually lose their luster): even small changes in nice activities (nuances,

details, refinements) keep things interesting, exciting, surprising, and add spice (just be careful not to get too bizarre);

- Continually look for new or additional activities to share in the relationship: it at least keeps discussions going and communication open;

- Continue to keep yourself in top physical shape and condition (be careful not to get fat, sloppy, gross, stinky, or otherwise uninteresting): maintain your *sexuality*;

- Continue to improve yourself mentally: whatever it takes and however you choose to do it (it could be as simple as reading and sharing what you've discovered). That activity alone will continue to make you an interesting person;

- Learn to unstress and practice it actively: taking frustrations out on your partner is a very inconsiderate and selfish thing to do;

- Use faith and/or religion as a shared cornerstone if it works for you; otherwise find another area of common, significant interest;

- Tactfully and diplomatically *negotiate* issues involving the household and the relationship (investments, finances, purchases, toys you *must* have, pets, and "rules"): this takes a lot of practice, effort, and it's worth it (no ultimatums, unilateral surprises, or sneaky activities);

- Stick with hammering out solutions to problems, friction points, and tensions: ideally, don't stop until you reach an agreement (at the very least, get issues and feelings on the table and start thinking about them);

- Don't be overly shy or sensitive (especially women, including discussing and disclosing pleasing and/or repulsive sexual activities);

- Infuse your gestures with as much creativity, excellence, and flexibility as you're capable of; and execute your attentions/niceties with taste and style; try to be entertaining, accommodating, and certainly attentive in conversations (too many *honest* compliments are much better than too few); go for fun, laughter, kidding, and playfulness.

CRITICAL COMPONENTS: EASIER SAID THAN DONE

When you're caught up in your day-to-day activities, it's easy to overlook (paradoxically) the most important area: nurturing the relationship. It seems to always be there, it seems to manage itself, and it seems to be fine: but it won't stay that way if you don't pay attention! Take it for granted and it will gradually begin drifting toward mediocrity, resulting in dissatisfaction and someone (or both) looking for ways to meet their needs outside that once mutually exciting and supportive relationship.

Ethics and *integrity* are critical. The concept of *trust* must be continually reinforced, and lying or cheating (to any degree, including omissions and secret agendas) eats at the essence of the relationship.

Communication is another critical component: including all forms (love notes, poems, cards, comments, discussions, negotiations). If communication is difficult for whatever reasons, try making a game of it with rules (content, method of presentation, timelines, etc.) Just making up the rules will enhance communicating and negotiating. If you think you're overcommunicating, you're probably *just* getting to where you should be. *Insist* on communication, and *force* it if necessary. Include a third party in serious matters, but it's always better if you can work things out on your own.

TROUBLE SPOTS

Here are a few symptoms that can devastate relationships (indicators of when outside intervention is probably advisable): *withholding intimacies as punishment (women), or overbearing sexual demands (men); unsatisfying or infrequent intimacies; ignoring, unresponsiveness, or lack of communication by either party (especially if there is avoidance in discussing sensitive issues); partners competing for attention; holding grudges; being totally self-indulgent (minimal reciprocity, or absorbed in/consumed by appearance); seeking attention or reinforcement by "coming on" to other people (disrespectful and rude); envy of partner's success and/or abilities; consistently wearing revealing attire (women); comparing and bragging about past conquests (men); using partner as a parent figure; being habitu-*

ally condescending (quips, put-downs, jokes, and/or complaining that the partner doesn't look like a model or actor); any form of emotional or physical abuse; promiscuity, perhaps even calling it "only sex"(no such thing); hetero vs. homo-sexuality; "kinky" activity as perceived by the partner, including heavy emphasis on pornography and/or nasty jokes; expecting/attempting to significantly change the partner's personality or beliefs; etc.

FULL CIRCLE

Isn't it interesting, that much of the subject matter discussed throughout this book totally applies to sexuality and managing your relationship?

Successful personal relationships require stability, maturity and effort. They also create a foundation for success in other endeavors: including your career. Success in your career also bodes well for your organization. It all ties together.

26

Assimilating Information, Creativity, and Constraints

"He who will not reason is a bigot, he who cannot is a fool, and he who dares not is a slave." *Sir William Drummond, 1585–1649*

EQUIPPING YOURSELF TO process information accurately and objectively is probably the single most *empowering* attribute to develop for enabling optimum performance and success in any endeavor. That involves developing excellent: writing skills (grammar, syntax, spelling, punctuation, organized structure), reading/research abilities (to obtain pertinent information), nonverbal assessment skills (including listening), deductive/inductive skills for determining meanings, verbal communications skills, and critical thinking (reasoning ability and attempting to grasp reality). It also means understanding computers and using application programs effectively. Develop and/or enhance these attributes any way you can and as quickly as possible: it's never too early or too late!

IF IT'S IMPORTANT, COMMUNICATE FACE-TO-FACE

Communication is a wonderful thing, but words, if not carefully chosen and diplomatically presented, can be misinterpreted, interpolated, and meanings can change dramatically from the intended message. When words are communicated in person, the chance of accurate exchange and transmission of information increases with the added dimensions of body language, inflections, intonations, emphasis, and Q & As. Written words must be chosen more carefully, since immediate clarification may not be available; and missing elements are as significant as stated ones.

Impersonal memos, e-mails, and letters may allow you to think through and organize your information, but effectiveness relies on your command and presentation of the right words for your intended purposes. E-mails and memos are notoriously blunt; and reluctant/introverted people can come off as rather bold, even if they don't mean it, with results easily emerging differently from those intended. Inefficiencies are likely with a poorly constructed or marginally complete memo, requiring clarification by phone or through more e-mails.

Face to face is still the most useful and preferred communication mode for important matters; and don't make the mistake of negotiating serious matters over the telephone, there are too many missing cues. Determine the most effective mode of exchanging information and insist on it.

SLIPPERY SLOPE

Finding accuracy in information is a never-ending, often daunting experience. We are always trying to understand problems and situations just a little more clearly; and it seems as though there is never quite enough information to be sure about very many things. Enter the slippery slopes of conjecture, ascribing intent, interpretations, second-guessing, assumptions, unsubstantiated opinions, and all forms of filling in the blanks. These are the domains of miscommunication, misconception, misunderstanding, and inaccuracy: areas to be carefully addressed and navigated (if not avoided) or they will most certainly create problems.

Differentiating between useful and useless information is an art form, especially with so much data available to us through a plethora of systems and technologies. The constants for effective communication (leading ultimately to effective problem-solving), however, will probably never change, and they include:

- Establishing what is factual vs. speculation, conjecture, opinion, etc.

- Using a reasonableness standard to identify/sort out important data.

- Employing objectivity to determine significance.

- Not being unduly distracted, at least initially, with hypotheses (although this "creative" tool can be helpful in organizing information once sufficient factual evidence has been discovered).

- Exploring and considering as many causal relationships as possible.

- Applying rational approaches and technologies to resolve issues.

REALITY AND REASON

"Few men have imagination enough for reality." *Goethe*

To understand *reality*, you must see it as a continuum of facts, consisting of a series of reasoned building blocks that eventually lead to realizations of significance and truth. Being able to recognize meanings in relationships of people, things, and events; and then optimizing discoveries and observations with constructive action (without wasting time on useless activity) is where you want to be.

Most of us like to think of *facts* as *reality*. And they may in and of themselves be just that. But facts are probably neutral in their existence. They may be perceived as objective and real, but they don't mean much to us until they are collated, categorized, labeled, described, organized, and given some kind of significance or value using (much less than objective) conclusions, opinions, and ascribing of intent. As a result, there are many potentially justifiable and even accurate realities, some more valid than others. So, by and large, reality is what you believe it to be; and if your reasoning ability is strong and objective, your sense of reality will be closer to the truth.

Facts are just pieces to the puzzle called "truth." Facts can be very elusive when they come forth in the form of circumstantial evidence, anecdotal experiences, marketing/media spins, inductions, and deductions that seem to have some level of validity. Facts, truth, and reality must be carefully sorted from their illusions: ritual, habit, common wisdom, expert opinion, generally accepted practices, persuasive discourse, interpolations, pitches, and believing you want to believe as true.

Isn't it interesting how if you were to pose the same set of facts to two different juries, how often you could end up with two totally different verdicts? All manner of dynamics come into play: dominant individuals, persuasive talkers, emotional responses, selective primacy of and emphasis on some facts more than others, experience and background of the jurors, the attempt to reason between right and wrong within the constraints of the allegedly factual evidence that is provided (and not knowing what may be missing), ascertaining motives and intent, resisting drawing conclusions outside the evidence, following the letter of the law (and jury instructions), and the edict to reach a consensus of opinion.

Facts, reasoning, judgment, individual feelings (perceptive constraints), and several perspectives converge to purportedly sort out the matter and determine the truth. The theory is that several opinions will cleanse and counterbalance irrelevant, spurious, and arbitrary arguments, resulting in disclosure of *reality*.

The description above doesn't exactly instill a sense of trust and confidence in the judicial process, does it? And, as should be expected, this (and any similar) committee process invariably errs more often than anyone cares to admit.

As in quantum mechanics, *reality* is very much a perception of the relationship of a set of facts to other things and events. Most certainly, facts that appear to indicate one thing may be easily interpreted to mean something else, and *reality* may be something altogether different from that.

Enter those fragile, limited individual perceptive constraints: personal experiences and frames of reference (what we've learned, think we know, and what we've been conditioned to believe). The more narrow the frame of reference, the more impressionable and less accurate the individual's *reality* will be. It is logical to conclude that ignoring reality is embracing mediocrity, and that an ignorant person has no understanding of, little use for, and no interest in *reality*. For most of us, it is an act of faith on our part to believe that even our own thoughts have any relation to *reality;* and many of us function consistently on our assumptions, belief in illusions, and reliance on embedded opinions and biases.

Also, people often rationalize random or unexpected events as happening for a reason or for a purpose. The reality is that there is only significance, reason, or purpose if you recognize, explain, and categorize it in a particular manner. The important thing is whether or not you learn something significant, useful, and real from an event or series of events. Since facts are what you interpret them to be, how you determine and deal with *reality* defines you as a person.

A key to being successful is to be alert to the multitudes of convergences, junctures, intersections, and intertwining of people, situations, and events occurring around us every day, and to be open-minded enough to find significance in those relationships.

It is incredibly *empowering* to use informed, logical reasoning to objectively sort out and determine what is likely to be real. To continuously improve, progress, and be successful, nurturing, developing, enabling, allowing, and demanding that mode of thinking is *imperative*.

A MATTER OF BALANCE

Too much information and you can overload. You may feel as though anything could potentially influence anything else, resulting in perplexity and confusion. Insufficient or incomprehensible information, and you don't have enough to grasp what you're dealing with.

With too little study (and usable information), you could easily feel that everyone else has assessed the situation more completely than you ever realistically could. That could cause you to gravitate to what others tell you (specialists, consultants, experts, etc.). In turn, that could lead to selecting and confirming a position you like, deferring to the opinion of a dominant personality or simply endorsing the opinion of one who seems most knowledgeable. You may fill in for your lack of command of the subject with what you already know: seizing on ideas that have general acceptance (safe conventional wisdom), and what you have a comfort level with. Or, you may draw conclusions that are politically correct (also safe): which fundamentally avoids negative considerations and assumes the positive, constructive, non-controversial (easy to communicate, be a part of and gain consensus) stance. The results will probably not solve the problem or contribute anything new to the body of knowledge. But your observations and conclusions could perhaps be the starting point for someone who can "take the problem and run with it." Clearly, your mind-set and personality (along with how much time you can or want to devote to the issue) will have major influences on how you deal with an issue.

If you are sorting through reams of information, complexities, intertwined issues, and/or opinions developed by others, it can also be easy to: inadvertently focus on minutia (small gaps in the streams of other's logic, if only because you can claim it as your own), and perhaps not be aware at how insignificant your observations may be; or to become paralyzed by the overwhelming amount of information, and not know where to start understanding and dealing with it. This is when bouncing your ideas or dilemmas off an informed but uninvolved colleague can help immensely: don't be shy about it!

The ideal balance is when you understand a situation or problem to the point of having a feel for how various components of the issue interrelate: when you can empathize with the situation, and put yourself into it with a reasonable level of comfort and confidence. With practice and concentration you'll sense when you're approaching the information redline (overload).

At the balance point, you can anticipate (deduce and/or induce) likely outcomes, influences, and causal relationships. This creative process can have enormous value in overcoming traditional misconceptions and common oversights and for generating viable new perspectives and solutions. The challenge is recognizing facts, neutralizing the distractions of your own personal biases, being able to turn your creative side loose, and then having the guts to communicate (diplomatically of course) potentially unpopular or sensitive observations. This is the essence of the *empowered* mind-set.

ENORMOUS UNTAPPED POTENTIAL

The mind's capacity and potential for processing information is far broader than most people will ever begin to realize or use. Balladeers can easily remember lyrics to hundreds of songs, and actors can memorize enormous amounts of dialogue. Add to that "hard drive" reservoir of information the ability to reason, relate, and conceptualize, and you start to realize that you have a potential megacomputer on your shoulders.

The challenge is to learn how to use as much of your mental capacity as possible. Unfortunately, there are hundreds of socially conditioned/learned restraints compartmentalizing your thinking. Seeking to unleash mental energies is, has been, and probably always will be a continuing quest (i.e., seeking truth and understanding) for anyone who tries to really think. Perhaps some of the following observations can provide a few insights on constraints and how you might start supplanting or overriding them, if only for your personal satisfaction.

"Use it or lose it" is a very disturbing reality for the purpose of this discussion. If you don't exercise your mind, it will atrophy (like unused muscles) and you won't even realize it. On the other hand, overuse of your mind doesn't seem to cause any known problems. And, for those too lazy to work at it, artificial stimulation (drugs) is like running an engine above the red line with no oil: it'll fry and lock up in a hurry.

In other chapters, we've touched on how to change and be more interesting, how to develop a presence, how to get unstressed, and how to get into the Zone: all of those suggestions apply here as well.

Where are we untapped or underutilized? Here are a few exercises and possibilities to jump-start your thinking:

- Research, collect, learn, read, contemplate, and memorize: try doing even a few of these and see how it stimulates your mental processes. And then, put all of that information to work through:

- Creative conceptualizing in any area you choose (problem-solving, writing, etc.): and look specifically for nontraditional perspectives. For example, novel legal theories are seldom used because the percentages for success seem stacked against them; but when they are used and they work, they become valuable precedents and create whole new frameworks, because someone executed an overlooked thought effectively! The same holds for any occupation or philosophy. Develop a creative slant or aspect to what you do, and your effectiveness may increase dramatically: it's worth a try!

- At least peruse writings of philosophers and abstract/conceptual thinkers. It can be as simple as reading through a topic in a collection of quotations: these can be excellent and efficient stimulants for thought.

- Be physically fit: your mind is not immune from bad habits, junk food, fatty deposits, pollutants, and anything else moving around in your body—treat it well.

- Objectively assess opinions divergent from your own, and do not summarily dismiss them because you don't think you like them. Give new ideas a chance, it adds to your repertoire and may have value when you least expect it (perhaps in an evolved form or variation).

- Become acutely aware of everything around you: notice little things, interact with interest (listen), and simply observe people. For example, becoming an amateur photographer is easy, and it instantly allows you to see the world just a little differently.

As you think about these possibilities, you'll develop a few of your own. Try them and see what happens. Here are a few quotes on creativity to stimulate your synapses:

"Discontent is at the root of the creative process...the most gifted of the human species are at their creative best when they cannot have their way, and they must compensate for what they miss by realizing and cultivating their capacities and talents." *Eric Hoffer*

"Knowing a lot is a springboard to creativity." *Charlie Rose*

"Periods of tranquility are seldom prolific of creative achievement. Mankind has to be stirred up." *Alfred North Whitehead*

"Proximity to the crowd, to the majority view, spells the death of creativity." *Abraham Joshua Heschel*

"What has been best done in the world, the works of genius, cost nothing. There is no painful effort, but it is the spontaneous flowing of the thought. Shakespeare made his Hamlet as a bird weaves its nest." *Ralph Waldo Emerson*

"Could Hamlet have been written by a committee, or the Mona Lisa painted by a club? Creative Ideas do not spring from groups. They spring from individuals." *A. Whitney Griswold*

LIMITED CONCEPTUAL FRAMEWORK = NO ASSIMILATION OF NEW INFORMATION

A limited belief system can only result in limited perspectives and less than optimal results. This applies to anything and everything: professional and academic intra-disciplinary wisdom; political platforms; theology; philosophies; athletic training; business practices; losing weight; hobbies;…everything!

Limited conceptual frameworks and the processes that cause them are ironically reinforced by the disciplines taught at universities, and the politically guarded jealousies of experts in subjects that should (in an ideal world) be totally integrated (psychology vs. sociology, or social psychology vs. anthropology, or osteopathy vs. general medicine, just to start). The other major limiting culprit is occupational specialization, which in a similar manner, focuses on one aspect of "the whole" at the expense of understanding all of the influences on the profession, occupation, business, industry, or economy (big picture).

It seems that each developing discipline must have its own vernacular, its own set of basic precepts (often with minor distinctions from other disciplines), its own set of leaders, and its own wise men. Eventually the dominant perspectives become locked in through all manner of social dynamics, and countervailing theories are resisted. Like specialized university disciplines, religions exhibit the same type of behavior. When viewed objectively, small differences often create very enthusiastic and assertive followings. Good examples include: the multitude of Protestant sects, and the seemingly minor differences between Catholics and Eastern Orthodox faiths.

CENSORSHIP: THE SOURCE OF EPIPHANIES

Subscribing to a generally acceptable body of information and its related practices (along with other mainstream thinkers) will get you through your social and/or university life effectively, probably with a good degree of comfort, security, and success. But eventually many people begin to wonder if that is all there is to life in an occupation or any discipline (resulting in feeling incomplete, searching for more, feeling lost, wondering if you've done enough with yourself, wondering how you fit into the scheme of things, and being unsure of where you're going).

This can result from operating within limited perspectives and out of date or inapplicable theories, and perhaps even feeling some pressure to conform and not stir things up. Some people eventually grow out of traditionally held precepts *and realize it!* But suddenly that secure comfort zone (protective cloak) is gone, after intense commitment and investment of time and energy within the conceptual framework and related support structure. The dilemma is where to go and what to do after this *epiphany*. If you are capable of these kinds of realizations, you are capable of continuing to grow, but it may be in a different (more tolerant) field, or it may be for your own fulfillment and pursuit of your interests rather than devoting your efforts to reinforcing someone else's theories.

Few dare to touch sensitive or sacrosanct ideologies (individual or institutional). It's too compelling to subscribe to established and accepted conventional wisdom vs. challenging it (even when overwhelming evidence and reasoning justifies a different perspective). In this way, individuals, disciplines and organizations censor information that is not compliant with prevailing thinking. New information often changes and disrupts many comfort zones, it challenges the validity of those who became prominent professing what is now the conventional wisdom, and the natural tendency is to resist any change. Attempting to suggest that someone's ideological foundation is faulty is tantamount to calling them narrow-minded idiots who don't know any better. Discussion, persuasion, facts, and logic obviously don't have much value if one attempts to change a deep-seated stance or conviction.

Devoted To Including or Excluding?

The answer is *both*. Organizations, ideologies, institutions, professions, and disciplines tend to inadvertently become bureaucracies, fervently protecting the status quo. Change occurs very slowly, and it requires independent individuals to precipitate them. These independent types, to be catalysts for improvement, risk being criticized if not ridiculed. Often their ideas are not accepted until someone within the power structure of that discipline adopts it as their own idea and declares it viable: after the originator (the threat) has been shipped off to another occupation or field of study. *That's* politics.

The same principles hold true for exclusive clubs, interest groups, societies, political parties, etc. By definition they: *exclude* people with philosophies divergent from their focus (banishing them if they get out of line), censor incompatible ideas, and reject even marginally challenging information or perspectives. Concurrently, they will *include* people who meet their standards, conform to their expectations, and demonstrate their commitment (usually $). Some even seek converts (militias, cults) and then work to control them. Eventually, most people find where they comfortably fit in.

Message: *Embracing and producing compliant diatribes will keep you in the mainstream, but it won't do much to improve the discipline, body of knowledge, organization, or the individuals therein.*

COUNTERACTING LIMITATIONS

Everyone has a limited frame of reference (stored/programmed information at their disposal). The important thing is to know it, acknowledge it, and consciously transcend limitations (it's called *keeping an open mind*). And it's easier said than done.

Message: *Receptiveness to (or even tolerance of) new and/or different concepts, cross-disciplinary thinking, and development of sound reasoning are the cornerstones of good judgment. Good judgment leads to reasonableness and open-mindedness; and those attributes lead to sound purposes, strategies, and actions. All of which together lead to optimum outcomes (being empowered).*

Think of it (your mind) as a well-written/integrated information system in a supercomputer, capable of assimilating multitudes of stimuli, with lots of filters for eliminating superfluous and extraneous noise: producing several options for solutions to any problem and/or isolating the best of all dogmas, philosophies, and disciplines. Then your only problem becomes sorting out which solution, approach, and/or philosophy is the most applicable and viable at that point in time.

Now *that's* the way to process and assimilate information! It gets you out of the useless protective mode, and lets you process (i.e., *think*): creatively assimilating and validating information rather than accepting what you're told/taught (and ultimately *do*) at face value. But first you must have a solid grounding and foundation in your chosen discipline before you can begin to understand enough to introduce viable new concepts with any credibility.

FREE SPEECH AND GOOD TASTE

No one can argue against free speech and information, it's the cornerstone of any true democracy. Having said that and meaning it, there should be limits. Probably the most appropriate and rational standard is *reasonableness.* Reasonable people know what's tasteful, harmful to others, lewd, or simply wrong.

As you partake in your freethinking and creative expressions, employ a *reasonableness* constraint when you disclose your ideas to others. Good taste is always an attribute you want to be admired for!

LANGUAGE: THE KEY PROCESSING FRAMEWORK

Our prowess at reading and writing is unquestionably correlated with how well we can sort, organize, and assimilate information. The more we read, the more words we have to categorize and understand concepts, abstract ideas, and other intangible thoughts. The fewer words you have to work with, the more limited your framework, and the more impressionable and susceptible you are to suggestions and tenuous perspectives.

If you add another language or two to your repertoire, it seems as though your depth of comprehension increases immensely. A descriptive phrase may have a very profound effect, feeling, and impact in one language but that impact can be easily lost in translation. You know you've mastered a language when this level of consciousness and understanding becomes apparent. You *want* a large repertoire of perspectives.

Suffice it to say, that the more you can develop your reading and writing skills, even if only in your native language, the more proficient you will be in processing a much broader band of information with greater understanding. You can only benefit from having more tools (words and expressions) at your disposal: enabling more efficient classifying and prioritizing of information.

Message: *The more variety of "descriptors" you have at your disposal, the better you can organize your thoughts and find relationships and similarities (even lessons) in seemingly disparate experiences. That's when your thinking, creativity, and information processing reach a truly proficient level.*

SUPERFLUOUS INFORMATION, TIME, AND "NOISE"

In this age of personal communication devices of all shapes and sizes (cell phones, pagers, computers, e-mails, and variations thereof) and information attacking us from seemingly every direction, sorting out important information from everything else is becoming increasingly important. Everything has a spin and everything is urgent.

When it comes to being "in touch," don't overload yourself with too much communication: it probably won't make much difference when it comes to success and impact. The important data always seems to get through. Remember, the more you're communicating, the less time you're spending actually doing something. And, the more you're communicating, the more time you're spending sorting out the useful from the useless stuff, and the more demands you'll have made on your time and energy. No wonder people are getting overstretched and stressed.

A professional colleague once made an astute observation. He spent years working 12+ hour days. After having enough of that, he experimented with *making* himself work 8-hour days. He discovered he could complete 99 percent of what's important within that time allotment: largely by eliminating superfluous distractions and making himself available only where he could have an impact. Others' demands/interests will always take up as much time as you allow.

INFORMATION THAT CONTROLS ORGANIZATIONAL/ BUSINESS OUTCOMES

Here are a few observations and points to consider on the systems/ information front:

- Be cautious about using business standards as performance incentives: improvements will likely occur in one or two areas at the expense of other important business functions; efforts and information/data collection will be focused heavily on the areas that will result in bonuses;

- For example: emphasize turns, and you may be facing an unexpected, negative financial "hit" when inventory reductions occur at the wrong time or in the least efficient manner, or when goods are moved at alarmingly low margins...but the "turns" will increase!

- The role of top management is to make sure all of the specialists in the organization (with their narrow perspectives and limited information) have a clue when it comes to the overall workings of the business: blending isolated information components into a sensible framework, and making sure everyone is focused on the purpose and goal of the organization.

- Regardless of politically correct corporate assertions and contentions about vision and honorable missions, every organization is driven by the financials. If you know, understand, and respect that fact, many things begin to make sense, especially in a for-profit organization. Financial information is the lifeblood of any organization. You can do without most other data, but not that;

- Monolithic business systems may or may not help run a business: it all depends on if there are competent people assessing all that data. Just remember that the system can only describe what's happened (assuming it's set up correctly and the data is accurate: no small concerns): it doesn't ensure success, it can't foretell the future, and it isn't responsible for the viability of products or quality of decisions;

- Be especially careful not to place excessive credence in or rely heavily on information generated by computerized models. These are averaging tools with their foundation in the past, not the future: their projections are an extension of the past, with lots of tenuous assumptions built in. Think about the accuracy of stock market trends, investment projections, and weather forecasts, and then decide how much you should rely on similarly based prognostications.

27

Change and Transition

THERE ARE A few personal characteristics that usually won't change much over your lifespan. These include your personality, the expertise you've spent years developing, your likes and dislikes, the way you assimilate information (think), and your habits. These characteristics will probably remain the foundation for how you do things, what you're interested in, and what you're capable of doing for as long as you exist. Everything else is in a constant state of transition. Fortunately, if you choose, you may be able to enhance and improve your personal attributes by changing a few behaviors, if only a little. But it's not always easy and you must really want to do it.

"All is change, all yields its place and goes." *Euripides*

"Any real change implies the breakup of the world as one has always known it, the loss of all that gave us an identity, the end of safety." *James Baldwin*

"Change is not made without inconvenience, even from worse to better." *Richard Hooker*

"Control over change would seem to consist in moving not with it but ahead of it." *Marshall McLuhan*

MANY KINDS OF CHANGE

It's ironic that as you're growing up, you can't wait to change, get bigger and get older. Then, after you've developed yourself to your optimum physical, social, and career state (probably in your thirties and forties) you do everything possible to not change much more. That's when you start changing indirectly. You try to stay relatively the same while everything around you continues to evolve. Essentially, through inaction, you may become obsolete and out of date. The fashion statement of the 1980s, for instance, is the dork of the 2000s if he doesn't update his ties.

Most people do seem to have an interest in the kinds of change they can precipitate and control. They take vacations to do things they don't usually do, and to get away from the normal, secure routine. Ironically, many repeat the same vacation places and activities: turning that into a routine as well.

Fifty percent of marriages fail, probably because something has changed and many participants didn't have a clue as the process was going on. Perhaps they didn't pay attention, no one wanted to work at it, one changed and the other didn't, things got too staid; and finally, perhaps it just became easier to change by starting all over. It's interesting how subsequent partners can be similar to the last one (so, w*hy change?*).

Many people change jobs because the opportunities may seem better elsewhere; but the chronic job-hopper eventually gets into a rut of too many impressionable jumps, resulting in little sense of purpose and direction. Others change cars because the excitement of the current one wears off, losing lots of money on car trades, and still never quite achieving satisfaction. Others turn to drugs for a break in their routine, usually with disastrous and unsatisfying outcomes.

Self-initiated change or variety certainly has an element of interesting (or even exciting) escape to it. It could result in improvements, a temporary respite from routine, or an unequivocal miscalculation and poor outcome.

Message: *Perhaps the changes that don't quite work out are a result of not having made good choices, not really understanding what you want or need, not anticipating likely scenarios, or not having executed the choice well. Any of these miscues could result in repetition of the same mistakes.*

CHANGES (IMPROVEMENTS) THAT CAN HELP ANYONE

We've established that change will occur whether you like it or not, in anything you do. In previous chapters, the notion of being a trendsetter vs. a copycat was suggested as one way to establish a presence and develop self-confidence; self-development and improvement plays a role in constructively changing perspectives and getting you motivated; and variations in relationship-based activities added spice. Changing a clearly negative situation, environment, or state of affairs always seems like the right thing to do. Any effort at improvement in these areas seems obviously constructive, but what else?

You are in a constant state of transition. If you accept this notion, roll with it, and capitalize on it (rather than denying and fighting it), you may be on to something pretty useful and satisfying. In other words, continually find ways to personally change and improve yourself and what you're doing: staying ahead of events. Here are just a few observations and possibilities:

- Living largely on past memories (long gone) is sad and a formula for docility. The better mind-set is to continue making memories: always studying, researching, and being on the lookout for a better way of doing the things you like, and/or becoming involved with new activities.

- Occasionally doing something very unusual for yourself can be quite a stimulating change and satisfying ego boost: a sailboard lesson, an excursion to a remote location, a photo safari followed by a lecture, an interview with a person you admire (followed with writing an article about it), researching something interesting and then giving a speech on it (if only at your social club), making something creative and then exhibiting it, etc.

- If you've been the silent type, take a course and begin articulating and expressing yourself; and when you feel ready, go to an open stage and do a poetry reading (it doesn't have to be your own writing). If you've been verbose, play the listener role for a while and see what happens; or, try out for a Shakespeare play and see just how good of a drone you can be.

- If you've been relaxed with your social graces (even with your spouse or partner), learn and adopt some manners, privacy, courtesy, and cleanliness: brush your teeth more, easy on the belching, cut out the bad language, and eliminate any other nasty habits you may have. In previous chapters we've discussed the benefits of developing a constructive "presence": do the same on the home front!

- Stop and assess whether or not you exhibit obnoxious behaviors and fix them (loud cell phone use in public, misbehaving kids, poor driving habits that precipitate road rage, being so overweight that you can't fit well in an airplane seat, or being otherwise annoying).

- Try giving gifts to loved ones at nontraditional times (as Robert Fulghum suggested in his writings): surprise them with expressions of appreciation through some creative, unconventional concepts, philosophies, and practices (they'll remember it more).

- If you've been narrow-minded, obstinate, self-absorbed, overreactive, or stubborn (and have realized it), work with a psychologist (or at least read a book) to get over it. Work at overcoming the obstructions that impede growth, improvement, and/or relationships.

- Develop a good sense of timing. Know when to: call someone, do something, express yourself, be somewhere, leave. It takes being empathetic and tuned into others activities and reactions. This area is well worth changing and/or developing if you don't have a good feel for it.

- If you really want a challenge, write down what you dreamed as soon as you are even partly awake and research their significance; or start some other self-discovery quest such as personality profiles, outward bound programs, or even seminars on the subject.

In other words, continue evolving, or risk being overlooked, taken for granted, or even avoided. If you feel you're in the ho-hum doldrums of sameness, complacency, and quiet desperation, you must at least *try* changing something. The goal should be to make yourself continually interesting, if only for your own self-esteem.

Changing Negative Energy

Competitive individuals such as athletes (especially martial arts experts) do this naturally: it's a great philosophy and *it works* (in the physical and mental world). Take disparaging information such as gossip, a put-down, or chiding *as a challenge* rather than internalizing it and letting it get you down. The correct mind-set is to reverse and convert the assault into energy/action that redeems and validates you. Questioning your self-worth and accepting even a little guilt can make you despondent, lowering the quality of your thoughts and actions.

Instead of getting angry or plotting how to superficially "get back," demonstrate primarily to yourself that they are wrong: change contempt, discouragement, or resentment into a stimulant and into a constructive goal. If and how you choose to address the "critic" is up to you. You may decide it isn't worth a confrontation. A poised and focused *(empowered)* mind-set will help you decide what actions are appropriate and effective.

MANY TRANSITIONS

There are many "rites of passage" that are largely inevitable and universally recognized as important, ritualized, and even institutionalized.

These include (but are not limited to): being born, circumcision, baptism, first communion or bar mitzvah, starting school, earning your first trophy, first date, driving, your first car, losing your virginity, graduating from high school, going to college or into the military (leaving home), graduating, drinking legally, being a crime victim (or going to jail), any life-threatening event, the first car accident, getting married (or un-married), having kids, getting a big promotion, getting rich (or going bankrupt), being on TV, having grandkids, getting very sick or injured, losing your parents, realizing you're old, and eventually passing away.

There are many more of course, and after each event, something is different. It's interesting to reflect on just how many life-changing events you've actually experienced, how they affected you, and how you handled them: it will tell you much about yourself. If you discover any pattern(s), it may help set some worthwhile goals. If you try, you will probably remember every defining moment in your life, except the first three and the last one.

WHAT CAN A NORMAL PERSON DO TO LEAVE A LEGACY?

Do something that lasts. It may not be perfection, but it can have a tremendous impact on your kids and maybe even on subsequent generations. It's as simple as documentation, and it can be invaluable. If it's a little creative, that makes it all the better. Here are a few ideas:

- Keep a scrapbook of your achievements and any documents such as birth records, school report cards, etc. The better labeled and organized the better.

- Organize old photographs into a logical sequence, and note what they're all about.

- Have someone videotape you doing things. When you get older, have someone in the family interview you on details about growing up, your family, mother and father, including all the details. Most important, tell your favorite stories, tell your favorite jokes, play/sing your favorite songs, and be yourself. Tell your story and even brag a little.

- If you can, write and self-publish a family history. Toss in a few old photos and it will become an heirloom.

- Do something very creative that reflects your personality: artwork, crafts, poetry, anything…and show/tell about it in your video.

Personally, I managed to do many of these things with my parents before they passed on. After they did, it was wonderful to see them as I knew them, and remember them so fondly. I had captured a little of their essence, at least for me for my lifetime.

THE FINAL TRANSITION

Let's assume for a moment there is an afterlife. Be cautious on relying on absolution alone to get to where you want to go. A reasonable assumption is that any supreme being would take into account the sum total of your actions to make determinations. In other words, don't leave your fate to *fate*.

Change Resisters

Individuals who resist change simply like things exactly as they are, and they probably feel they have a comfortable level of control over the situation(s). However, they are fighting a losing battle. Always expect things to change!

Enter a significant (inevitable) event or episode totally out of your control. It's usually negative, you don't want it, it is totally unsettling, most people would rather not even think about the eventuality, and now you have to deal with it (upending your routine and introducing new stresses). That's how many people see *any* kind of change.

By and large, changes in areas very important to most people (jobs and income; work assignments; faith; professional knowledge, skills and abilities; family relationships; health; etc.) tend to be received less than enthusiastically, primarily because so much personal energy has been devoted to establishing and stabilizing them. But changes will most certainly occur in these areas as well, so anticipate them!

On the personal/social level, if you want to: freeze time and live in the good old days. If your circle of friends participates, reinforces, and encourages the lifestyle, and you enjoy it, then there's probably no reason to change!

However, when change resistance involves and affects others, such as in the work environment, its manifestations are annoying at best and can damage the organization at its worst. The insufferable bureaucratic is the classic example, along with those who would censor new information or discoveries in order to preserve their control and prominence in a discipline or in any endeavor.

Message: *Resisting change in the organizational setting is, for those who don't realize it, tantamount to filling out your own pink slip.*

Message: *On balance and in the long run, for any individual or organization, too little (or too slow) change isn't nearly as beneficial as leaning heavily toward a constructive, never-ending, pursuit of refinement and improvement.*

28

Power, Influence, and Persuasiveness

OUR LIVES ARE interlaced with illusions of accuracy, truth, ethics, integrity, and intent/motivations. Trying to sail through this sea of fog is often a daunting and exasperating, if not stressful, continuing experience. Sailors call a successful navigation being in *the Slot*. We call it being in *the Empowered Zone*.

Empowered individuals understand the fundamentals of influencing and persuading others, in all areas of their lives. More important, they can recognize when efforts to persuade and/or influence are directed at them in a disingenuous, unconstructive, wasteful, unsolicited, deceitful, or ineffective manner. Since much of what we do involves influence and persuasion in many variations, this chapter summarizes much of what we've explored heretofore, facilitating tying it all together. Different aspects of this interesting area have been touched upon in previous chapters, most notably in: *"Negotiating," "They Speak with Such Power and Conviction,"* and *"How Do You Define Yourself?"*

Although alert individuals understand these concepts very thoroughly, many can still nevertheless be influenced by seemingly sincere gestures. The following discussion will address a few areas that any individual who wishes to be objective (in any forum: business, social, or personal) needs to be acutely alert to, aware, and cautious of.

Much of this exploration will focus on sales/marketing types by whom we seem to be assaulted daily; but that is only because they are most experienced in trying to influence us, and most people use their methods and strategies to find compliance and acceptance in all other situations. The goal in this discussion is not to make you jaded or negative, but to strongly encourage development of constructive objectivity and use of reason so you aren't duped and taken advantage of.

NEEDS AND VULNERABILITIES

The first order of business is to be especially aware of your own vulnerabilities and personal needs. Good marketers will probe to discover any such needs, and if they are discreet and accurate in this discovery process, they'll often be successful in exploiting them. This runs from swarming people with compliments or admirations (vis-à-vis their own alleged inabilities in areas such as sports, creativity, appearance, success, etc.) all the way through kickbacks to greedy physicians for admitting patients to a certain hospital, and many points in between. If the recipient wants to be admired, recognized, or serviced in any manner, they consciously or unconsciously become vulnerable and susceptible to influence, attention, suggestion, and persuasion.

A good marketer will create a perceived need even when one may not exist (Sony and its Walkman for an example). An extreme example is the drug dealer providing drugs to an addict: the addict is dependent and keeps coming back, because the easy solution to his problem is the dealer.

IT TAKES CREDIBILITY + RECEPTIVENESS

To persuade or influence anyone, it helps immensely to have (or are perceived to have) credibility, ethics and integrity, trust, and presence on your side, for starters. On the other hand, the recipient of your persuasive efforts can and will be influenced to do something if the person: wants to; can justify or rationalize the request; feels some obligation, guilt, or pressure; has a need; has been compelled to act; and/or is somehow vulnerable *(see "Protecting Your Assets")*.

In other words, there are many ways to try and get want you want. Sales/account management types go to schools regularly on this topic and practice related tactics hour by hour. Fortunately, with the advent of impersonal Internet-based RFQs and auction-style shopping for goods, services, and prices, the days of the traditional sales/account managers and their glad-handing routines may very well be numbered.

But since sales types are still around and since many other people use their techniques and principles, lets review a few of the key ones.

STANDARD PRACTICES

Lots of *compliments* tend to work very effectively at winning over many people. Interestingly, even if compliments are inaccurate, the positive impact is still there. Perhaps some people will do anything for flattery and recognition, even if they know they're being lied to. One possible explanation is the recipient may rationalize that for someone to even try to give them a compliment, it shows they must be really interested and impressed by them (a major vulnerability). If a rapport develops on this basis (accurate compliments or not), the deceptive tactic worked.

Gratuities and gifts have been covered in other chapters, and it's important to realize that these efforts are also very effective. The obligation to respond favorably (reciprocate) after you've received something of perceived value or pleasure is a strong tendency with many people, and they often try to outdo the giver. To most people, *quid pro quo, "I'll scratch your back if you'll scratch mine"* thinking is a matter of fairness, goodwill, and courtesy. Good sales/marketing people will determine quickly what you like, respond favorably to it, and work it.

Persuasive efforts may involve simple conversation and indulgence of the person, i.e., listening to them even if the recipient couldn't care less: a need is being served. This is a very powerful technique, since the more time a sales type remains in your presence, the more likely they'll get a concession. This is obviously true in dating or flirting situations as well.

Often a gift or contact is as simple as a card or, a follow-up call, offering to find some basic business facts, providing industry information, a lunch, reminders that the persuader is there (ostensibly for you).

Or, persuasion may cross the ethics and integrity line as discussed in previous chapters. Apparent recent examples involved the Salt Lake City Olympic scandals, where several high-ranking individuals were allegedly influenced to select Salt Lake City as a Winter Olympics venue through a variety of gratuities, and instances of "influencing" judged events were discovered. A common workplace theme might be a woman who feels grateful for having been hired for a promotion, succumbing to the sexual advances of the hiring party. Needless to say, the fewer gratuities and fewer feelings of obligation, the better for objective business.

Time has been touched on as a strategy. *"If you don't take advantage of this offer now, it may not be around tomorrow."* Or, *"I'll be traveling for the next few days and difficult to contact, and I know there are others interested so I don't know how much inventory we'll have...."* We've all heard those calls for closure. The less time available, the more likely you are to act. This explains why labor negotiations tend to find closure just before a strike deadline. It also explains why enamored couples can become quite passionate just before a sailor leaves for a tour of duty: that opportunity won't be around for a while.

The *"personal"* aspect is an especially important area to exercise restraint. Any and all business arrangements *must not* be on a personal level. Even though from the sales perspective, relationship building often works for the marketer, it may not be in the best interest of conducting business for *you*. A notable exception would be international business relationships, where diplomacy, cultural awareness, correct protocols, and correct social graces/courtesy are essential elements in most ventures.

The "personal" approach involves the persuader "identifying" with you, trying to show similarities, sharing interests, emphasizing commonalities (places you've lived or gone to school, people you both know, etc.) and building a familiar, close rapport. If they can't find similarities and common experiences, they'll often make them up. If they talk about their crummy golf game, it's to make you feel superior and flattered. If they make any kind of a connection, they've entered your personal space. A woman may be exceptionally attractive and appealing, and your attraction to her can be a *distraction* in conducting business activities. Good marketers will always be affable, neat, and tidy. They thrive on first impressions, and they work hard on having an effective presence. Beware if you find yourself giving anyone the time of day on the strength of their looks for business purposes.

Articulation is an important method to keep any "seller" in your

presence. Enthusiasm, and energetic, positive, helpful, sometimes entertaining, "constructive" dialogue are effective, standard practices.
Close cousins are *persistence* (once they are in your office, you'll have
to pry them out: that *five minutes* of your time is really an hour in their
time) and *optimism*: the world is a rosy place, you certainly want to be
a part of it, and they'll show you how to be there. Also, the *"everyone's
doing it, so it must be good, don't miss out on it"* message is almost always
there in some variation.

All marketers will try to achieve some *closure* or a *deliverable* of
some kind, or at worst it will be a gracious request for some kind of a
concession or commitment by you (like a follow-up meeting or session with you and your boss, or making some kind of future plans).
They'll ask for it (or suggest it) more than once and in different ways.
The manner in which they ask makes a lot of difference to people
as well; and if a personal rapport has been established, saying "no"
becomes less likely. Once even a *maybe* response is garnered, that is
as good as *yes* to a marketer, it may just take a little more effort and a
little longer to "close."

Message: *Once you let any interactions, negotiations, or business discussions out of your control or if they become personal or emotional (need-
based) in any manner, your impressionability takes over and you become
vulnerable.*

INFLUENCE

"Influence" is an interesting persuader, particularly when it's there
without any reasonable entitlement. Encounters with the police, the
boss, or others who have a level of control over you are easy to understand. You will typically do (or at least accept) what they say as
somewhat valid. We've explored the shortsightedness of how people
who have titles are often instantly perceived by many as brilliant and
omnipotent. It is also interesting how individuals who've had success
in one narrow field are often deemed experts in totally unrelated fields.
A good example is the perception that actors who play physicians or
attorneys know something significant about medicine or law. But,
that's exactly how narrow and impressionable many people can be;

and that fact (in various forms) accounts for the high success rates of superficial sales techniques. An old sage friend of mine had a favorite saying: *"I don't know which is worse: the one who lies or the one who wants to hear the lies."* I always feel a little saddened by individuals who allow themselves (usually inadvertently) to be taken advantage of, only because they aren't aware of other's agendas.

In summary, here are a few characteristics of people who tend to generate *influence* and *persuasiveness*:

- Having control over scarce and wanted resources: goods, money, talent, skills, information;
- An ability to rally people around a cause, philosophy, or project, and being able to control them;
- Being able to solve problems for and/or meet the needs of someone, or a group;
- An ability to make people feel like they are special, or that they are getting a bargain;
- Less positively, an ability to create or point out a need or dissatisfaction and assert they have the solution, or that they can do better: usually exploiting emotions and vulnerabilities;
- Touting credentials, achievements, titles, connections, and/or formal authority (power);
- Making assertions with passion and conviction, charisma, attractive appearance, and/or presence.

THE AUTHORITARIAN PERSONALITY

Another aspect of influence also rests within individuals commonly referred to as having *authoritarian* personalities. These are people who are very structured in their obedience to authority. In its extreme, it is unquestioning loyalty to rank and/or higher expertise or status. This also happens to most of us temporarily when we see a doctor. In the military or in religious hierarchies, obediently following orders is essential and required.

When it comes to formal structures like the military, that's just the way it needs to be. But when it comes to any other matters, another adage comes to mind: *"The only way to maintain competence is to constantly challenge that competence."* That perspective should apply to all bodies of knowledge and to all day-to-day encounters.

Assertions, requests, or directives that don't make sense or don't have a reasonable stream of logic *must* be challenged, regardless of the institution or the reputation, title, or status of the individual. Challenging and debating are among the best learning techniques, but it takes some backbone (as in the case of a student wanting to challenge a statement, but not wanting to offend the instructor).

Message: *To blindly accept what you are told to do or think without applying reason to test the validity of an assertion is to hand your mind over to someone else.*

PERSUASIVE PRESENTATIONS

Persuasive presentations (verbal, visual, or written) are ones that don't waste time, they maintain flow and interest, and they don't insult the intelligence of the recipients. To wit:

- Unless *"by way of background"* has critical significance, forget it;
- Highlight the salient arguments on all sides of an issue fairly and objectively;
- Forget about hypothesizing about intent and motives, just present the facts and observations (opinions/conclusions may or may not be useful);
- Outline viable solutions, with the up and downsides, including the costs, timelines, and probabilities for success;
- Make a definitive recommendation for action.

And that's really all it takes to get to the core of most issues. If you are truly *empowered*, you will have already acted on your proposed recommendation, the results will have been successful and cost-effective, and there won't be a need for making a presentation, other than to report that the matter has been resolved.

PERSUASIVE INTERACTIONS

A case in point: *If you interact with a colleague and quickly understand a troubling issue, objectively assess and present logical options to resolve it, even matter-of-factly suggest the best resolution, and then move along without any expectation of (or tacit demand on) the recipient, then you've just established credibility and you've made the recipient feel better. If your solution works, your future persuasiveness is enhanced with that person and with many others he/she knows (reputation).*

NEGATIVE PERSUASION

This is what politicians do when they get in trouble, when someone is accused of a crime, or when someone is caught doing something they shouldn't have been doing. In its most blatant form, it's called *lying*. In a less blatant form it's pleading *the Fifth*, and cavalierly implying *"prove it if you think you can."* At other times it takes the form of *denial* together with the assertion that there was a *misunderstanding* by whoever discovered it. Denial can be emphatic and vitriolic, discrediting and raising a question of integrity on the part of the discoverer or accuser (unethical motives, psychosis, political agendas, etc.).

It never ceases to amaze how much compassionate, unquestioning support can be garnered with simple denials, coupled with the representation that the person (the accused) has been somehow wounded, and misunderstood and deserves sympathy. After all, they suggest, they are, ostensibly, basically "honest" people caught up in an unfortunate set of circumstances, and we of course all make miscalculations. Recent examples include the Clinton and Condit escapades. In more extreme cases the victim is verbally attacked and discredited in the media.

For politicians there are no percentages in admissions, especially if they are guilty. If red herrings or any reasonable doubt can be thrown into the issue, let someone else prove something. If they're lucky the matter will gradually dissipate, the voting public will eventually forgive and forget, and the matter will go away. From the practical perspective, if protecting a political career is the goal, then why not try various smokescreens, especially if there is culpability; they may just work.

For all the rest of us, copping a plea is probably more practical and more redeeming. For those trying to protect a marriage, honesty and facing any transgression(s) are the only viable solutions. Any other gyrations or evasive maneuvers only serve to exacerbate suspicions, confirm guilt, and raise tensions.

PERSUADING BUREAUCRATS

When it comes to applying policies, rules, regulations, and laws, bureaucrats often need instructions on what to think and do. If you're seeking a favorable interpretation, use precedents, logical arguments, simple and/or visual explanations, and lots of conceptually viable alternatives to either confuse or win them over. Here's a typical example: *In one place where I worked, I habitually backed into a parking space on a busy street, enabling easy and safe egress into rush hour traffic. This practice was apparently unlawful, based on the ticket I was issued. I showed the judge a video of the light traffic when I parked and the heavy traffic when I left, arguing my actions were motivated by safety and not disregard for the law. I prevailed with simplicity, logic, and easily understood visual facts and details.*

The same concepts apply to most governmental or regulatory issues: at some point reasonableness will usually prevail, provided your position is based on sound principles that also allow the bureaucrats to save face and not diminish their power with new precedent (although it may take a couple of appeals to get there).

With regulatory agencies the bully factor is a reality, and they seem to thrive on it. The key is to stand your ground, follow through correctly with all of the administrative processes, and be consistent in presenting the same arguments. Make sure your arguments have plenty of details and nuances included (settlements are often spun from surprisingly insignificant minutia), and supplement your position with novel legal theories. Once again, when bureaucrats begin realizing they may create new, unfavorable (to their power) rulings and precedents, they can become surprisingly reasonable. In some instances, however, especially righteous ones, you must become a bully yourself, case in point:

A local school district was given land for a school by the developer, who installed a light industrial park. The plot was next to a residential neighborhood, but kids would have to cross a railroad track and a golf course to reach the school. The new school would have 800 kids, within 100 feet of a 24/7 factory that had 1,500 employees. The street would have tractor-trailer, school bus, car pool, and employee traffic in addition to kids walking and on bikes. It made no sense to anyone except the school board and the town administration, both of whom were polite in dismissing repeated requests to change the location of the school.

After I went to a TV news station and made my case, other TV stations, radio, and print media picked up on the story and controversy. I focused my comments on school safety and the risk factors for all involved. Within a few days the developer and town administration found a parcel in the middle of a residential development and traded school sites. My company bought the original plot and built a large warehouse. The town and school administrators praised each other endlessly on their intergovernmental cooperation.

In dealing with utility companies (gas, electric), persistence is the key. As a matter of practice they will repeatedly reject claims for reimbursement of losses that were clearly their responsibility. Eventually they'll settle, but you can't let up, and plan on four or five meetings and hearings. The same is true for hospitals, insurance companies, airlines, phone companies, local governments, water services and any quasi-governmental organization. Never resort to threats or emotional outbursts: that is all the reason most bureaucrats need to disqualify the validity of any claim. Stay cool and matter of fact, even if you want to slap them silly.

Your assertions must have a "hook": a creative, compelling, logical, reasonable argument, and you must be able to present it rationally, calmly, and succinctly. With those elements in hand, you'll usually prevail. If you are perceived as a potentially harmful, credible witness if you were to sue, you are in control and *empowered*.

There is nothing wrong with being affirmative and even aggressive in protecting your interests. It's fairly easy to adopt that mind-set if your position has merit, principle, and integrity. Here are two more cases to illustrate these points:

The first case involved a Department of Labor charge. I was working with the hospital CEO to make sense out of a potential $6 million claim by the government for an alleged variety of wage and hour infractions. In mediation, the government was willing to settle for $4 million The CEO was nervous with my assertive stance against what seemed to be largely a bluff. I took a risk, offered to settle for $1,000,000. with payments issued only upon written request and application within a one-month period. The final settlement cost was in the $250,000 range.

In another case, a notoriously and extremely liberal administrative law judge was about to hear an unemployment case that had serious implications for the hospital I was representing if the former employee prevailed. The employee had been fired primarily at will and also for abusing a patient. The employee was threatening retaliatory discharge and discrimination lawsuits, and a favorable ruling could provide momentum for his threatened claims (collateral estopple). I sat opposite the administrative law judge at the end of a long hearing table (power position). When he asked about my role, I stated that I was there in behalf of the employer to observe the fairness of the proceedings. I stated that if I had problems with the process, I would reserve the ability to review the situation with the law judge and his supervisor. He checked with his superior, who instructed him to proceed with the hearing. At the end of the hearing he asked if we needed to meet with his supervisor, and I told him I'd wait until after I saw his ruling. The determination was favorable to the company.

RELIGIOUS ORGANIZATIONS

If working with a religious order, and asking for a ruling or an interpretation, the same basic principles apply, except that bullying won't work here (they can simply tell you to go...somewhere). Mainstream religious groups don't like to be challenged, and they resent a layperson interpreting holy manifests: that's the province of the ordained. In the Middle Ages one would be excommunicated for even entertaining the thought. This area may involve issues such as interreligious marriages, annulments, participants in a baptism, and a plethora of other possibilities, depending on how much one wishes to follow the letter of the religious law. Left to their own devices, religious orders have no inducement or inclination to interpret protocols liberally, and they too will make every effort to not set new precedents. It theoretically opens the door to losing some ecclesiastical control.

The most compelling argument one can make would have to be based on its uniqueness (so as not to set a precedent), on its individual merits and nuances, and perhaps the salutary effect of time. Also, arguments would have to be encased in a religious framework that doesn't create controversy. Often, a significant donation can take care of the issue fairly expediently. *Empowered* thinking in this arena suggests not embarking on religious permission with the intimidated attitude of a supplicant, because that's where the clergy prefer you remain, but rather with diplomatic insistence and persistence. After all, mortals make even religious-based interpretations and decisions.

INFLUENCE IN MATTERS OF THE HEART

This area uses all of the tricks of the marketing trade: embellishing the product, attention-seeking/giving in all forms, compliments, lies (and many halftruths), gifts, and everything else you can think of. Unfortunately the sense and reason aspects get lost quickly in lieu of passions, emotions, and hormones. The adage *"All's fair in love and war"* usually accurately represents the attitude of the participants.

In trying to influence a spouse, just know that everything is emotionally charged and usually carries some sensitivity. It's best to tread diplomatically and with the *imperative* that any issues are discussed actively and thoroughly. If an argument ensues without resolution of a matter, it's often still a good catharsis, relieving tensions and stresses at least a little (as long as it doesn't get physical or condescending).

INFLUENCE AND THE BOSS

This matter is covered thoroughly in *"Supervisor-Subordinate Relations,"* so please review those discussions for a few insights. One way *not* to positively influence the boss, and often overlooked by subordinates, is to inadvertently delegate work *up* or back to the boss, who was relying on you to complete it: bad form!

Another area subordinates take too lightly is getting *buy-ins* by other staff for their projects or programs. If you're looking at restructuring the organization, you're probably out of your element unless the president is your dad. For other support-garnering efforts, be careful not to overstep your role and end-run your boss: or you may not have any support of *any* kind. Confer with your boss about whether or not any support even needs to be sought for your assignments.

INFLUENCE AND TELEMARKETERS (ET AL.)

This one is easy, and it includes phone contacts, TV, mail, door-to-door, the Internet, etc. This is a great time to practice saying *no* emphatically. Don't worry about being rude: the solicitor has already offended you by attempting to extract money from you and by intruding on your time, space, and activities. They deserve to be verbally abused. Don't forget, the longer they have your attention, the more likely they are to get a commitment out of you. Be very clear, don't waste your time, and learn to say *no* very clearly.

POWER AND INFLUENCE

When all is said and done, in most matters you have as much *power* as you think you have and as much as others perceive you as having. If you act like you have *power* and if you have lots of confidence, if you can resist influences that would deter you, if you've prepared yourself for any endeavor, and if you have a presence, you are *empowered.* The results may even surprise *you.*

Just as important, *empowered* individuals have identified, cultivated, and capitalized on their unique attributes. It may sometimes take a while to find your center of excellence, but it's well worth the quest.

If you look back through history, those who stood out, made significant contributions, and gained recognition and prominence all had different and usually better ways of looking at the world around them and at what they were doing. The most successful ones weren't doing things just like everyone else. If they were, they would have been like everyone else.

Message: *Whatever you choose to do, do it with style, high expectations, and don't let assumed constraints discourage you.*

29

The Relentless Pursuit of Happiness

WHAT IS HAPPINESS?

IN CONTEMPLATING THIS topic, it became apparent just how elusive, abstract, esoteric, fleeting and temporary, contradictory, and perplexing *happiness* can be. Maybe *trying* to be happy is the problem, and perhaps Eric Hoffer summed it up when he stated: "*The search for happiness is one of the chief sources of unhappiness.*" As we explore this subject, a possible conclusion may be that a concerted quest for happiness in and of itself should probably be left to the Don Quixotes of the world, and the rest of us should consider it as an outgrowth of pursuits we are motivated to address.

Webster's Collegiate Dictionary defines *happiness* in terms of good fortune, prosperity, well-being, contentment, and/or pleasurable, satisfying experiences. Much of the perplexity occurs when someone generically asks, "Are you happy?" Wow, how do you deal with that one? The real, truthful answer is an equally baffling question like: "*With what, whom, and at what time of day?*"

The sages don't seem to help much in sorting out this concept. Their ideas seem to be all over the map. The sixteenth to nineteenth-century philosophers liked to equate happiness with virtue, health, and a clear conscience, while Ogden Nash suggested that happiness could emanate from having no conscience at all. Many speak of happiness in terms of no debt, having money, doing something excellent, doing something worthwhile and preferably what you like, as well as improving yourself. Hellen Keller represented this orientation very

286

well when she wrote: *"It is not attained through self-gratification, but through fidelity to a worthy purpose."*

Another school of thought suggests that happiness comes from giving, a relationship with God, serving others, having someone to love, and something to hope for. Many philosophers indicate happiness is a journey and not a destination, others state that it is quality of thoughts and intelligence, while a common folk idiom states, *"Ignorance is bliss."*

Yet another perspective, such as one advocated by Storm Jameson, states: *"Happiness comes of the capacity to feel deeply, to enjoy simply, to think freely, to risk life, to be needed."* Mark Twain spoke of happiness in terms of a *Swedish sunset* and Charles Shultz thought of it as a *warm puppy*. And Anatoly Karpov contended, *"Happiness should always be a bit incomplete. After all, dreams are boundless."*

So, I'm sure any or all of the foregoing astute and probably valid observations will seem to make sense to somebody on the grand, philosophical level; but what about happiness on the daily level?

PERPETUAL HAPPINESS

There is probably no such thing, unless you're into deluding yourself. There are and/or will be many unhappy things that will happen to everyone, and to be happy about them is beyond natural.

A case in point is the born-again individual, walking around with a sustained grin. Besides looking totally out of touch, these people are so dependent on support outside of themselves that their whole well-being depends on an abstraction, and that seems very fragile. Perhaps if someone needs this kind of support in the short-run while they get their confidence back, then it's okay. But if a person's reliance on any external support fades, then something else equally tenuous will probably take its place (probably something just as extreme like cults, politics, or drugs).

It's understandable that marketing and sales types are perpetually optimistic if not happy, because a less than happy and successful face to potential customers and clients wouldn't serve them well. But once again, it's often an orchestrated illusion.

In other words, if you're continuously happy, then you probably don't understand your whole situation (or you've opted not to). The reality is that if the preponderance of your experiences on a day-to-day basis is positive and satisfying, then you can (if you really want to) call yourself *happy*. Or, one big happy event can make up for an otherwise bad day. It all seems to be a matter of balance, and that balance is amorphous. The following section brings *happiness* into the practical world.

WHAT IS HAPPINESS FROM THE SCALED DOWN POINT OF VIEW?

Here are a few ways people are made happy and pursue happiness on a real, daily basis. Whether it is right or wrong, this is what people do; and as usual, you can probably add a few more thoughts to this list:

- Buying something you really want, especially if friends will be envious.
- Being recognized for an achievement and/or doing something outstanding (work, athletics, hobbies, etc.), or simply improving on your personal best in anything.
- Getting more money (gift, wager, promotion, bonus, other winnings…).
- Being complimented or flattered and feeling special.
- Feeling secure and conforming within yourself and/or your social group (club, gang, social circle, church…).
- Having friends to do things with, and who will listen to your troubles.
- Having your personal needs satisfied, whatever they are.
- Escaping from your troubles with alcohol, drugs, or prescribed meds.
- Resolving your troubles.
- Going on a great vacation to escape from a boring routine, using the spa and being attended to, and seeing new and interesting things.
- Flirting and having your sexuality reinforced and validated.
- Doing something risky for the adrenaline rush, and surviving it.

- Running/exercising and feeling good from the endorphins.
- Having a deep spiritual relationship, not feeling guilty, knowing you are a good person, and feeling secure with yourself.
- Being in love, and experiencing other positive rites of passage.
- Being able to comfortably pay your bills and feeling financially secure.
- Feeling confident in yourself and in what you do.
- Getting revenge and/or retribution for a wrong (much maligned concepts discussed a little later).
- Appreciating the beauty and artistry in creative works, and the awesomeness of nature, one little encounter after another.
- Interacting meaningfully with your children, family, and sensing the closeness.
- Achieving your goals.

A compelling argument can be made that happiness really resides primarily in the foregoing, albeit these are occasional experiences and not in all of those detached theoretical abstractions so many scholars/philosophers like to try and compartmentalize it into. Happiness is many different things, constantly changing as we change. The challenge is to empower yourself to appreciate and understand when you experience it.

HAPPINESS IN PERSONAL RELATIONSHIPS

When wondering what the source of happiness is in interpersonal relationships, people usually don't want to hear the correct answer: *that happiness must emanate from within you.* W. H. Auden stated it fairly correctly, although a bit bluntly: *"No human being can make another one happy."*

It is unreasonable to expect someone else to anticipate, know, and cater to your needs, and be right on target most of the time; it's too much pressure and it's way too selfish. It is unreasonable to expect someone to make you happy on a continuing basis: it's difficult and it can be exhausting. Like in a marriage, it isn't that your mate doesn't love you anymore, it's just that paying the bills and romancing can be stressing, and too much to expect. Expressions of affection will happen occasionally, not continuously, and there's nothing wrong with that. The same holds true for an occasionally unintended or misdirected quip, comment, or criticism. Happiness in a relationship is made up of many little mutually reinforcing and forgiving encounters, and the good stuff you want isn't always going to be there when you want it to be. If you're mature you'll understand and allow for that. Remember that selfishness is a sure way to unhappiness.

If you're an interesting, caring person, you've done your job in a relationship. If the other person doesn't appreciate you, move on, it's their problem and not yours. If you expect to be perpetually entertained by someone else, you're expecting too much and you'll never be fully satisfied…you will become selective in what you like, the other party won't know it, and you'll end up rejecting the well-intended individual: because you're too into yourself! This is where reciprocity really means something.

Can a person be too perfect? If you're smart, you'll consider the alternatives, and if that's the person's only fault, there's probably something misaligned in you.

WHAT ABOUT LOVE?

There can be many real conflicts here. While love can make you very happy, it can also make you very sad if it is one-sided, unfulfilled, or if you feel deceived. It's easy to get resentful and even calloused after being rejected one or more times by someone you love. Love is very closely related to happiness, and perhaps as in the quest for happiness, *searching* for it leads to confusion. This is where love and lust become ironically intertwined. The difficulty comes when one person (usually the man) pretends to have an emotional connection with someone, convinces her of a true interest, but whose motive is more in the realm of conquest, scorekeeping, and boasting. From the woman's side, the difficulty comes when she involves a man physically, he commits emotionally, and she decides he's not what she really wants (or someone more interesting comes along). Wow, those and similar situations are as emotionally charged up as they come!

If one person or the other sees the partner as a compromise, and feels they need or deserve more, they can never be really satisfied or happy. It's probably unfair, to someone, to continue that kind of relationship. But if there are kids involved, the obligations change big-time. Then the primary casualty will probably be affection. If there is another person in the picture (as in a love triangle), the matter becomes supercharged (egos, emotions, morals, everything!). No really happy endings are likely here.

KIDS HAVE THE RIGHT IDEA ABOUT BEING HAPPY

Their formula for happiness seems to be right on, and we should be so lucky: simplicity, playfulness, and creativity. They're always searching for ways to entertain themselves, and they can make themselves happy by playing with the simplest things. A persuasive argument can be made that we shouldn't have to grow out of this mind-set.

We're all born with a natural tendency to explore, but gradually those impulses are contained and controlled with rules, regulations and expectations. Open curiosity gets diverted into other obligations, habits, places, jobs, and people we associate with, and we become more and more narrow, and much less playful.

Unhappiness in kids seems to come from feeling insecure and afraid of bigger kids and the rest of the great big world they don't really understand, if only because they're so little. They're always looking for ways to not be scared. Case in point: *My little six year old boy and I were having fun chasing and scaring a large, quickly growing puppy. The first time it was fun, but the second time, my little boy said: "Maybe we shouldn't do that to Abby (the puppy)." I asked "Why?" and he said, "She's a baby and babies are afraid of lots of things."*

When it comes to imagination and letting your creativity loose to feel enjoyment and happiness, we should take a lesson from our (or any) kids at play.

ANTI-HAPPINESS: DECEPTION AND CONFLICT

Since deception in its many forms leads to conflict upon discovery, in a practical sense *deception* and *conflict* are too closely related to distinguish. Either or both of these cause-consequence bedfellows are the antithesis of happiness. The final chapter addresses conflicts in more detail, but it's worth touching on the subject here as well.

Deceptive unhappiness can come from many sources: an expensive but sloppy home renovation, a medical misdiagnosis and a cover-up, defective tires that lead to accidents and, you guessed it, more cover-ups. Closer to home, it could be your teenage daughter lying about where she stayed last night, the neighborhood bully acting nice and then beating you up again (if you're little), your spouse secretly spending all of the discretionary cash on a useless toy, or your girl-friend claiming you made her pregnant when you didn't. Everyone has experienced all levels and forms of deception along with the accompanying unhappiness.

If you *really* want to make *yourself* unhappy, frustrated and per-plexed, try reforming a liar and deceiver. Eric Hoffer put this issue into perspective when he said: *"It is doubtful whether we can reform human beings by eliminating their undesirable traits…elimination comes to nothing more than substitution. Envy takes the place of greed, self-righteousness that of selfishness, intellectual dishonesty that of plain dishonesty. And there is always a chance that the new bad trait will be more vigorous than the one it supplants."* So, the issue becomes, how can you make yourself happier when faced with deception and conflict? This is where an *empowered* mind-set becomes a wonderful ally, stabilizer, unstressor, and balancer.

Given you are faced with a very unhappy situation involving de-ception, conflict and lots of negative feelings, assertively confronting and exposing the deceptive person can be a very gratifying aspect of the solution, at least helping to mitigate a bad situation. But to enjoy (and be happy with the result) you must outsmart the perpetrator and you must do it legally, cleverly, with class, and effectively (not through a barrage of pejoratives, expletives, physical assaults, and emotional outbursts). Your goals must be restitution, justice, and fairness. If you can shame and embarrass the liar a little along the way, then the solution may reach 110 percent. After all, someone needs to find the wherewithal to stand up to these types of people, don't they? So why not you, why not now, and why not affirmatively? You won't change them, but at least you may feel a little invigorated.

REVENGE AND RETALIATION

This brings up a very different assertion about the maligned concepts of revenge, retaliation, retribution, and even vengeance (to a degree). There is most certainly an element of happiness when you realize those "ends" after you have been wrongfully treated. As long as revenge and retaliation aren't extreme, they are probably a satisfying if not happy aspect of justice and even fairness. We are conditioned to believe that revenge and similar aggressive "solutions," along with anger and resentment, are wrong, asocial, somehow deviant, and even immoral. That is fundamentally inaccurate and wrong! It's exactly what we do in war. In some societies, acts of passion up to and including murder are excusable in cases of betrayal, murderers are executed, and white-collar criminals are made to pay heavily for their mistakes. Until you have balance and fairness well in hand, don't think too much about forgiving and forgetting, it just isn't in the natural order of sense, logic, and fair play (unless you like to be abused, or if you're the perpetrator).

SEX AND HAPPINESS

This topic personifies the elusive, transient, sometimes-satisfying sometimes not aspects of *pursuing* happiness. Most men equate even fleeting sex with happiness, and most women use sex to look for happiness. As an old adage suggests: *"Men use love to get sex and women use sex to get love."* In reality, matters aren't quite that absolute, but there is an element of truth, suggesting: be cautious, careful, and beware, but most important, *learn to communicate openly, honestly, and effectively* in this delicate and sensitive area!

The operational terms to be very conscious of in this area, besides communication, are: genuine, continuing *affection* and *intimacy* (and not just physical). Without those aspects, sex becomes mechanical, and while temporarily feeling good (usually for the guy) and giving the illusion to the woman that there's something meaningful developing, it can be a very awkward, unhappy, incomplete, and even tense after the fact. In other words, the song that says: *"If you can't be with the one you love, love the one you're with"* is very shallow, immature advice. But then, if you are shallow, you probably don't know the difference and you may really think you are *happy* even in meaningless encounters.

IN SUMMARY

The primary way to realize happiness is first being capable of objectively seeing situations and relationships for what they are, appreciating their significance, and enjoying the little, real experiences we encounter every day. In other words, your *empowered* understanding creates *happiness*. Also, consciously bringing creativity and playfulness into your activities can lighten up your attitude and allow *happiness* to occur.

Conflicts and the Search
for Perfection

"A gem cannot be polished without pressure and friction, and a man cannot be perfected without trials." *Chinese proverb*

WHAT IS PERFECTION?

PERHAPS THE MOST appropriate synonym for perfection is *truth*. Almost every logical person would concur that perfection in almost anything is probably impossible, except perhaps as a philosophical opinion or belief of what is absolutely "true." Perfection can be a very abstract concept.

In what seems to be an imperfect world, it is commonly accepted that humans are quite fallible in their thinking, efforts, and pursuits. Humans are not infallible, yet they seem to believe that perfection is attainable. If they can't attain it in life, they conceptualize it through their religious beliefs. An environmental perspective holds that the world as it is (or has been) may indeed be perfect given its natural balance and interdependences; and that humans are compromising an otherwise logical, beneficial, and useful series of relationships. Maybe randomness, chaos, and natural adaptive creativity are perfection in the natural order of things, and that's as good as it can get. Those are certainly interesting speculative concepts, but we'll stick to human issues as we understand them.

Imperfection and fallibility for humans, for all intents and purposes, probably mean we aren't in a paradise free from wants, needs, toil, suffering, immorality, pain, insecurity, conflict, wars, and all other forms of discomfort. Nor, some would argue, do they deserve to be.

Bringing this stream of logic closer to earth, in a *perfect world* there would be peace, no crime, no hunger, and there would be respect for one another and justice for all. We'd also like to see illness and accidents eliminated. Taking it down another step, imperfection means we all can't be, and aren't, *rich*.

At a truly practical day-to-day level, perfection probably really is synonymous with truth, fairness, honesty, and attaining a comfortable balance between our own and the competing influences and interests (demands) levied upon us from every corner of our lives (i.e., conflicts). Taking this logic further, perhaps our search for perfection is really a matter of how well we *empower* ourselves to deal with conflicts in our quest for truth and fairness. This has been the essence of the messages throughout this book.

DEALING WITH CONFLICT: A FEW INSIGHTS

Many years ago, Charles Schultz, asserted through one of "Snoopy's" aphorisms: *"No problem is so big or so complicated that it can't be run away from!"* As amusing and clever as it sounds, it is definitely the way many people deal with conflict: avoidance. A quantum leap from that philosophy is the *empowered imperative*, to wit: if you want to be successful in any aspect of your life, you must face conflicts head-on, take control of the situation as best you can, and don't let up until you have attained a reasonable level of balance, justice, fairness, being made whole, or whatever the situation demands.

The following list explores a few aspects of conflicts. These points are a synthesis of earlier discussions, by no means all inclusive, and one or any combination of them may be helpful in formulating a viable approach to a specific conflict you may be dealing with:

- Probably the best-equipped individuals for dealing with conflict are effective *negotiators*. Study their methods and attributes and your ability to deal with conflicts will improve considerably. Reasonableness, diplomacy, the ability to compromise, and assimilating information objectively are very important.

- Psychological conflicts such as guilt (see *Epilogue*), denial, defensiveness, cognitive dissonance, and any number of other possible internal distractions seem very elusive and too conceptual to understand, maybe because you can't really see or touch them. Robert Louis Stevenson summed this issue up the best: *"You cannot run away from a weakness. You must sometimes fight it out or perish; and if that be so, why not now, and where you stand?"* In other words, face it and fix it now!

- If you are emotionally involved in a conflict, get rational, impartial advice. You may think you can be objective, but you need someone to keep you in check. Left to their own devices, at some critical point your emotions will impede resolving a conflict.

- Emotions are a powder keg in most interpersonal disputes, and emotional outbursts, cathartic as they may seem at the time, simply light a fuse and raise tension for everyone involved. If you can find a way to get past the emotions, wait them out, or at least legitimately put them aside (usually a very difficult thing to do), your ability to resolve any conflict will improve dramatically.

- Finding a solution as quickly as possible must be a primary goal (within the context of first neutralizing emotions), and exploring all possible ways to find the best solution should be equally important.

- *Intentions* or *why* something happened may not be nearly as important or relevant as you think, often creating an unnecessary distraction and leading to unsatisfying speculation. Getting at the truth via facts is about as good as you can do. And, as Frank Lloyd Wright stated: *"The truth is more important than the facts."*

- Conflicts within yourself and your priorities are pretty important, and sorting them out constructively is critical because a pattern of frivolous decisions will begin distorting your future and/or your effectiveness. Understanding who and what is important to you and why is the foundation for everything that you'll do (or let happen to you). Allocating your time according to your priorities is mandatory.

- It is imperative that every aspect of a conflict is considered and understood. Most important, you must know or at least empathize with the perspective of the other party. If the conflict is within yourself, you must understand right/wrong, causes/consequences, and the implications of chosen actions/solutions.

Only then can one begin to objectively formulate a balanced remedy.

- Withholding valuable, relevant information or insights is often a formula for sustained and/or irreparable conflict. This is especially true if someone feels taken advantage of at a later date when all pertinent information is eventually discovered or disclosed.

- Using a neutral third party may be very useful if an impasse is reached or if communications are strained. In personal matters this can be clergy, a social service worker, a therapist, a counselor, or a doctor. In business circles it may be a factfinder, mediator or arbitrator, and in serious matters, civil court.

- Conflicts concerning which social groups you want to be affiliated with vs. ones you should be associated with, must be governed by your interests, whether or not you'll learn or gain anything useful, whether or not the social exclusivity is gained through belittling or victimizing others, and whether or not membership will alienate you from constructive relationships. Be very careful whom you choose to hang with, it shapes your character and it can limit and censor your perspectives.

- Political conflicts are usually more ideological than practical, with posturing and showmanship taking center stage in an effort to persuade and cajole financial support, with the real deal-making taking place where you can't see it. In the extreme, political conflicts include war and variations thereof. This subject is covered in a later section.

- In family conflicts, it's all too easy to have family members take sides and inflame/confuse matters by adding too many extraneous opinions to the stew. Once families take sides, feelings get entrenched and positions get hardened, obstructing matters rather than helping. Confusion can also result from peer groups and casual thoughts of close friends who can't really understand the situation but are quite willing to give advice.

- A cooldown period or time-out for a few days can be helpful at times; but continued focus and hammering at issues is usually the best approach. Keeping at it means regrouping if one approach doesn't work and trying something else. Always have plans *B* and *C* ready to go (options).

- Poorly executed communication is often at the heart of interpersonal conflict, resulting in misunderstandings and often-unintended escalation of emotions resulting from poor taste in jokes, insults, quips, and/or comments. Sensitivity, tolerance, tact, and respect go a long way.

- If at all possible, interpersonal conflicts must never be allowed to reach a physical contact stage. Verbal brutality isn't much better, and should be avoided, even though disparaging labels often help the injured party organize the injustice in their mind. As in a war, everyone loses something: someone gets hurt, someone gets sued, feelings are out of control, others are pulled into the fray, and things only get worse.

THE DECEIVER/LIAR

At the heart, root, and core of many conflicts is the ever-present deceiver/liar. They come in all forms and sizes, and it's important to recognize, understand, and deal with them as the situation dictates.

Little "white" lies (if there is such a thing) are all around us constantly, and sorting through them can even be fun given the right context. But for chronic, habituated, or even recreational liars, it's very difficult for them to know where the line between fun and harm falls: after all, they are deceivers, and they'll lie to themselves probably more than to anyone else (it's called rationalizing).

An argument that is often made by the deceiver is that if a deception isn't discovered and doesn't hurt or harm anyone, then it's fundamentally innocuous. Other arguments include: the deception wasn't significant (only one dollar was stolen), that the person needed something more than the other, or even that it was to the benefit of the deceived person (such as telling your spouse she is attractive as soon as she wakes up).

Generally, the liar looks for ways to not be held responsible for an error, to avoid punishment, to cover up something they innately know is wrong, to continue doing what they shouldn't be doing, and they'll often go to great lengths to save themselves from shame, guilt, or admonishment. Sometimes they'll blame others, withhold information, suggest bizarre theories as a distraction, bring others in to support them, and mitigate their involvement any way they can. If they are successful, they've been reinforced; and if others support them, they've been validated and gain confidence; allowing the behavior to repeat itself. Is there a genetic predisposition to lie? Early success at it certainly provides at least social reinforcement, and it seems logical that it is at least partly "wired in" with the personality.

THE DISCOVERY PROCESS

"The cruelest lies are often told in silence." *Robert Louis Stevenson*

Others can sense inconsistencies, especially if similar events re-occur, and then at least subliminally become cautious and start look-ing for those inconsistencies. It isn't long after someone is "tuned in" to a liar before they start sharing their observations with others, and everyone starts comparing notes. The liar continues to spin inconsis-tencies, others collect them, and since it's harder to remember a lie than the truth, the liar continues to dig a credibility hole, and, often without realizing it, develops a reputation. Others are careful around the liar and don't generally challenge his statements.

At some point, since they can't help themselves and continue misbehaving, they are discovered through an error they can't wiggle out of, or someone just gets tired of "observing" and gets in their face if only because "it's time." That's when the liar can become aggressive to preserve his own dignity, resorting to even more emphatic strategies to avoid responsibility. Now the liar is in a survival mode and anything goes, from threatening lawsuits to being boisterous to pointing the finger and looking for scapegoats, to becoming totally submissive to garner sympathy and support, and many other tactics in between.

People take sides for or against the individual, and a range of subconflicts and opinions ensue, often taking attention away from the liar's transgression and focusing on the liar's personality as well as what should or shouldn't be done. The key is to not let the deceiver/liar off the hook under any circumstances because of extraneous reasons such as their likability and/or because they can generate excuses or aggressiveness.

In perhaps what will be unheeded advice to the liar, if you are caught lying: admit it, get everything out in the open, make reparations, and make the best you can of it. Then get counseling, stop misbehaving, stop lying, and make other lifestyle or job changes that may give you a fresh start.

> "Delusions, errors, and lies are like huge, gaudy vessels, the rafters of which are rotten and worm-eaten, and those who embark in them are fated to be shipwrecked." *Chinese proverb*

TRYING TO MAKE THE SITUATION WHOLE

> "Since nothing is settled until it is settled right, no matter how unlimited power a man may have, unless he exercises it fairly and justly his actions will return to plague him." *Frank A. Vanderlip*

In most conflicts, whether personal, business, or interpersonal, a few questions that should be considered include: *How much do I want to solve the conflict? What is real and what is assumed? Do I really understand the situation? What are the alternatives? Do I need help in figuring out the situation? What is fair, just and right? How much damage have I really suffered? Is there room for compromise? Can/should a relationship continue? Will consideration ($) adequately resolve the conflict or is something else important and appropriate?*

In many conflicts, often the only viable way to make one party or the other "whole" is an economic approach. Facts may lead to some level of truth; and then placing a reasonable value ($) on an error, a wrongful act, or unfulfilled agreement may be the only possible relief. There is no way to restore behavioral characteristics such as confidence, trust, integrity, ethics, and honesty with an assertion or promise to that effect, nor is there a way to contract morals. Those aspects will have to find their own way in their own time, if at all, once they have been compromised. And in cases of wrongful death or incapacitation, not much can be said.

- If you are in a conflict and you have been clearly wronged, don't make the mistake of taking a "win-win" attitude from the onset. Even in a *win-win* situation someone still wins a little more than someone else; and an early win-win attitude/approach suggests you've philosophically conceded (again) to someone who may have damaged or hurt you. Establish what you want in a solution and go for it with reasonable flexibility.

- Platitudes, clichés, abstractions, conceptualizing, philosophizing, labeling, diatribes, and even apologies often don't mean much when trying to resolve a serious issue. Stay away from patronizing comments like *"Let's forgive and forget," "It's time to move one," "What's done is done," "Both sides are at fault,"* and similar dribble. Try to find tangible remedies, otherwise promises and rhetoric alone may soon leave you feeling that the solution was inadequate and incomplete.

- Understand that *revenge* is a real and honest need, and it shouldn't be belittled as many psych-types like to do. Discrediting revenge and retaliation doesn't make the feeling go away or make matters better, but it can inflame the one who wants or needs it. It is really a cry for justice, although those who aren't directly or emotionally involved tend to give it a dirty, malevolent label. These emotions need to be channeled into viable remedies as quickly as possible.

- Business conflicts are usually relatively easy to identify and deal with legally or through negotiations (unless there is a serious cover-up). It's almost always a matter of money.

- Taking preliminary steps toward a legal action may be a viable method for forcing interest in negotiating a settlement, but be prepared to file the lawsuit and don't bluff. If the complaint is ready to go and the other party knows it, you've demonstrated that you're serious.

- With interpersonal or cultural clashes, a line must be drawn somewhere, someone eventually has to suck it up and admit some level of wrongdoing, and then the psychology of remediation becomes a possibility.

- Negotiated results may never reach the optimum level of fairness you would like to see, but you can come close with persistence and some creativity. At least explore shaping a package of solutions that preserves dignity and protects financial interests.

- Open communication is always a critical ingredient in resolving any conflict. Once communication is truncated, assumptions, speculation, and second-guessing fill the void: usually in a negative way.

IRRESOLVABLE ISSUES

How people see themselves in a conflict is interesting and important, since it sets the stage for determining if there will be a mutually acceptable solution, if a solution must be dictated (as by a court), or if there will be any reparations at all.

If principles, dogma, morals, integrity, and similar intense faith-based or behavioral issues are involved (religious conflicts, marriages, or inter/intrafamily issues), attempts at reconciliation can be extremely difficult. When one side of the conflict is totally committed and then somehow deceived or disparaged, personal feelings are intense. The deceiver will argue that there was some mitigating situation or some defensible reason for what happened, and the party holding the moral high ground isn't about to concede anything. No easy answers or simple resolutions here, matters of pride, dignity, and respect are in the forefront. For resolution to occur, the responsible party would need to make big dramatic concessions and admissions at the expense of their own dignity: something that doesn't happen often.

If a person sees someone who has harmed them as a criminal, a negotiated settlement is extremely difficult. A criminal on the other hand will rationalize and often see himself as an enterprising person, themselves victimized, trying to survive in a hostile world. The real victims are simply symbols of the success they couldn't achieve legitimately but were somehow due. Clearly, the gap between criminal and victim is huge and probably impossible to breach, especially if the crime is brutal and/or debilitating. Monetary compensation is unlikely, and the situation can never be made completely "whole," if only because of the psychological trauma.

In family, interclan and interethnic disputes, deep emotions, habits, traditions and the lack of civilized communication always hamper any peacemaking attempts. If there has been brutality or killing, feuds can rage for generations, easily becoming international issues when the sides become populous enough. Hatreds become institutionalized, inbred, and very difficult to broach. Gangs display a similar dynamic, although with much shorter timelines. These cases make the case for preempting and resolving conflicts early, before they grow out of proportion.

Issues of morality, crime, kidnapping, preventable deaths, and war are the most unfair and irresolvable conflicts. Dealing with them requires support, lots of time and a very empowered mind-set. Fair closure in these situations is highly unlikely

INSTITUTIONALIZED DETERRENTS TO FAIR CONFLICT RESOLUTION

In earlier discussions we've touched on the inadequacy of the legal/ justice systems in criminal matters. The same holds true in civil cases. In either case you will be as successful as the quality of your legal representation (with the burden of related costs).

Two very real deterrents to fairness have evolved in recent decades as many states have adopted no-fault auto insurance and community property divorce laws. Proponents argue that courts would otherwise be inundated with relatively small but complicated claims that are costly to adjudicate, locking up justice for years. But in "simplifying" the system in these areas, they have inadvertently allowed potential wrongdoers lots of latitude at the expense of the other party.

Case in point: *I was processing a $750 auto damage claim with my insurance adjuster, who happened to be a very open conversationalist. In the course of a few minutes I learned she was splitting up with her third husband, living on a very nice ranch from her previous husband, and driving a nice car from her first husband. She stated, "I love community property" as she was apparently counting the money she was about to receive from her third husband while extolling the virtues of the law.*

In other words, the moral, ethical, and probably legal promissory aspects of marriage yielded to legalized fraud. Similarly, with no-fault auto insurance, a poor driver who causes a collision also causes the good driver to share in the costs of the poor driver's mistakes.

No-fault and community property laws may have succeeded in making life more convenient for bureaucrats who couldn't find a better solution, but they also provided a victory for those who are good at deception. There are novel and legitimate legal approaches that are possible to offset the negative impact of these allegedly neutral statutes, but it will (again) require a resourceful and usually expensive attorney.

However, the most intense institutionalized deterrent to fairness is *war*.

THE PINNACLE OF IMPERFECTION: JUSTIFYING WAR

"Never think that war, no matter how necessary, nor how justified, is not a crime." *Ernest Hemingway*

Someone can always justify and show a reason why war is the right answer. Here are a few random thoughts on this difficult subject.

- It is easy to justify war when your people are starving and the only way to live is to conquer someone for their food. They die and you don't, in a struggle for survival.

- If war is used to secure scarce resources and land in lieu of using economic agreements, then it is really a form of theft. It's tempting to steal if you have nothing to trade. Perhaps war is a way to politically cull the population when there are too many people to support and appease.

- If war is retaliation for killing or stealing, is it a form of justice to continue killing and stealing? It is unquestionably an easy way to bond together a group with a renewed common interest: hatred for an enemy, clustering for security, unifying and rallying. All have a primordial, bloodthirsty, low-intellect appeal. Mao Tse-tung recognized this circular, self-perpetuating logic when he stated: *"Often war is the only way to prevent war."*

- At a practical level, war is obscene, disfiguring, disabling, and grotesque, involving previously uninvolved people. The loss of sustenance, friends, and relatives the uprooting of people from their homeland, and the impact on children are among the worst of horrors.

- War provides an opportunity for some people to excel. Politicians suddenly have a righteous cause, and they can demonstrate leadership in a time of crisis. Certain portions of the economy that have grown stale can be rejuvenated. Individuals can garner recognition that would be otherwise impossible: as heroes or martyrs. Others who have simply been bored with their lives can find a diversion. Unfortunately, war destroys many more people than it helps: economically, mentally, and physically.

• People with integrity who understand the practical aspects of war seem to want to avoid it, and often it is (ironically) in the hierarchy of the military. But getting caught up in the moment and the frenzy of retaliation and retribution is so compelling it usually can't be avoided.

• What happens to religion and its impact at this point? Individuals become disillusioned, some become ruthless killers and exploiters, and everyone wonders how God could allow such atrocities. The dying and grieving may be somewhat consoled; but organized religions become political, choose sides and show their duplicity if not hypocrisy. Also, it is easy to be a pacifist if you haven't been touched by the horror of war.

• There is much to be said in favor of winning over enemies with ideologies rather than annihilating them. Americans probably don't know how to do that yet…our philosophies are too fragmented to mean much, it would take too long, and economic initiatives wouldn't be understood or realized for generations by groups intent on hurting us. Giving victims of war restitution and food probably only breeds more resentment, although it must be provided. But Americans must find and employ effective words and concepts and take the time and effort needed to make them work. Otherwise we may see ourselves increasingly more isolated.

There are probably no totally logical "truths" in war, and each side has its righteous perspectives. If good faith diplomacy and outside intervention cannot resolve a conflict, then war becomes an option, albeit an extreme one. Suffice it to say that if physically attacked without provocation (a discussion unto itself), forcing a balance and making the situation whole in whatever way possible, including war, is unquestionably the appropriate precept. Having mercy on the innocents may be the only redeeming characteristic of war.

IN SEARCH OF PRACTICAL PERFECTION

"Aim at perfection in everything, though in most things it is unattainable. However, they who aim at it, and persevere, will come much nearer to it than those whose laziness and despondency make them give it up as unattainable." *Lord Chesterfield*

"A man can do his best only by confidently seeking (and perpetually missing) an unattainable perfection." *Ralph Barton Perry*

Probably as close as we'll come to perfection is occasionally being in *the Zone* at whatever we do, and experiencing the best we can be for at least a transient, fleeting moment. A feeling of perfection can also occur when we have an epiphany or when we achieve something we've been striving for, after enduring/resolving all the challenges and conflicts along the way. A level of perfection is also embodied and satisfaction is felt in all those rituals and rites of passage we experience throughout our lifetime. We see perfection through acts of our sports heroes, whose records are indeed an act of perfection until someone does a little bit better. We seem to realize there are degrees of beauty and perfection in creative works such paintings, writings, sculptures, and photographs. We see beauty/perfection in nature. And we often appreciate excellence, if not perfection, in speeches, performances, and in demonstration of incredible talent, ability, and achievement in many forms and venues.

What seems *should* be most important, however, is that feeling of perfection that comes with everyday, often small and continuing experiences, through our ability to understand and appreciate their significance. Here are a few examples of practical perfection (never without conflicts) that many of us have experienced, and to which you can add many more:

- Truly falling in love, mutually (and better yet, staying that way).
- Having and raising kids.
- Nurturing the strength of family.
- Sharing time with loved ones.
- Maintaining loyalty, morality, and integrity.
- Recognizing and appreciating the good things in our lives while

resolving the bad.
- Continuously searching for truth.
- Striving to achieve whatever you really want.
- Bringing out your creativity.

IN SUMMARY

The continuous search for excellence and perfection, truth, and fairness are the cornerstones of *empowerment*. If in some fashion the foregoing essays may have helped in your quest to improve your organization, your career, or yourself, then my purpose has been achieved. Fare thee well and all the best to you.

> "Anyone entrusted with power will abuse it if not also animated with the love of truth and virtue." *Jean de la Fontaine*

> "You all have powers you never dreamed of. You can do things you never thought you could do. There are no limitations in what you can do except the limitations in your own mind as to what you cannot do." *Darwin P. Kingsley*

Epilogue

1. IT SOUNDS THEORETICALLY APPEALING, BUT IS IT POSSIBLE TO ACTUALLY HAVE AN EMPOWERED ORGANIZATION?

It isn't common, but it can happen. My personal experience bears it out. Six senior managers bought a division of a Dutch multi-national company. That little company, with $30 million-a-year revenues, grew to $100 million in three years, allowing three of the six owners to divest and retire. The company then grew to $200 million in the next four years, allowing the other three to do the same.

Although each partner was an independent type, and some didn't really like each other that much, all were: very intelligent, experienced businesspeople who had exceptional judgment; multiskilled (filling in where needed without "turf" battles) and exceptional performers, with excellent technical *and* interpersonal abilities; focused on expanding and then selling the business (two times as it turned out); dedicated to that purpose; intent on running a lean/clean organization with excellence as a standard; willing to take the financial/performance risks; and not preoccupied with useless bureaucracy, infighting, or other distractions. It was an unusual *convergence* of six truly *empowered* personalities. It was a great run while it lasted, and now each partner has gone his (and her) own way.

That experience contributed greatly to the theme and content of this book. Accordingly, this book is dedicated at least in part to my former partners.

2. HOW WOULD AN EMPOWERED MIND-SET MANAGE A MONOLITHIC, AUTHORITARIAN ORGANIZATION LIKE THE MILITARY?

Speaking of the military and its role in national security issues vis-à-vis protecting our country from very destructive national problems, and the military's search for its role in the new world order, how long can the military deny the obvious? They must affirmatively and effectively address drug trafficking, illegal immigration, organized crime (including street/school gangs), and terrorism. If those aren't all critical national security issues, then *hello* Mr. President and Congress, time for a reality check!

The trade-off may very well be a slight threat to privacy, but if a person isn't doing something illegal, they shouldn't be too concerned (some of the militant militia types would disagree, but maybe they can be included in these efforts, and channeling their energies more constructively). In our country the development of a police state isn't very likely. It's about time authorities swarmed and took control of these insidious and destructive problems.

The local authorities certainly haven't had much success! Let's really put the military to work protecting our external and internal freedoms, interests, and security. There's nothing wrong with the military exercising a police function (other countries do it), and it would be worth a constitutional amendment if it were needed. This would be a way for the military to earn its keep as well as begin reengineering and constantly improve itself (expanding its scope of activities, and tempering that ultimate predatory machine with civil intelligence and discretion).

3. HOW WOULD AN EMPOWERED PERSONALITY APPROACH MANAGING AN EDUCATIONAL INSTITUTION?

Let's address all levels of education. All levels of this industry could use a significant attitude adjustment. Here are a few examples.

Pampered professors need to do more work: rather than delegating teaching assignments and research to grad students, and then publishing books that their students are obliged to buy, for which the professors receive royalties (often with additional stipends from corporate or federal grants: with much of the research the real work having been done being by yet more students). The professors then go on speaking campaigns for honorariums, *and* to promote their books and consulting services, of course. Sounds like a bunch of conflicts of interest or some kind of racket, doesn't it? Students working for tiny hourly salaries call it extortion. It can be a very cushy, self-serving arrangement, especially if the professor is tenured and can't be fired.

Online teaching is making life even easier for professors; and somewhere along the line, the product (education) has become diluted and less complete. There's lots of room for improvement at universities: starting with eliminating the chronic inbreeding and incestuous development of their administrators. The oft-present intellectual pompousness, arrogance, and demeaning attitudes toward students could use a little toning down, too. The frequent infighting between professors could use some attention as well. It seems as though higher education has become too busy with extraneous activities to execute their core mission effectively: preparing people *well* for becoming successful in their fields and careers.

When it comes to education *below* the higher level, administrators need to seriously focus on beefing up the curricula and expecting students to perform. We must return to a well-rounded, classical education for kids (languages, math, sciences and arts, civics, etc.). Also, school administrators need to learn to use much more discretionary judgment in dealing with problem behavior and in setting their policies. Perhaps public schools could, and should, learn a few lessons from effective private schools.

In the realm of education, too many of those in power (legislatures, politicians, board members, administrators) speak and think philosophically rather than practically. They are often too timid to experiment and try different approaches (as is needed for different schools, different populations, and different needs) rather than search for statistical indicators and try to apply generic programs that simply don't apply to too many kids. Active involvement of the teachers is critical, as is a better review of how effectively money and other resources are used/allocated.

Quality of teachers and their pay are an issue. Teachers are developed by teachers, and so are school administrators: they all come out of the same cookie factory and as a result they are so similarly conditioned they may not recognize a viable alternative solution if they were looking at it (after all, they are the experts).

A good example of a poor policy is the notion of "zero tolerance": it's easy to administer, sounds good to the political board, and it's a mistake in many instances (leading correctly, to lawsuits; but only because an administrator couldn't or wouldn't make a reasonable vs. a by-the-book decision).

4. HOW WOULD AN EMPOWERED MIND-SET ADDRESS A HOPELESSLY BUREAUCRATIC ORGANIZATION LIKE A TRADITIONAL STATE-RUN SOCIAL SERVICE AGENCY?

If any bureaucratic organization in any industry (such as a social service agency, public or private) were to hire and put a proven entrepreneur in charge, with appropriate expectations, standards, measurement/auditing controls, and substantial performance incentives (including a considerable base salary), and then let them manage, there would be many improvements in the system and in results. The first order of business would be to replace bureaucrats with interested, motivated workers.

The reason this will *not* happen (or not be executed effectively) is because board members or other political hacks envious of the compensation package would maneuver for the positions themselves, get the jobs, and then not perform. Eventually the governing board would declare it was an unsuccessful experiment, and dump the concept.

5. HOW WOULD AN EMPOWERED APPROACH DEAL WITH PROBLEMS IN OUR CRIMINAL JUSTICE SYSTEM?

Once again, the first order of business would be to eliminate or at least minimize all aspects of the bureaucracy, thereby and concurrently increasing the competence of the staff.

Probably the single most significant, conceptual obstacle to effectiveness in this area is self-imposed *constraint*. Once a significant (ostensibly precedent-setting) judicial decision is issued and seems to impede justice, the various components of the criminal justice system (police, prosecutors, judges, attorneys) all seem to lock up and back off, giving criminals the loopholes they are so adept at using. When the justice system backs off, it restricts itself, probably for fear of lawsuits by criminals. Effectiveness diminishes one step at a time, and the criminal appears to have more rights and protections than the victim.

The *empowered* approach in this area would be to: outsmart the criminals on a daily basis; take more risks in arrests and prosecutions; not back down under any circumstance, emphasize doing what's right; and create new precedents that enhance enforcement/prosecution. In other words, aggressively reverse the trends. Also, lobby for and pass legislative improvements; and use the untapped (and often idle) resources of the military as soon as, and as much as, possible.

6. HOW WOULD AN EMPOWERED APPROACH DEAL WITH RISING HEALTH CARE COSTS AND QUALITY OF CARE?

The insurance industry would need to be heavily regulated, if not eliminated (it's an expensive middleman that often meddles in and delays needed treatments, usually to make money, although they would contend it's to save money).

If politics, bureaucracy, and litigation could be reasonably controlled, a compelling argument could be made for socializing this exceptionally important area in its entirety, including pharmaceuticals (it's almost there already with Medicare and many other regulations/limitations). The keys would be (again): effective, competent leadership; incentives for researching and developing treatments/medications; eliminating cumbersome/ineffective controls and regulations; and providing effective incentives for practitioners to perform well, at all levels.

7. WHAT WOULD HAPPEN IF EVERYONE HAD AND USED AN EMPOWERED ATTITUDE?

Everyone would be functioning at a higher level with greater expectations, continuously improving, and there would be much less unethical activity. People would be well versed in many subjects, they would have multiple skills, they would be better adjusted and everything would be better (maybe we'd even have *world peace*). Obviously it won't happen, but it would be nice.

8. "GUILT" IS A REAL EMOTION, HOW CAN THE EMPOWERED MIND-SET JUST "BLOW IT OFF" AND TAKE IT SO LIGHTLY?

John Crossan, a former Catholic priest, in his book *A Long Way From Tipperary*, commented on guilt very effectively, to wit:

> Guilt is totally inoperative for me, and I suggest it should be for all of us.... Get rid of it.... Think of it as spiritual waste product, and more important, it distracts us or excuses us from absolutely necessary attitudes as honesty and integrity, clarity and accuracy, accountability and responsibility.

If you feel guilt, fix it, get over it, confess to the one(s) you've hurt or wronged, and make them whole. Don't let guilt hang over you; you're probably not a bad person. Just the process (and good intent) of pursuing a remedy will make you feel better about yourself. Ask yourself, "What am I feeling guilty about?" Is that something a valid matter; or is it (the "guilt") an artificial, fabricated, out-of-date, inapplicable, unreasonable, unnecessary issue or formality that no one really cares about (or something that doesn't matter)?

Maintain and continue to carry your guilt if you wish, but you'll also continue to feel inadequate (as we humans often have a tendency to do). If God says you are inadequate, what's the use of trying? After all, fate put you where you are, and fate will determine what you'll do, right? What an incredible demotivator! Do you really like that notion?

Instead of feeling guilty, actively pursue tangible, real, reasonable remedies and improvements.

9. HOW CAN PEOPLE IN THE LOWEST OCCUPATIONAL LEVELS EXERCISE AN EMPOWERED ATTITUDE? WOULDN'T IT BE CONSIDERED CAVALIER OR DEFIANT?

People who have the lowest socioeconomic status often have the most pride, dignity, humility, honesty, integrity, and drive. In many instances they need those attributes to survive: working many hours (and/or several jobs), having large families to support, very little time for recreation or self-improvement (schooling), and being tired from all of their obligations. You can't help but admire them.

In many cases these people innately have or demonstrate an empowered mind-set to the extent possible. What they need is time to continue improving themselves without being exhausted and to be able to pay attention to what they're learning. This is a serious point for social service policymakers to consider.

10. HOW WOULD AN EMPOWERED MIND-SET ADDRESS THE "UGLY AMERICAN" IMAGE SO PREVALENT AROUND THE WORLD?

On the international, world-class level, Americans must make the effort to become much more cultivated culturally, more informed, and much more respectful. This precept can be applied here at home as well as abroad.

Our foreign policies need to help strengthen third world economies and not simply exploit their resources and low labor rates; and we need to be less duplicitous about favored nation status and our proselytizing about human rights. Our marketers have elevated lying to an admired art form, raising a legitimate question about our values.

Similarly, chasing the high standard of living we feel we must have through exhausting workloads and time spent on the job seem to be eroding the fabric of the family. So many marriages fail because everyone seems to be filling their needs outside the family, kids are basically raised alone or in single-parent households, and they learn to act like their parents.

The rest of the world sees us as what we are, an economic power and bully, they admire us for our wealth and internal governance/security, they are frightened by our military ability, but they wonder about our ethics, and they can't stand our arrogance and pompousness.

Maybe a good place to start would be for all of us to demand ethics, integrity, and excellence of ourselves and to truly respect all others.